Love, Sex, and Desire in Modern Egypt

Love, Sex, and Desire in Modern Egypt

Navigating the Margins of Respectability

L. L. WYNN

University of Texas Press ◆ Austin

Requests for permission to reproduce material from this work should be sent to:
   Permissions
   University of Texas Press
   P.O. Box 7819
   Austin, TX 78713-7819
   utpress.utexas.edu/rp-form

♾ The paper used in this book meets the minimum requirements of
ANSI/NISO Z39.48-1992 (R1997) (Permanence of Paper).

Library of Congress Cataloging-in-Publication Data

Names: Wynn, L. L., 1971– author.
Title: Love, sex, and desire in modern Egypt : navigating the margins of
   respectability / L. L. Wynn.
Description: First edition. | Austin : University of Texas Press, 2018. | Includes
   bibliographical references and index.
Identifiers: LCCN 2018001199
   ISBN 978-1-4773-1704-4 (cloth : alk. paper)
   ISBN 978-1-4773-1707-5 (pbk. : alk. paper)
   ISBN 978-1-4773-1705-1 (library e-book)
   ISBN 978-1-4773-1706-8 (non-library e-book)
Subjects: LCSH: Ethnology—Egypt. | Egypt—Social life and customs—
   21st century. | Egypt—Social conditions—21st century. | Sex role—Egypt—
   21st century. | Women—Sexual behavior—Egypt—21st century. | Women—
   Egypt—Social conditions—21st century. | Man-woman relationships—
   Egypt—21st century.
Classification: LCC GN648 .W95 2018 | DDC 306.0962—dc23
LC record available at https://lccn.loc.gov/2018001199

doi:10.7560/317044

Contents

Acknowledgments

I wish to thank the many institutions and individuals who supported me financially, intellectually, and emotionally as I wrote this book. When the research began it was supported by Princeton University, the American Research Center in Egypt, and a US Department of Education Foreign Languages and Area Scholarship (FLAS) fellowship. Later research and writing was undertaken with funding from Macquarie University and an Australian Research Council Discovery Project grant (DP120103974). In addition to Macquarie University, I also wish to thank Yale University, the American University in Cairo, and the University of Sydney for providing me with institutional homes during my sabbaticals, which gave me the space and intellectual inspiration to write this book. Jim Burr at the University of Texas Press has been enthusiastic about this project from the beginning, and I am really grateful for his support.

I gained valuable feedback on portions of this manuscript during invited seminars I gave at the Australian National University, Oxford University, Princeton University, Tufts University, the University of Auckland, the University of Exeter, the University of Sydney, and Yale University. I thank them all for hosting me and for their intellectual engagement. Members of the Sydney Women's Anthropology Group (SWAG), including Gillian Cowlishaw, Holly High, Vivienne Kondos, Alison Leitch, Rozanna Lilley, Diane Losche, Jeannie Martin, Yasmine Musharbash, Kalpana Ram, Cristina Rochas, and Rosemary Wiss, gave me valuable critical insight and support during the writing process. I thank them all, and I mourn Vivienne and Jeannie.

A host of individuals all over the world either read early drafts of chapters or the entire manuscript, provided stimulating intellectual conversation that helped me take my writing and thinking in productive and new directions, provided emotional support, or told me what I was doing was rubbish and thus helped me figure out how to improve. To Nada Abaza, Oumnia Abaza, Zeinab Abaza, Tom Abowd, Lila Abu-Lughod, Justine Aenishaenslin, Paul Amar, Mohammed Anwar, Mohamed Ashour, Jumana Bayeh, João Biehl, Amahl Bishara, Jim Boon, John Borneman, Isabelle Clark-Decès, Aaron Denham, Robin Dougherty, Greg Downey, Alex Edmonds, Marwa Elshakry, Danny Fisher, Angel Foster, Layla Gamal, Gennaro Gervasio, Carol Greenhouse, Kevin Groark, Ghassan Hage, Abdellah Hammoudi, Max Harwood, Saffaa Hassanein, Zahi Hawass, Anna-Karina Hermkens, Chris Houston, Shakira Hussein, Yvette Hymann, David Inglis, Rigel Inglis, Saiph Inglis, Marcia Inhorn, Siobhan Irving, Konstantina Isidoros, Lucy Iskander, Michael Jackson, Bridget Jay, Maryam Khalid, Laleh Khalili, Hanan Kholoussy, Rena Lederman, Alex Lipman, Chris Lyttleton, Anne-Corrine Mahiou, Gabriele Marranci, Lindy McDougall, Francesca Merlan, Elijah Moloney, Nefissa Naguib, Mohammed Nasr, Katy Natanel, Rachel Newcomb, Eddy Niesten, Amal Osman, Sarah Pinto, Noor Al-Qasimi, Payel Ray, Melissa Rochfort, Larry Rosen, Carolyn Rouse, Alan Rumsey, Anwar Esmat El-Sadat, Rania Salem, Clemence Scalbert-Yucel, Kirsten Scheid, Mohammed Sarawat Selim, Banu Senay, Omnia El Shakry, Chris Stone, Tom Strong, Andrew Thomas, Jaap Timmer, Susanna Trnka, James Trussell, Katia Tsiolkas, Liz Tysoe, Marc Valeri, Debbie Van Heekeren, Chris Vasantkumar, Eve Vincent, Shiraz Visinko, Stephanie Woerde, Chris Wright, Corion Wynn, Don-Raphael Wynn, Jared Wynn, Jeff Wynn, Louise Wynn, Valerie Wynn, Elisa Wynn-Hughes, and Carol Zanca, I owe you each a debt not easily repaid. Any remaining faults and errors in this book are mine.

I dedicate this book to David, Saiph, Rigel, Alex, and Elijah.

CHAPTER 1

Foreigners Like Things Looking Old and Dark, Not Shiny

I didn't go to Cairo to study love and desire. It happened because that was what everyone I knew wanted to talk about.

Of course, that is a cliché of anthropology. Anthropologists don't consider a complete overturning of our research topic to be a failure. We consider it proof that we are doing exactly what anthropologists are *supposed* to do: letting our research be shaped by what we find in the field, not by what we go looking for.

But despite what everyone was talking about, it took more than a decade for me to decide to write about love and desire, sex and gender, and respectability. Over that decade, I watched my friends in Egypt date, fall in and out of love, get married, and have extramarital affairs. I wrote down their opinions about the collapse of my own marriage.

I watched a revolution sweep the country. I watched as mass demonstrations played out in the bodies of women and men, as sexual experimentation became intertwined with political activism, as sexual assault became a tool of a dying regime, and then as Egyptian activists rose up to challenge gender norms and sexual violence.

Eventually, I started to write about love and desire and the moral codes that hedge these about. Finally, I thought I had begun to grasp the concepts.

And then I had to rethink everything I thought I knew about love and desire when, a decade after documenting what I thought was a great love story, one of my closest friends in Egypt revealed that her lover had helped one of his relatives rape her. That she had continued to love him afterward. That she had loved him until he had abandoned her. In my shock, I realized that I understood nothing about love if I couldn't explain the relationship between love and violence.

Violence is not central to this account—in fact, it is decidedly pe-ripheral—but it is nevertheless one potential aspect of relationships that cannot be ignored, not only because it has its own cultural logic but also, critically, because it pervades the international political economy of representations of the Arab world and Arab masculinity.

Though I didn't consider it my topic when I started my research in 1999, all my informants were talking about love and desire, sex and gen-der, and respectability, so I wrote down what they said in my field notes. Here I reconstruct long-ago conversations from these detailed notes. I rarely recorded these conversations, not only because they were in-formal but also because they often covered sensitive topics, since love and desire are highly moralized issues in Egypt. Though I present them here as verbatim dialogue, they are in fact approximate reconstructions from handwritten notes, which I then typed up with details and com-mentary a few hours after the original conversations occurred.

Setting the Scene

In the great tradition of setting the scene (Clifford and Marcus 1986) by writing the anthropologist into the story while promising that what is to come will not (only) be an exercise in navel-gazing, let me begin by re-lating the circumstances that led to this particular book.

I started working on this book when I got completely fed up with having to fend off the advances of an old man. My marriage was fall-ing apart in painful, emotionally draining, and expensive phone calls at night (this was a few years before voice over internet protocol programs like Skype), and by day, the seventy-year-old who was my chief infor-mant in the village of Nazlet el-Semman kept putting his hands on me, and no matter how much I squirmed away from him and made pointed remarks about my husband back in America, he kept doing it. I couldn't stand it anymore, and as usual, I wasn't up for a direct confrontation over the matter, so I retreated and started working on something com-pletely different.

That is the story in a nutshell.

I had been living in Egypt for about two and a half years, first study-ing Arabic and then doing my dissertation research. I was researching the politics of Egyptology and, specifically, the conflict between the Egyptologists who worked on the Giza Plateau and the villagers of Naz-let el-Semman next to the pyramids (Wynn 2007, 2008b). The villagers claimed that the land-grabbing Egyptologists cared nothing for living Egyptians and were only interested in what they could find buried underneath them. As part of my investigation into the villagers' perspective, I had been introduced to a powerful old man in the village. I will call him Abu Ahmed. (Of course, all the names in this ethnography are pseudonyms, and I have changed identifying details to protect people's privacy; those whose lives I describe most intimately were consulted about what details to change or hide in order to conceal their identities.)

Abu Ahmed was a freelance tour guide who seemed to know everybody, Egyptologist and villager. He was well educated and knew a great deal not only about ancient history and the monuments but also about the contemporary social life surrounding the monuments. When he introduced me to his elderly wife over tea at his home, I felt safe and welcome.

But in the second week or so of visiting Abu Ahmed and touring the village with him, he put his hand on my back to guide me into a stable to meet the owner. I noticed the touch and put some distance between us. On the way out, he put his hand on my upper arm, as though to guide me along the uneven ground. The ground wasn't *that* uneven. I immediately stepped out of his reach, hoping to communicate my discomfort without confrontation. But that afternoon and the next day, he continued to put his hand on my back, my shoulder, and my arm. I kept jumping out of his reach more and more abruptly, making, I thought, my displeasure clear. I found ways to mention my Arab husband back in America, and in other means tried to communicate my status as a Respectable Wife—alluding, for example, to a curfew my husband had set for me, to his impending visit, to his concern about my proper behavior. Abu Ahmed kept touching me.

After a couple of days of this, I took an evening bus back to my apartment, hot and tired and miserable. I knew I could look forward to another battle with my husband that evening. I could imagine exactly how the conversation would play out, based on dozens of similar ones. I would call him in the United States or email him and tell him about my day. That would include an account of Abu Ahmed's advances. My husband would chastise me for not doing a better job of keeping the old man in line. He would complain that I must be somehow communicating that I was not a respectable woman, that I was someone who could be touched. I would tell him that I had done everything I could do, short of a confrontation that would destroy any chance of using this valuable informant for my research. What is more, I was afraid that if

I offended Abu Ahmed, he might block my access to other villagers I wanted to interview.

Then my husband would accuse me of prostituting myself for my research. I would tell him that I was sick of him calling me a prostitute, and I didn't see the point of telling him about my research if he was just going to take everything I said and use it to insult me. He would remind me that he was telling me this for my own good, because he could see things from the Arab perspective, and he could show me how the Egyptians saw me.

Wasn't I an anthropologist? Didn't I want to learn how to behave in locally meaningful, proper ways? Wasn't I married to an Arab man, and didn't I aspire to being a respectable Arab wife? Why couldn't I do my research with respectable married women? Why did I have to keep talking to all these men?

Looking back at my field notes from this period, I see that this conversation repeated itself many times. We were both exhausted from arguing about the same thing, and yet the issue was never resolved. It drove me crazy, but I loved my husband and I wanted to save my marriage. Besides, I *was* an anthropologist. I *did* want to learn how to behave in culturally meaningful ways and be seen as a respectable woman. My husband was teaching me. The lessons were taught in painful, daily email exchanges and phone calls that were emotionally wrenching for both of us.

Yet no matter what I did, no matter how I tried to wear the respectability of my marriage like a thick cloak, some men made sexual advances toward me. Those who did were a minority. Most of the men I knew in Egypt always treated me like a sister or a respected colleague. Yet somehow, it is the ones who didn't that I remember. It happened enough that I had gotten used to it and come to expect it. I no longer thought of it as sexual harassment, which seemed like a crude concept to translate across cultures.

These were in the days before the Egyptian anti-sexual-harassment campaigns that are reshaping Egyptian understandings of the term. In 2017, as I am finishing this book, the word *al-taharrush* (harassment) is commonplace in Cairo, thanks to the efforts of local activists. (And Paul Amar [2011], Vickie Langohr [2015], and Aymon Kreil [2016a] have all written about the history of Egyptian activism around the concept of sexual harassment and its development as a linguistic concept.) However, when I first lived in Egypt around the turn of the millennium, I never heard the term and there was little awareness of the issue. Instead, *[handwritten:]* to anthropologists often speak about their personal lives like this? Or this novel and/or useful later in the book? it seems unprofessional.

Foreigners Like Things Looking Old and Dark **5**

Egyptians whom I knew used the word *mu'akkisat* as a catch-all term for both "flirtation" and "harassment," depending on whether the meaning attached to its use in context was positive or negative.

I thought of these sexual advances as a way that men were testing boundaries and hierarchies, gauging the truth of my claims to be married, enacting culturally encoded roles of masculinity and femininity—or, to put it in more emic terms, having a bit of fun or paying me a compliment. I had developed ways of dealing with it. If I could tactfully deflect their advances—and I was getting increasingly good at this—I could usually get what I wanted for my research. As a poor graduate student, I had not much to offer people in exchange for their social knowledge, other than friendship and help in typing something in English. If all I had to offer in exchange for some men's time was the diversion of letting them "flirt" with me, then I was willing to let them flirt. Indeed, I had come to think of it as the price I sometimes had to pay for my research. (My experiences are neither unusual nor specific to the Arab world; as Katherine Clancy, Robin Nelson, Julienne Rutherford, and Katie Hinde reported in 2014, a majority of anthropology graduate students they surveyed reported having been sexually harassed in the field, and 20 percent reported having been sexually assaulted.)

But whether the concept of sexual harassment is cross-culturally meaningful or not, my husband wasn't as sanguine about it as I was. It infuriated him, and he blamed me for putting up with it. I was incriminated simply because they did it. In his view, I must have been doing something to invite it, or at least to not discourage it.

Perhaps what my husband was recognizing was that, as other anthropologists have done (e.g., Golde 1986), I was coping with sexual harassment by using my sexuality and men's advances instrumentally to gain knowledge. He knew I was not exchanging sex for money; his accusation that I was a "prostitute" was metaphorical.

It might be tempting to interpret my husband's reaction as part of an Arab cultural complex of honor and shame, but that would be grossly simplistic. It wasn't some culturally ingrained, knee-jerk impulse for him. His concentration on shaping and controlling my behavior, so overwhelming when I was in Egypt, was almost nonexistent when I was in the United States. He was alone and powerless as, from a distance, he watched me awkwardly fumble through fieldwork. He wanted to help me be a good anthropologist, and he wanted to keep me safe from predatory men.

Anthropology has a very peculiar methodology. The ethnographic method requires that the American anthropologist who wants to learn about Egypt doesn't do so by reading books or distributing a survey and analyzing responses. She uproots herself and moves across the globe to a dusty megalopolis, she learns a different language, she leaves behind her family and her own culture, and she immerses herself in the families and culture of the people she is writing about, becoming not only an observer but a participant in that culture. The ethnographic method also asks the anthropologist to suspend her own values and cultural beliefs enough to learn about another culture without judgment—or, at least, to set aside that judgment long enough to learn other worldviews. I was eager to explore a range of different moral codes and subcultures in Cairo, and for me, that meant learning about more than simply the dominant bourgeois ideal of respectable femininity that my husband urged me to embrace. He wanted me to learn about a particular set of cultural values that he endorsed. But I wanted to learn about more than just his idealized version of Arab culture. I wanted to learn about all the ways that people defied those dominant cultural ideals and yet still managed to find a place for themselves in Egyptian society.

As I chafed at my husband's restrictions and his remonstrations, the love that made all this conflict endurable was wearing thin for both of us. Also, the more limitations he put on whom I could talk to for my research, the less I was convinced of the anthropological value of learning the lessons he was trying to teach me. Why should I be a respectable woman, if I had to drop the whole part of my research project that focused on belly dancers? What if I wanted to know for my research what it meant to be *not* respectable? Since I had never been given any reason to worry about my personal safety, I couldn't see what was so bad about being not respectable, if the only consequence was a bad reputation. If all I had to fear was sexual harassment, and that was already the reality of my everyday life, then what was the value of being a respectable woman, with the attendant constraints on movement and behavior?

So I came home from that day of failing to set boundaries with Abu Ahmed with all this on my mind, frustrated and miserable and fed up. Abu Ahmed had urged me to call him the next morning to set up a time we could meet the following afternoon. I could not bear another hot day of trudging around the village with a lecherous old man if it meant that I had to not only fend off the old man's roving hands but then also listen to my husband call me a prostitute yet again.

If I was going to be accused of whoring for my research, then I might as well enjoy the metaphorical sex.

And so at that moment, I decided that I had enough data on the conflict between Egyptologists and villagers. I no longer cared if the ethnographic context for my village study was thin. I wasn't going to put up with Abu Ahmed anymore.

For my last six months of fieldwork in Cairo, I started investigating a completely different subject. I had already been writing down what people said about love, desire, and female respectability. But now, I decided, I would focus exclusively on these fascinating topics. I started closely observing and writing about people's relationships, their theories about how women should ideally behave, and how they actually *did* behave. As I documented the ways that women's and men's behavior is morally judged, stigmatized, and rewarded, I increasingly defied my husband. I socialized with belly dancers, and in many contexts I became a decidedly *not* respectable woman, though in other contexts I still clung to my respectable persona and hid the fact that my marriage was falling apart.

The material I have written about in this book emerged organically out of the conversations I had with my friends and research participants while I was engaged in a completely different research project about tourism in Egypt. It was not planned, and I did not deliberately go out recruiting a particular typology of research participants. Instead, I observed closely and listened to the conversations of those people I was already spending time with, and I asked follow-up questions. I paid attention to the things that interested them, and what people all wanted to talk about, I found, was love, desire, and social respectability and how those things were intertwined. I asked questions about the things that interested me, such as how these related to money and intimacy and what it meant to be a "respectable woman" or a "prostitute." I continued to ask questions over the years to come, and by the time I finished writing this book, over a decade had passed, during which I had written hundreds of pages of field notes on people's ideas about love, marriage, desire, affairs, and gender roles and on how these related to social norms and ideas about social respectability. This "slow ethnography" allowed me to see how people's ideas changed over time, shaped by important life events.

It is a convention of anthropological writing to have the first chapter of a book be a careful theoretical formulation of the topic and a systematic literature review. Typically, only after writing a theory-dense introductory chapter do we break out the stories that illustrate our theories.

But I want to invert that formula. Since I didn't go into the field with theories about love and desire but, rather, came to theorize these concepts through what I unexpectedly documented, I want to begin not with theory and a literature review but with an extended passage of ethnographic narrative. I will build from there to show how the slow accretion of data in the field became the foundation for my understanding of love and desire in terms of mimesis (a performative engagement with gender norms and national stereotypes), kinship (the mutual obligations that men and women feel toward each other, encompassing deep-seated feelings about what they owe to others and what is owed to them), and gift (the norms of reciprocity that govern intimate exchanges of sex and money). The thematic thread running through both the ethnographic narrative and all these different domains of theory is the simulacrum of social respectability.

Women and men engage with socially acceptable gender roles, creating narratives of self that simultaneously participate in those social ideals and defy them, emphasizing or hiding behaviors according to their need to present different social personas, but also claiming social respectability *no matter what their behavior.* Even sex workers and belly dancers—not considered respectable women by dominant social norms—call themselves respectable and demand respect from those around them. Meanwhile, as we shall see, others criticize women's behavior and call women prostitutes, whether or not they sell sex (or even have sex at all). What this demonstrates is that women's and men's moral status is a simulacrum, in the Baudrillardian sense: a copy that has no original, a substitution of the signs of the real for the real, which is thus *more real than the real.* I focus in particular on a woman's respectability as a representation that circulates, divorced from the original referent, independent of her actions, and constructed through intersubjective encounters. Women and their kin create idealized moral histories for themselves, and the fact that these are simulacra opens up possibilities for creative maneuvers not only in the social construction of their moral identities but in their pursuit of love and desire.

But before we elaborate on this theory, let us begin with the ethnographic story, stepping back in time to the turn of the millennium, to the very start of this research project, when I was getting to know about the love and desire of two women and two men: Ayah, an upperclass university student in her early twenties who had recently gotten engaged to middle-class Zeid; Kerim, Zeid's upper-middle-class friend; and Sara, a poor woman in her midtwenties who lived in the Cairo slums and who was in love with a married man named Ali.

Ayah, a sophomore at the American University in Cairo, asked if I could help her type a paper in English for one of her classes and promised me that afterward, she and Zeid, her fiancé, would take me out for dinner and dancing. She arrived at my apartment out of breath from the three flights of stairs and almost as soon as she saw me, she burst out in gasping, choking laughter.

"What?" I asked her. Her eyes were tearing; her laughter verged on hysterical. "What is it? Tell me!" I insisted.

She wiped her eyes. "I was in the taxi," she finally said, "and the taxi driver started talking to me, right? He was telling me about some old film. I wasn't really paying much attention, but I kept saying, 'Yes, yes,' to be polite.

"Then all of a sudden he says to me, 'Then Rushdy Abaza grabbed Faten Hamama's breast, he took it in his hand and started squeezing it like a fruit. It was big as a cantaloupe and just as juicy.' I didn't know what to say! I was just staring at him. Then he says to me, 'And speaking of melons, I'd like to get a handful of yours!' And he reaches his arm back behind him and he starts waving it around, trying to grab me while he's driving at the same time."

My eyes were wide. "What did you do? I hope you hit him!"

"No, I was too shocked! I just shouted at him, 'Please, please, don't do that!' and squeezed myself into the far corner of the car where he wouldn't be able to reach me. Then when he arrived, I got out of the car and threw the money at him and ran away."

"*What?*" I squeaked, appalled. "After all that, you *paid* him?"

"I just wanted to get rid of him, and if I didn't he would start arguing with me. And who knows what he would say about me on the street?"

There it was in a nutshell: the negative side of Ayah's aristocratic manners. She was from one of the old, elite, landowning families who had lost their property in the days of Abdel Nasser. Whenever anyone heard her last name, their eyebrows would go up a couple of millimeters. It was like being introduced to a Kennedy or a Rockefeller. She was raised to be perfectly proper and polite. It was impossible for her to be aggressive with a stranger, and she hated confrontations.

But Ayah's response was more than just a conditioned aversion to confrontation. Her question—"Who knows what he would say about me on the street?"—showed her fear that if she confronted this man for his gross violation of Egyptian social norms, he would flip the blame back onto her and it would affect *her* reputation in the neighborhood, not his. When it comes to sexual behavior, women's reputations are far more vulnerable than men's.

Women are also more vulnerable to having their freedom curtailed as a result of men's misbehavior. "Don't tell Zeid," Ayah warned me.

"He'll freak out and he won't let me take taxis anymore, and then I'll be stuck at home whenever my sister has the car."

When Zeid got to my house it was nearly midnight. He breezed past me into the room, giving me his standard greeting, "Hi, daaaaaaaaar-ling" in an exaggerated British accent. He didn't bother to kiss my cheek or even to shake hands, even though he hadn't seen me in a month. Zeid was charismatic, witty, and brilliant, and he was also completely bored by social niceties. People frequently considered him rude. He could be quite charming if he wanted to, but if he decided it wasn't worth the ef-fort, he would just yawn in your face. He had a lot of nervous energy and was always talking on his mobile phone, and he could never hold still while he was talking; as soon as the phone rang, he had to jump up and start pacing back and forth with his long legs, back hunched over as he gestured dramatically into the phone.

Ayah was irritated with him because he had arrived so late, and she was worried that we were going to be too late to get a seat at the club. She stared at him balefully. Feigning oblivion, he went over to kiss her. "My little cat," he said in Arabic, "you look lovely."

She brushed him away, pointedly looking at her watch.

"Such a little duck you are!" he simpered mockingly.

She flared her nostrils and picked up her papers.

"You still aren't done?" he said. "What have you been doing all this time?"

She put down the papers again. "And what have *you* been doing? Out with Ayman and Kerim again?"

"No, I was at work!" he said, rather defensively. "I was rushing to get over here on time, and look, it seems I didn't need to hurry after all, since you two are still working."

Ayah ignored him and resumed dictating her sociology paper to me. It was on cultural gender roles in Egypt, offering a feminist critique that drew heavily on the work of Moroccan sociologist Fatima Mernissi. She read out loud in English while I typed:

> A double standard applies to social norms for men and women. A man can do whatever he pleases without facing social stigma: he can stay out with his friends and come home late at night; he can date, smoke, drink, and even have premarital sex without people looking down on him. The last two (drinking alcohol and having sex outside marriage) are strictly prohibited in Islam, but culturally, they are tolerated behaviors for men. If a woman drinks, people will talk about her negatively behind

her back, and if she loses her virginity before marriage, she is considered practically unmarriageable, which is what drives the whole industry of hymen-replacement surgery. But if a man drinks, people look the other way, and if *he* has sex outside of marriage, they applaud his virility. In short, men are practically granted unlimited privileges and independence, whereas women's lives are constrained by rules of . . .

Zeid interrupted to disagree in Arabic. "That's not true, men are socially stigmatized for doing these things, just like women. A man who drinks too much gets called *khamragy*, and that's definitely an insult."

"No," she replied, "men only get called *khamragy* if they drink too much, like if they are drinking all the time and always getting drunk, but women would get that title if they drink at all. And besides, you know very well that it's much worse for a woman to be called *khamragy* than for a man to be called it."

"I could never drink or smoke in front of my father!"

"Yes, but a woman can't drink or smoke in front of *anyone* except her female friends. You would never let me smoke and drink in front of your friends."

"Well you *don't* drink and smoke, whether in front of other people or not, am I correct?"

"I'm speaking theoretically," she said. I kept a poker face. I knew she smoked at home with her sister.

Zeid still disagreed stubbornly. "No, the same rules apply for men as for women."

"Oh really?" said Ayah. "So then why do I have to be home by midnight at the *latest* if I'm not with you, but you don't even *meet* your friends until 12:30 a.m.? And God only knows when you come home! You sit there with Ayman and Kerim eating sandwiches from that disgusting roadside stand in Mohandiseen, and nobody says anything about you, because that's just what men do. Meanwhile, take Rasha. Just because she likes to go out driving around at night when she's bored, you know she has a bad reputation, and she hasn't ever even *kissed* a man! She's *that* innocent, and still people call her a prostitute just because she goes out late at night!"

"Well she *is* a prostitute. And retarded too." Rasha was Ayah's neighbor. She was pretty, blonde, and slow-spoken, and it wasn't clear to me whether Zeid really thought her mentally deficient or if he just disliked her. Probably the latter.

"No she is *not*, and you cannot imagine how sensitive she is when people say things about her. She's really so innocent, can you imagine?" she said, turning to me. "Thirty years old and she's never even been kissed!" Ayah put a hand over her heart.

"Okay, whatever. I doubt it," Zeid said, sneering. "But just finish the paper so we can go do something."

Ayah continued to dictate, and Zeid continued to interrupt and argue with her, and she decided to retract several points that he convinced her were too outlandish. Eventually he wandered into the study to make some free phone calls on my landline.

When Ayah finished dictating the paper, we went downstairs and got in Zeid's car. Ayah and Zeid both sullenly ignored each other as Zeid navigated through the empty back streets, past the pink Turkish embassy and the government buildings on Parliament Street. I spoke to break the silence. "So how is work, Zeid?"

"It's really hectic, you know. I'm so tired all the time."

"If you're so tired," Ayah interrupted, "why do you always stay out late with your friends?"

Ignoring her question, Zeid appealed to me in the back seat. "Look, Lisa, you can judge between us, we both know that you're fair and objective. Do you agree, Ayah?"

Ayah tossed her hair back. "Yes, let Lisa judge."

"Okay, I'll tell her my side first. Ayah thinks that 'going out' means going to a fancy place like Pomodoro. That means at least four hours for dinner and dancing. Ayah doesn't regard a quiet dinner with friends as 'going out,' so I have to always come up with some big night out to satisfy her. And to tell you the truth I'm getting really sick of Pomodoro. It's just these spoiled, rich assholes spending their fathers' money and they don't have anything else to do with their lives so they drive over there in their BMWs and Porsches and act pretentious. You see the same damn people there every night. Like stupid Clapping Guy, always standing on a table clapping and blowing his whistle in time with the music. He's like the orchestra leader for his whole stupid band of rich asshole clappers."

Ayah forgot that she was supposed to be telling me her complaints and spoke directly to Zeid. "You always say that you're busy and don't want to go out, and I swear I try to be understanding, but in the end, I find out that you go out anyway with the guys from work."

She twisted around in her seat to speak to me. "Like last night. Zeid was complaining about how he was so tired and that I dragged him all the way out in the horrible summer traffic. So I went home and then later I called him on his cell phone and I expected him to be at home in bed, and guess where he was? He was with Kerim and Ayman! That's after he kept yawning and complaining about how tired he was, but obviously he wasn't too tired to go meet *them*."

Zeid didn't respond, and the silence in the car was tense. I watched the multicolored neon lights of the feluccas reflected in the Nile. Finally Ayah turned her head and said to me, "I'm sorry to always drag you into our fights."

"Don't worry," I told her dryly. "I'm honored that you feel comfortable hanging out all your dirty laundry in front of me. It's good material. Later on I'll write about your fight in my field notes." Zeid snorted out a sharp laugh.

I thought about their argument. I suspected that there were other factors playing into this whole drama, factors that nobody could articulate. First of all, Zeid was probably broke. His father had had to pay for Ayah's *shabka* (gold jewelry, including her diamond engagement ring) and *mahr* (bridewealth), which his family had to give her when they got engaged. It was a large sum of money, and the expense came right on the heels of Zeid's sister's big engagement party, which meant his parents were also having to buy furniture in time for her to get married in the winter. It was the responsibility of the bride's family to furnish the new couple's flat, which the groom's family provides.

So when Zeid complained about going out, it was partly because he was broke and couldn't afford to take Ayah out for expensive dinners all the time. I didn't know whether he actually preferred to hang out with his male friends instead of Ayah, but it was much cheaper to eat at grubby outdoor places, places that weren't considered respectable enough for entertaining a fiancée. But he couldn't admit this directly. He might admit to being broke and not liking to ask his father for money, but he would never admit that this was at the root of his troubles with Ayah and their arguments about going out. Appearances are important, especially in the engagement period, and he didn't want Ayah—much less her family—to think that financial matters were a serious problem for him, or they might doubt his suitability as a groom. She was from an upper-class family; Zeid's family was solidly middle class. This was the time to prove himself. And Ayah would never suggest paying for their dates, nor would he ever accept such an arrangement. It would be shameful, a challenge to his very masculinity.

We arrived at Pomodoro, a restaurant-bar franchise with a small dance floor built out onto a platform that extended over the Nile. It was a hangout for Cairene elites of all ages, from students to aging business-men, who sometimes brought their wives but more often brought their mistresses. Pomodoro was unique among Cairo nightspots because it had a constantly rotating coterie of attractive foreign waitresses from South Africa and Europe, which went a long way toward ensuring its popularity.

We squeezed through the press of bodies at the door and I spoke to the maître d' in English. Even though I spoke Arabic, it was always my role to speak English here, since foreigners got preferential treatment. We found Kerim in a booth near the door. "Lisa!" he exclaimed. "Zeid told me you were back. Thank God for your safe arrival!"

"And may God keep you safe," I replied. We clasped hands.

"I missed you so much while you were in the US! How is your husband?"

"He's good, praise God; he sends you his greetings."

"May God keep him safe."

Once we finished this ritualistic exchange, we could speak more in-formally. "What's it like to be back in Cairo? Hot enough for you?"

"It's good to be back. I miss my husband, but it's good to see you and Zeid and Ayah."

I had just gotten back after a one-month trip home to visit my hus-band and family. In the first year I was in Egypt, when I was study-ing Arabic, I used to make a point of never talking about my husband. I didn't want to be an object of pity, always moaning about how home-sick I was. But then Kerim had commented on how strange it was that I never mentioned my husband. Didn't I love him? Didn't I miss him? Then why did I never mention him? Was I really married? After that, I made a point of talking about him and carrying around pictures to show people.

We all sat in the booth. Zeid sprawled on the zebra-print cushion next to Kerim, stretching his long legs out under the table. He was wearing a dark suit because he had come straight from work, but he had removed his tie and undone the top two buttons of his shirt. Ayah was wearing trousers and a sleeveless shirt. Her bare tanned arms looked good, and Zeid couldn't resist them. He put one arm around her and started squeezing the back of her upper arm. She frowned, rolled her eyes, and said without looking at him, "I know, fat. But not too fat." But he kept pinching her arms and said in a sarcastically simpering voice, "My darling has fat arms!"

She looked even more disgusted and pulled away from him, and as she did, he reached out to grab another handful of arm and squeezed. She pushed away his hand and said, "Ooph! You are very annoying! I know, now you are going to say that I have to start going on my diet again."

Zeid maintained a slightly wicked smile on his face and just said, "Who is my little duck? My little chubby duck!" Ayah moved to a chair on the other side of me and picked up a menu. She had a sullen look on her face, and Zeid kept smiling. I wondered if he had teased her deliberately to stop her from ordering an expensive meal. Ayah always ate salads when she was dieting, and salads were the cheapest items on the menu.

A waitress came over to take our drink order. She was petite and extremely fair, probably a natural blonde, but she had dyed her hair jet black and wore it in a short bob, which, with her coloring, produced a strange effect. She looked like a little punk china doll with her nose ring.

After she left with our order, Kerim said, "Do you remember the other really pretty blonde woman who was working here before?" We didn't. "She was very beautiful, an Englishwoman. Or maybe South African. Anyway, she married a friend of mine. He used to be a big playboy and drink a lot and run around, but now he mostly stopped drinking and I think the girl converted to Islam. She's living here with him."

"Why don't you try to marry a waitress from here?" I asked Kerim. I knew he was looking for a bride, and he often commented that he wanted a blonde.

"No *way.*"

I was surprised at how vehemently he had spoken. "Why not? What if she converted?"

"No way," he repeated, banging down his glass for emphasis.

"Why?"

"No matter what she's like with me, I'll never be able to forget that she used to be a waitress at Pomodoro. Fifteen years from now, I'll still always look back and remember how she had started working at a place like this where she was on display for all these men, and probably all my friends were flirting with her. . . . I'd never be able to get that out of my mind. I wouldn't ever be able to respect her, and I have to respect the mother of my children."

[handwritten margin note: good background necessary for respect]

"What about 'love conquering all' and making you forget the past?"

"People who say that aren't thinking about the long term. They're the ones who end up getting divorced. Okay, yes, maybe love conquers all in the beginning. He's infatuated with her, and he thinks she'll change and start living a respectable life. But then later it's going to start driving him crazy. He'll always be jealous. He'll always be worried about what she's doing when he's away. It will start to eat away at him, and they'll start fighting all the time." He put down his glass emphatically. "Marriage is a serious thing. Have an affair with a waitress from Pomodoro—good for you. But you're crazy to marry her. Marry someone who you will always respect."

"So why did your friend marry that waitress?"

Kerim shrugged. "Not everybody thinks like I do."

The waitress had brought drinks while Kerim was delivering his monologue on Pomodoro waitresses, but he was speaking in Arabic and figured she wouldn't understand. He cheerfully flirted with her while she took our dinner order. Ayah ordered a salad. Zeid's phone rang. He answered, then handed it to me. "It's your husband."

I took the phone. "*Habibi!* [My Love!] Hi!" I had given him Zeid's number because I didn't have a mobile phone. It was the first year they had appeared in Egypt, and they were really expensive.

"Who are you out with?"

"Zeid and Ayah and Kerim."

"Just those three? It doesn't look good, Lisa. It will look like you and Kerim are a couple." My then-husband was Arab and acutely concerned about my reputation, even among Egyptians he had never met.

"But we're not sitting together. I'm sitting next to Ayah." I walked out of the noisy restaurant to talk, wobbling in my platform heels as I paced over the cobbled driveway outside Pomodoro, where two black BMWs, an Audi, several Mercedes-Benzes, and a Jaguar were parked. (Zeid had parked his ancient Eastern European beater down the road.) Men in dark suits and women in cocktail dresses and lots of bling were pouring past me into the restaurant. I felt glamorous to be speaking on a mobile phone. It was only last week that I had even learned how to use one. Zeid had lent me his phone to call someone, and I dialed the number and then waited and waited but nothing happened. He had had to explain to me that you have to hit the call button after dialing.

"It's already one in the morning there, isn't it?"

"Yes but things don't even get going until twelve thirty. It's a weekend. And it's summer, everyone stays out late in summer. We'll go home at two o'clock."

"Who drove you there?"

"Zeid and Ayah."

"Okay." He sounded satisfied. "*Khaliki muhtarima* [Keep yourself respectable]," he said by way of ending the interrogation. "I love you."

I went back in and returned Zeid's phone to the center of the table. "My husband says hi," I announced.

"That's nice that he checks up on you; he must really care about you!" Ayah smiled at me. "You know, if a man doesn't show his jealousy, you don't feel that he really loves you."

I sat down next to her and she lowered her voice a bit. "Like Nellie and Ahmed." These were two friends of hers who were in law school who rarely came out with us because they were both studying all the time. "You know, I have never felt that he really loves her. I don't know. He just doesn't act jealous. When I'm with her, he never calls to ask what she's doing."

I thought about that. "Hey, by the way, Ayah, how do you say 'beak' in Arabic? Like a bird beak?" She looked at me curiously and told me.

The conversation shifted to extramarital affairs. "A man is always looking for a wife who is devoted to her children and family and who would never play around on her husband," Kerim observed, in a continuation of our earlier conversation about the suitability of marrying a Pomodoro waitress. "But a lot of men cheat."

men cheat, women loyal

"But," I said, "if the men are cheating, they have to be cheating with someone, so there obviously are women out there who the men are cheating with, and probably their wives who they imagine to be so pure are also cheating on their husbands with some other men."

It seemed perfectly logical to me, but Zeid looked extremely put out by the idea. It was not his idea of how the world worked. He scowled and ate another bite of food.

"No," Kerim argued, "the man is careful to chose someone to marry who would never cheat, and then he finds a different kind of woman to fool around with. The kind of woman he can date, he can take her out with him, but he won't marry her."

"What kinds of women are these?" I was thinking about my husband's admonition that I "keep myself respectable" and wondering which category of women Kerim would put me in. He seemed awfully judgmental, and though I didn't much care for my husband's constant haranguing about how I needed to see to my own reputation, Kerim's comments were making me think that maybe he was right.

"You see that woman with the long wavy black hair sitting at the end of the bar?"

"The one wearing the skirt with the slit up to her thigh?"

"Right," he said in a conspiratorial voice. "That woman is well known for being very wealthy and loose. Her father died and she inherited a lot of money and she has her own apartment and she has sexual relation-ships with men just for pleasure. She's a prostitute."

"A prostitute?" I interrupted. Kerim had been speaking in Arabic, but he said "prostitute" in English. I was confused. If she had sex just for pleasure, how could that make her a prostitute?

"A *sharmuta*," he said reluctantly, rolling his eyes. The term was used throughout the Arab world (though in rural Egypt the term refers not to a woman of ill repute but to a fabric rag used for mopping floors), but the word in Arabic was too rude to say in polite company. It translates bet-ter as "whore," which doesn't necessarily connote taking money for sex, but for some reason Egyptians rarely said the word "whore" in English.

I looked over at the woman again. She was talking cheerfully to a man with beefy arms, the sort of pumped-up man that skinny, geeky Zeid passionately hated for spending time in the gym. "How do you know? And how do you know her, anyway?"

"I know some of the men who dated her. They told me. But apart from that, it's obvious by the fact that she has her own apartment. A re-spectable woman does not live alone."

"I live alone," I pointed out.

"You're a foreigner."

"So people will think that I'm not respectable?"

"No, of course not, everyone knows that you don't have a choice. You can't live with your family, and anyway, people here know that family ties aren't so strong in the West and people don't live with their families."

"I'm very close to my family!" I exclaimed. My Arab husband had warned me to always talk about my family so that people would think I was respectable. Kin relations anchored a person. Someone without kin was someone who couldn't be trusted, someone who might do anything. I kept family pictures in a little photo album in my purse to show peo-ple, to establish my credentials as kin to good people.

Kerim leaned back and laughed. "Lisa, I'm not talking about *you*. Don't get so defensive."

"Well, maybe that woman just likes to have her own place instead of living with her mother."

"Yes, and *why* does she like to have her own place instead of living with her mother? Because she wants to live in a way that she can't live if she's with her mother. Which means she wants to bring men home with her. A respectable woman doesn't live alone. She lives either in her par-ents' house or in her husband's house.

"So you see," Kerim continued, "there are two kinds of woman, like I told you. A normal woman has a sexual relationship only in the context of a respectable family life. The other class of women are like that woman, they are *sukhna 'awi* [too hot]. And they're always going to find trouble because they can't keep their desire under control, and men pick up on that, so they find themselves in the category of women who men want to play around with but will never marry. Then they get older and older, and they get a reputation, and then they find that they can't get married at all. A woman like that one at the bar, she's lucky, because she can move out and live her own life. It's not just because she has money; it's also because her father died and she has no brothers so there's no one to protect her and make her live respectably. But most women are forced to choose between either becoming an old maid, living in their parents' home, or else marrying someone they don't love who doesn't know their history."

"Maybe she'll find someone she loves who doesn't know about her messing around."

"Of course he'll know."

"No, no!" I said excitedly. "There are operations to restore a torn hymen, and all kinds of other tricks that I heard about."

Kerim winced at my discussion of female genitals, completely inappropriate for conversation in mixed company. "I'm not talking about that. She can try those tricks with someone she doesn't love. But if she loves someone, then she won't be able to control herself with him and he'll see that she's too hot [*sukhna*] with him, and he'll figure that if she's like that with him, she was like that with other men, and then he'll never marry her."

"So she's stuck in a loveless marriage?" I frowned.

"It's better than staying at home an old maid—at least she'll have more freedom. If she stays with her parents, then she's always living in someone else's home, never her own."

"And if she's married, it's easier for her to keep playing around, anyway," interrupted Zeid with a leer.

"You know," Ayah interjected, "my mother always warned me that it was better for a woman to marry someone who loves her than to marry someone she loves. Then he will always take care of her and not lose interest. And she can learn to love him with time."

"Is your mother speaking from personal experience?" Zeid asked sharply.

Ayah's face suddenly became hard, and she just stared at him. She was angry not only at the words themselves but also at the way Zeid had said them, at the disapproval in his voice, at his tone, which he usually reserved for criticizing Ayah's sisters and friends like Rasha but which should never be used to talk about her mother. Zeid stared back and then looked away under the force of Ayah's gaze, realizing that he had erred.

"In any case," said Kerim, politely pretending that this small altercation had not occurred, "it's true that whoever loves less in the relationship has more power. If a woman loves her husband more than he loves her, then he'll cheat on her all the time and she won't be able to say anything because she'll be afraid to lose him to one of those other women."

We watched a group of women in short skirts come in the door. "What about the women he's having affairs with, does he love those women, too?" I asked. "Or does he love only his wife? Or does he love those women and *not* his wife?"

"Of course he doesn't love them," said Zeid. "He loves his wife. The others, he's just using them, just playing around with them. It's all about sex. He doesn't respect them and he doesn't love them."

"He might love them," said Kerim.

"Maybe some men, but in general, a man doesn't love his mistress, and even if he loves her a little, he'll never love her the way he loves his wife," Zeid argued.

"Why? What makes you so sure?" I asked.

"If he loved her, he would marry her. If he doesn't want to marry her, then you have to ask why? Obviously he doesn't love her, or he wouldn't take advantage of her, sleeping with her outside marriage."

"Maybe there are other reasons why he can't marry her," said Ayah. I didn't realize that she had still been listening.

"Like what?" Zeid asked tauntingly.

She gave him a look of exasperation. "Maybe she's married, or maybe he doesn't want to hurt his wife. And anyway, unless he's lower class, it doesn't look good for him, socially, to marry more than one woman. People really look down on that."

"They are two different kinds of love," said Kerim.

"There is love, and then there is sex. Don't confuse the two, brother," said Zeid.

"No," Kerim argued. "It's not just a question of sex. If he just wants sex, he can have sex with his wife, or if he wants something kinky he can go to prostitutes or whatever, but he doesn't have a long-term relationship with his mistress just for sex."

"For what, then?" asked Zeid, disdainfully.

"Maybe he doesn't really feel comfortable with his wife; maybe she's too formal and uptight. Or maybe she's proud and he doesn't really feel like a man, like he's in control. Or maybe she is neglecting him for her work, or maybe she loves her children more than she loves him."

Zeid was shaking his head. "If he really loves a woman, he won't make her not respectable and he won't keep treating her like a prostitute; he'll marry her."

Ayah also disagreed with Kerim. "It's not about love and it's not because he's feeling neglected," she said. "It's about conquest and it's about living a fantasy. He wants to imagine that he's still a young man, able to catch pretty women, instead of facing the fact that he's a father and he has responsibilities at home. He wants his wife to give him children, and then he complains when she gets fat because she's pregnant. Or maybe he feels old and he wants to prove that he can still catch women, and he wants to show off to his friends so that they think he's very manly. That's why all these men like to take their mistresses out dancing with them at places like this, so that everyone can see him with her. He doesn't think of her reputation, and he doesn't even worry about it getting back to his wife; he goes around with her right here in public."

I could see Ayah and Zeid holding hands under the table. Zeid's argument that a man could only love his wife, never his mistress, seemed to have improved Ayah's mood after her earlier irritation with Zeid.

We left the restaurant at 2:30 a.m. Zeid and Ayah waited until I was up the stairs of my building before driving off. Alone in my apartment, a wave of loneliness hit me. I thought of Ayah and Zeid, holding hands under the table, and felt a pang of longing for my husband. Whenever I came back to Egypt after a trip home, my emotions oscillated wildly. Often I was content. I would plod along with my life and not think about anything except how to stay cool. But other times the depression would come back suddenly and settle in like a weight on my chest, hemming in my breathing, digging little claws under my skin. Sometimes it didn't talk to me; it would look out from its perch on my chest and see what I saw in silence. Other times, especially when I was alone, it would stare me in the face and argue with me.

"You're all alone here in Egypt. Two more years away from your husband and your family. Your career, your fieldwork: what is the use of that? What kind of life is this, anyway?"

I closed the shutters to the balcony and crawled under the mosquito netting with my laptop, hoping that I hadn't let any mosquitoes in with me. I turned on the computer and started typing up field notes in the dark.

The next morning when I woke up it was already hot again, and I was sweating in my nightdress. I pushed the mosquito netting aside and stared out the window, waving away a fly and wondering how to be an anthropologist. How could I insinuate myself into people's lives, when everyone was so busy?

The phone rang from inside the bedroom and I ran to answer it.

"Hello?"

Silence.

"Hellooh!"

Finally the caller spoke in a husky voice. "I love you." It was the prank caller. He called about two or three times a day, but usually in the afternoon. Sometimes he said, "I love you," and other times it was, "I want to fuck you," and probably, I thought, it depended on what stage he had reached in his masturbating.

He had spoken in heavily accented English, but I responded in Egyptian Arabic. "*Inta labis badlat firakh?*"

There was a pause, then a disconcerted voice said, "What?"

I enunciated very clearly and spoke slowly in Arabic: "Are—you—wearing—a—chicken—suit?"

Silence.

"Because I really only want men who wear chicken suits. I'm talking with feathers and a beak. So please, don't call again unless you have a chicken suit. Then we can talk. Don't forget. Chicken suit. Feathers. Beak."

I hung up the phone and grinned, pleased with myself. The thought of the chicken suit will definitely put a damper on his amorous mood, I thought. Then the phone rang again.

I scowled, turned off the ringer, and then stood by the window, hoping a bit of a breeze would waft in. The air was clear that day, no smog, and I could see out as far as the Mokattam Hills.

I'll go to the antiques shop, I thought suddenly. There was a shop in al-Hussein district, not far from Mokattam, and I liked to sit with the workers there and pick through the antiques. I felt relieved to have a plan for the day. I could fill up half a day sitting with them, and I could take notes afterward and that would count as fieldwork. Surely the people who worked in the shop would have something to say of anthropological significance.

When I got to the shop, I found it was a sweathouse. The electricity was out. There had been a small fire the night before, they told me, two stores down, and the shop owner had turned the electricity off for everyone to prevent disaster. It wasn't dark, because they had opened a trapdoor in the roof to let in light. But no electricity meant no air conditioning and no fan, no air circulation at all. It was sweltering.

I sat on a chair and started fanning myself with a postcard. Sara was there, and Nesma, and George. The shop owner hadn't arrived yet, so it was just the four of us.

Sara was in a terrible mood because of the heat, and she looked like she was about to cry. "I can't take it. It's giving me a headache—how can anyone work in such conditions?" Finally, she got exasperated and took off her long-sleeved shirt, revealing a white camisole underneath. George adjusted his glasses and stared pointedly. Sara turned her back on him and said, "Just pretend today that I am a foreigner," and went on fanning herself. I hiked up my long skirt to the knee. Sweat was trickling down my legs.

Nesma looked over and shrieked, "Allah! Look how white and plump her legs are!"

"I wish I were brown," I said, ignoring the plump comment. I knew she meant it as a compliment.

Nesma scoffed. "Who wishes to be brown? I wish I were white!" She pulled out a pocket mirror and a black magic marker and drew a beauty mark on her dark upper lip. Then she adjusted her headscarf.

Sara looked over and saw George still watching her. "What are you looking at?" she demanded sharply.

"Nothing." He pushed his glasses back up on his nose and said to the room in general, "You know, Sara is a man. She looks like a woman, but don't be fooled. Really she's a man." Sara kept working with her head down and didn't respond.

"What do you have to say to that, Sara?" I asked. "Are you a man?"

She raised one eyebrow. "And do I look like a man?"

"So why do they say you're a man?" Sara didn't answer. On the other side of the room, George was repairing the clasp on a small silver chest.

"She's tough," he said to me. "She looks feminine, but in fact, inside she's tough and strong like a man; she thinks like a man."

"So this is a negative or a positive thing?" I asked.

George looked up from the chest and considered a moment. "It is positive."

Nesma leaned over and said to me in a stage whisper, "George just says that because he's scared of Sara." She reached over my head to a shelf above the desk for a bottle of metal polish and a rag.

"Don't polish too much," George warned her. "The foreigners like things looking old and dark, not shiny."

I grinned. "That's true! Don't waste your time polishing."

Sara said to me in a low voice, "Yesterday I saw Ali."

"Who is Ali?"

"My beloved!" she blurted out indignantly, as if I should have known.

"But I thought you both ended things! Weren't you all sad about that before?"

"We're always like that, on and off; that's the history of our relationship. But now we're back together again." She touched her cheek. "I wore a blouse like that one to see him, but transparent." She nodded at the blouse she had taken off and hung over the back of her chair. "He got *sooo* angry! He slapped me and then he ripped it off me and tore it into pieces. I had to go home wearing only the camisole I had on underneath." She smiled, still touching her cheek. I stared at her.

he slapped me, grinning

"Didn't you get in trouble with your family when you came home like that?"

"I made sure nobody saw me." She took a sip from her Pepsi.

"But didn't the neighbors see you?"

"I don't care what the neighbors say."

"How obnoxious of Ali! He needs to control his temper. How dare he hit you!" She just smiled, leaving me even more perplexed.

"After he ripped off my shirt," she said, "then he kissed me . . ." Her voice trailed off, a smile still playing around her mouth.

"He's married. Do you think you have any future with him?" Sara shrugged and tied her hair in a ponytail at the nape of her neck.

I persisted, still fanning my sweating face with the postcard. "Would you ever agree to be a second wife?"

Sara clicked her tongue and moved her head in a gesture that meant no.

"Does he have children?"

"He has two."

"Does he love his wife?"

"Of course!" Sara frowned. "Who has a wife and doesn't love her?"

"I'm sure it's possible," I said dryly.

"Of course he loves her, but she gives him problems. She's always complaining and causing arguments."

I felt a trickle of sweat roll down the back of my knee and suppressed an urge to scratch at it. "So it's okay to date a married guy?"

"Yes. Why not?"

Nesma said mockingly, "They're the classic star-crossed lovers. Romeo and Juliet, Antar and Abla."

I glanced at each of them in turn, but Sara didn't seem concerned about the fact that Nesma had heard her talking about Ali. I was surprised that she was speaking so openly about her love for a married man in front of her coworkers.

"Ali loves his wife and children," Sara said firmly. "And I love his kids too!"

"Oh, please." I rolled my eyes. "And I suppose you love his wife as well. So as long as you're already part of the family, why don't you just marry him? Why not be a second wife?"

"Not the second, nor the third."

"Why not?"

"Because people look down on that. They would accuse me of taking him away from his family. Of course, it's not forbidden; he can marry up to four." She fanned herself. "But the way Egyptians see it, it's wrong to take him from his wife and especially to take him from his children."

"So look for someone else you can marry and make yourself respectable."

"I'll never leave Ali. I can't love anyone else. I'll love him till I die." She spoke loudly enough for everyone to hear.

"You're stubborn and you're irrational," called Nesma from the dark corner of the shop where she was clearing cobwebs off some brass lanterns.

But Sara just ignored her. "I had a lot of other people go to my mother and propose, but I can't stand anyone else. Anyway, I'm pushing twenty-five; soon I'll be an old maid. After a few more years it'll be too late for me to marry anyone else. All my neighbors have gotten married, even the ones who are younger than me. Even if I do marry someone else, I'll keep loving Ali. And I'll keep seeing him."

George shook his head. "She's crazy." Sara ignored him. "You're crazy, O mother of corruption," he said loudly in a singsong voice, peering cross-eyed at a clasp he was holding close to his face and manipulating with needle-nose pliers, as his glasses slid almost off the tip of his nose.

Nesma flopped down on a folding chair and untied her headscarf, not caring if George saw her curly hair underneath. "She needs to find someone else to love who can make her forget Ali. She needs to marry someone else and put him out of her mind. There is no good in this relationship. It has no future, and only bad will come of it." She rewrapped the scarf and pinned the loose end. "Anyway, the guy is no good. He doesn't really care about her; he's just playing with her. She's the one that pursued him. He knows that he's got her, and so he's not interested—he's just using her. Man is naturally a hunter. He loves the chase. He doesn't like an easy catch. She made it too easy for him, and now he can't take her seriously." Sara frowned but kept silent.

While Nesma had been talking, the man who worked in the store next door came up to chat with his neighbors. He had a large round belly and he was dabbing sweat from his upper lip. He kissed George on both cheeks and clasped hands, then waved genially at the women in the room. "God, it's hot in here. What are all of you talking about?"

"Love," I offered. "Sara says she can love only one person."

"On the contrary," he said, trying to balance himself on a small stool. "Love is so big that it encompasses more than one person."

"And are you married?" I asked him. He nodded. "And do you think you could love someone else besides your wife?"

"Of course! I'm looking for another wife! But don't tell the first one that."

"You'll marry two women?"

"What do you mean, two? I'll marry three or four! Islam says we can marry up to four. Why not marry all I can find?" He grinned.

"Oh, please!"

He said, "Look, it's like food. You're hungry, you want to eat. My wife is an orange. Orange is nice, very sweet. But sometimes you get sick of only having orange. Sometimes it gives you indigestion. You need to taste other fruit: banana, fig, mango, custard apple!" He laughed loudly.

I was indignant. "Say your wife gets sick of orange, should she go find herself some banana? And maybe some mango and fig? Depending on whatever is in season, of course."

George, who had finally finished sorting out the problem with the clasp, laughed. "Ha! She's right, what if your wife wants to try banana, what are you going to do then? I'm sure she's sick of orange by now." Big Belly laughed genially, unconcerned with the idea. His stomach jiggled with his laughter.

Sara gave him a disapproving look. "Before you go looking for another wife, you need to lose some weight. You can't go looking for another bride in that condition."

"You know, if you find yourself another wife, or three more wives, you're going to have to buy lots of gold," I pointed out, feeling clever to know this detail about *shabka* and marriage in the Arab world. "It's going to be very expensive."

"No, it's easy to find women to marry, and you don't have to buy them gold, because they're just so happy to be married. Everyone wants to mess around with women these days, go out with them, but nobody is serious and wants to marry them. So when I propose to them, they'll be so happy to get married that they won't require gold."

"Okay, but they're still expensive, because you have to put them all in a different apartment, and don't tell me that apartments don't cost a small fortune here."

"Why should each have her own apartment? I'll just put them each in a different room of one apartment. That should be enough for them to have their own space."

George peered over his glasses and said sarcastically, "Why don't you just put them all in the same room? One room should be enough for everyone. Each can have a corner of the room and call it her own space."

Sara looked at Big Belly and said, "Just lose some weight first, please. That stomach of yours is disgusting." He patted his belly and stood up to go, still laughing.

"How long have you been married, anyway?" I asked him.

"Seven months."

George said, "He's thirty-five and his wife is only eighteen, and she's young and pretty and naïve."

"You've only been married for seven months and you're already looking for someone else? Give it some time to at least get tired of your first wife!"

"I'm tired of orange! I need to taste the other fruits!" He wiped away tears of laughter.

After he left, I asked the others curiously, "Is he serious about another wife?"

Sara tossed her head and said, "Are you kidding? His wife would cut his throat if he took another wife, and he knows it! She's not so naïve as George thinks."

2nd wife conclusion

- At what social class does the matter of respectability shift? Or is Sara just "unrespectable"
- Can women's jealousy be a sign of love?

CHAPTER 2

Mimesis, Kinship, Gift, and Other Things That Bind Us in Love and Desire

Defining Love and Desire

What are love and desire? In her book *Desire/Love* ("It's like being kissed hard on the brain by an angel with a strap-on," declares the cover blurb), Lauren Berlant offers these definitions:

> Desire describes a state of attachment to something or someone and the cloud of possibility that is generated by the gap between an object's specificity and the needs and promises projected onto it. . . . This means that your objects are not objective, but things and scenes that you have converted into propping up your world, and so what seems objective and autonomous in them is partly what your desire has created and therefore is a mirage, a shaky anchor. . . .
>
> By contrast, love is the embracing dream in which desire is reciprocated. . . .
>
> But there is a shadow around this image: who is to say whether a love relation is real or is really something else, a passing fancy or a trick someone plays (on herself, on another) in order to sustain a fantasy? This is a psychological question about the reliability of emotional knowledge, but it is also a political question about the ways norms produce attachments to living through certain fantasies. (Berlant 2012, 6–7)

Berlant's definition of desire has helped me think through the persistence of Sara's desire for Ali, her continued love for a married man who hit her and refused to marry her and give her the social respectability she craved. Sara's desire for Ali was a partially reciprocated fantasy, an attachment generated in the space between their (sometimes violent)

[handwritten margin notes: "desire", "love", "does she crave it fr. seems wrong to me"]

romantic relationship and the needs and promises of love, affection, and the possibility of future attachment—perhaps marriage as a second wife. When he slapped her for wearing a transparent blouse, that violence was itself part of that tantalizing promise, possibility, and fantasy. To her, it signaled the jealousy of a man in love, a violence born of passion, the instinct of a man with his female kin: controlling, punishing, possessive, but also loving (Ghannam 2013). In that slap, Ali was feminizing Sara and masculinizing himself at the same time; the combined violence and sexual charge of that moment, hinted at in Sara's wistful expression as she remembered it, "socialized each other into the links between gender, sexuality, love, and power . . . patriarchal connectivity inscribed as love" (Joseph 1999, 116).

Here I am paraphrasing Suad Joseph's analysis of a slap given by a loving brother to his sister in Lebanon—a slap that bothered the anthropologist even as the sister being slapped declared that she didn't mind—"it doesn't even hurt"—and that she would like a husband like her brother (Joseph 1999, 115). Joseph analyzes this slap in terms of "patriarchal connectivity" and love. Like Farha Ghannam, who carefully analyzes male violence, particularly toward female relatives, and the circumstances under which Egyptians consider such violence an illicit action versus an appropriate expression of masculine concern for female kin, Joseph sees this slap as alerting us to the complex emotional terrain of power enacted in the intersubjective creation of gender roles and intimate relationships and the ways that violence and love can be intertwined. Or, to return to Berlant's analysis, Sara's fantasy of attachment was a psychological phenomenon within the individual that, at the same time, raises political questions about how social norms around gender roles produce particular types of fantasies of attachment.

While Berlant's definitions of love and desire are productive, in this ethnography, my goal is not to impose my own favorite definitions of love and desire onto my research material but, rather, to excavate my informants' own definitions of love and desire. The problem, as we can see from the previous chapter, is that my informants had a multiplicity of definitions that were often contradictory. Not only do their definitions not agree with Berlant's, but they don't even agree with each other's. Kerim and Zeid and Ayah debated whether a man could love only a respectable wife or also (or only) a mistress he desired, who herself might represent not only sexual novelty but also an escape from the heavy duties of masculine responsibility. Here, there was little consensus over whether love (*hubb*) is contiguous with sexual desire (*raghba*) or only with respect. Ayah's mother advised her daughter that the balance of power in a relationship was determined by who loved less, and Kerim agreed, but Zeid protested.

There are a great many words in Arabic for love and desire. The words that my informants most often used for love was *hubb*, and for desire, *raghba* or *'ayiz* (wanting). Other Arabic terms for love, desire, and passion include *hawa*, *shaghaf*, *'ishq*, and *shauq*, which all have slightly different connotations. They appear frequently in pop culture (*hawa* is more commonly used than *hubb* in songs, for example) and in literature but not as commonly in colloquial, everyday speech. In the Qur'an, terms used to talk about love are *hubb* (which can refer to romantic love but also love for God, wealth, and sin, as well as God's love for people) and *muwadda* (which connotes fondness and affection, both between groups and between individuals) (Mahally, n.d.). But in general, "love" is a good English gloss for the Arabic *hubb*; both can equally be used to talk about one's love for kin, romantic love, and the way one feels about an excellent flavor of ice cream.

In short, the linguistic possibilities for talking about love, desire, and passion in Arabic are many: a range of words, all evoking rich cultural histories, are like open boxes into which multiple concepts and experiences can be packed.

The conversation recorded in chapter 1 between four friends in a nightclub illustrates the difficulty in finding beliefs about love that are culturally shared. Nevertheless, we can see from that discussion that there *are* concerns in common: a concern to understand the relationship between love and desire and respect by debating the nature of the feelings that a man feels for his wife and for his mistress, or by categorizing women according to the constraints that personal inclination and kin placed on their sexual desire. As Michael Jackson has pointed out to me (personal communication), "What We Talk about When We Talk about Love" (the title of a 1981 Raymond Carver short story) is not just love but a language for talking about our lives, our aspirations, and our disappointments. Talking about love is a way that people make sense of their world.

[margin note: Common concerns]

Globally, discos and nightclubs are sites for nonnormative domesticity, structuring the availability of intimacy outside kinship (Lyttleton 2014). The Pomodoro nightclub was a site for Ayah and Zeid's courtship ritual, allowing them a degree of public intimacy as Ayah enacted her own sense of respectable femininity, deferring to her future husband's authority and showing that she was a modern yet respectable upper-class woman who went out at night but dressed modestly, while Zeid demonstrated his respectable masculinity by showing concern for her family and neighbors (however badly expressed) and proving his wage-earning potential as her future husband. They were both engaged in a courtship ritual that was moving toward a respectable, normative, heterosexual relationship of marriage. Nevertheless, to some extent the courtship and the courtship site were both nonnormative because, prior to their recent engagement, Ayah had hidden similar excursions and her relationship with Zeid from her father, who would not have condoned his daughter going alone to a nightclub with a man to whom she was not engaged. Even after their engagement, Ayah did not tell her father about her late-night excursions with Zeid, telling him rather that she was "going out with friends." My fifth-wheel presence lent legitimacy to their excursions, since my being there with them kept their dates from appearing too intimate, in case anyone who knew Ayah's relatives spotted them and reported back.

Ayah and Zeid did not perfectly live up to the Egyptian ideals of femininity and masculinity, nor did they always agree on their roles. Ayah rebelled against Zeid's attempts to assert his masculine authority in judging her friend Rasha's moral status and her mother's philosophy of marriage. Zeid felt that Ayah's demands for expensive excursions were not in line with his ideal of a supportive, passive fiancée (even though her assertiveness and independence were part of what he adored about her). And Ayah felt that, by providing too few excursions, Zeid failed to sufficiently prove his ability as a future breadwinner and attentive husband. But their love and affection for each other bridged these gaps in their performance of culturally idealized—or "respectable," a term that was ubiquitous in all their discussions—feminine and masculine social roles.

This particular nightclub was a site not only for extrakinship intimacy but also for debating the nature of intimacy itself. This cacophony of Cairene theories and beliefs about love and desire, gender and respectability, sexuality and morality illustrates that culture is not a set of unified, shared beliefs but, rather, "the organization of diversity" (Wallace 2009; see also Abu-Lughod 1991). Anthropologist L. A. Rebhun, writing about love in Brazil, offers a definition that acknowledges this multiplicity of (sometimes contradictory) ideas, experiences, and affects:

> Love is not a singularity. . . . Its use as a gloss for deep emotion covers a
> great variety of sentiments bound together in the continuous stories of

longtime acquaintance, interpersonal interaction, and mutual interdependence. A declaration such as "I love you" made between lovers might better be described as a characterization of a stance or attitude of the lover toward the beloved than as a description of a steady state of singular sentiment. (Rebhun 1999, 59)

Rebhun sees love in terms of not only affect but also the social roles that one plays: "Any named sentiment has an associated role. In addition to feeling anger, one acts angrily; in addition to feeling love; one acts like a lover" (ibid., 30). This is also an important insight for understanding love, which my Egyptian informants so frequently described in terms of kinship roles.

But even this definition doesn't fully encompass the meanings of "love" that appear in the ethnographic exposition up to this point. For my prank caller, for example, "I love you" alternates with "I want to fuck you," and here love is not a declaration between lovers or even a feeling per se but rather a word spoken to heighten the autoerotic experience and harass a woman.

Where my informants' attempts to define love do agree with Berlant's analysis is in terms of the imperative to define and narrate. Berlant notes that "the difficulty of determining love's authenticity has generated a repository of signs, stories, and products dedicated to verifying that the 'real thing' exists both among people and in other relations" (Berlant 2012, 7). We can see this impulse to authenticate and verify in the debate among Zeid, Kerim, and Ayah over the meaning of love, or in Ayah's discussion of the semiotics of jealousy as an expression of love.

Desire is complexly entangled with the concept of love in this ethnographic narrative, making it hard to place neat boundaries around them or to define them as discrete terms. At one point, Kerim describes too much *love* (*hubb*) as that which leads women to lose control and give in to sexual desire, while at another, he describes women who can't control themselves as those who have an excess of sexual *desire* (*raghba*). (Notably, desire is described with a temperature metaphor: someone with too much desire is "too hot." The metaphor translates easily into English, which has similar metaphors.) For Sara, desire and love seem to be inextricably linked and perhaps synonymous: she can only desire (*'aiza*) the man she loves and vice versa, even when she knows that that desire is not a likely route to a marriage that will secure her status as a respectable woman.

Running through these narratives of love, desire, and respectability we see the themes of mimesis, kinship and gift.

The mimicry of (or the failure to mimic) expected gender and social roles, for example, is a recurring theme, whether as the pressure Zeid feels to perform the role of a man ready to support his future wife (and her demands for expensive social excursions) or my anxiety over playing the role of loving wife in order to secure my status as a respectable woman. (As we will see in the following chapters, the tourism economy makes mimetic role-playing around gender and sexuality even more complicated, as men and women engage not only with each other but also with their imaginations of how someone from another country expects a man or woman to behave.)

Kinship and responsibility toward kin is another recurring theme. The closer Zeid and Ayah get to marriage, the more right he feels he has to critique Ayah's and her friends' and female relatives' behavior, as he prepares to take on the role of protective and controlling male kin. Ayah's love for Zeid is demonstrated, in part, by respecting his demands as her future husband as he declares whom she may socialize with and by acknowledging that he would have the right to tell her she couldn't take taxis any longer if he believed it wasn't safe. Meanwhile, as my husband attempts to do the same from across the globe, my Egyptian friends nod approvingly at this evidence of his love. Constraint—preventing a wife from staying out late at night or a fiancée from smoking or a girlfriend from wearing a too-revealing blouse—is seen as synonymous with care, and jealousy (*gheera*) is the language through which a man expresses both romantic love for a girlfriend or wife and brotherly care for female kin (Joseph 1999).

Closely related to kinship is the gift economy—that is, the circulation of valuables outside a commodity exchange. In this economy, property (goods and money) mediates social relations. Men display their social status by spending on women. In so doing (or in implying their ability to do so by flaunting their wealth), they signal not only their interest, love, and desire but also their ability and willingness to take on the responsibilities of particular masculine social roles (Ghannam 2013).

The thread running through all these theories is the work that people do to construct and deconstruct moral identities, the slippages that occur when these roles are not played very well, and the way everyone copes with the gap between the cultural ideals and the reality of how different people inhabit (or reject) those ideals. Zeid works to perform his role of capable fiancé, even as he chafes at the demands Ayah places on him and deflects accusations that he is not capable enough. Ayah hides her smoking and the taxi driver's attempted sexual assault in order to play the role of respectable fiancée. I engage performatively (calculat-

dramance!

ing where to sit, how to talk about my husband, and when to break out the family photo album) with an imagination of local expectations about how a respectable woman would behave in a completely unrespectable situation, living alone in a city an ocean away from her husband.

As a foreign anthropologist, my attempts at playing appropriate social roles are more fumbling than my friends', but we are all playing roles that engage with our understandings of the social expectations around us. But while the terms "role" and "perform" might evoke a falseness or lack of authenticity, I am not using them in such cynical ways. Rather, I am evoking Judith Butler's (1999) sense of gender as performed and Connell's (1995) as reflective, generative, multiple, and contested. Gender is produced with reference to cultural ideals but is articulated anew with every individual performance, and it is also internalized as part of our authentic self: not only is gender our identity that we perform for the world, but it is also our internal subjectivity (Bourdieu 1977), embodied in the way we move and interact with the world and the way we feel—especially the way we feel love and desire.

Gender and love and desire are, in short, identity and subjectivity, continually created and re-created dialectically with the social world around us. Our understanding of those cultural rules that inform our subjectivities and help us craft and present socially acceptable identities are assembled and reconfigured intersubjectively, through our interactions with others. My understanding of the cultural rules is shaped when I express concern about what people will think about my living alone, and my friend Kerim reassures me that it is okay because I am a foreigner. Ayah's understanding of the cultural rules is reinforced when Zeid calls her friend a prostitute because she goes out alone late at night, thus conveying his expectation that Ayah had better not go out without him. Zeid's understanding of the expectations on him as a male-provider-in-training is reconfigured when Ayah complains about his sandals and late-night excursions with male friends.

Meanwhile, talk about and criticism of other people's behavior similarly works to communicate people's perceptions about the rules for maintaining a moral social identity. As theorists of gossip and rumor have pointed out, talk communicates social norms and disciplines those who deviate from them (Stewart 1996). Talking about the "prostitute" at the bar who lives alone and thus must not be a respectable woman signals to everyone else at the table that people are always watching and making judgments and passing them around. The man who goes to nightclubs every night and stands on the table clapping because he is supported by his rich daddy and doesn't have to work hard to build his career is not a respectable man, ready to marry and support a family, Zeid tells us, reminding others that Clapping Man is Zeid's own polar opposite and is of lesser moral value in spite of his greater economic worth. These judgments communicate ideals and discipline us all into conforming with them.

Unni Wikan makes a useful distinction between the general *kalam innas* ("people's talk," which might also be glossed as "rumor") and specific instances of talking (gossip) in Cairo:

> Gossip . . . is different from the people's talk in that it has both a face and an origin. Whereas *kalam innas* arises without anyone quite knowing where or how, gossip has a definite source: someone has gone and told what she has seen or heard. *Kalam innas* is like the wind which suddenly starts to blow, perhaps from several directions. Gossip is like a cold gust from one particular corner. (Wikan 1996, 121)

In this nightclub scene, men strategically alluded to the general, faceless rumors about unrespectable women as a way of warning their female friends that they too could become victims of this wind that blows from several directions, even as they also shared specific gossip about women.

Just as Marilyn Strathern (1981, 370) describes for Hagen men in Papua New Guinea, there is a disjuncture between "categorical denigration of females and contextual evaluation of particular women." Harsh judgments are tempered by the love and affection of friends and lovers: Kerim reassures me that I don't look like a prostitute, even though I calculate that I must look like one to someone at another table who isn't making allowances for friendship. Ayah loves Zeid and admires his work ethic, as she has told me (and him) many times, even if she also complains about it. George shows a grudging admiration for Sara's stoical masculinity and Nesma teasingly but tolerantly celebrates Sara's expressions of love for a married man. Talk disciplines, but it also creates boundaries around friendships and gives cohesion to groups, binding people together in a shared dialectic of judgment and tolerance. As Butler (1999, 22) notes, gender identities "come into being and dissolve depending on the concrete practices that constitute them," and it is these concrete, constituting practices that this ethnography examines.

Significantly, there is often a disjuncture between the moral identities always being constructed and the reality of the actions behind them. Rasha, who has never kissed a man, goes out at night and gets called

[handwritten margin note: What goes into consideration when fact is known to be different from general POV here?]

a whore by her neighbor's fiancé. Ayah successfully hides her smoking from her father and her fiancé and thus preserves her identity as a respectable woman. Sara (as we shall find out later in this book) is sexually experienced but successfully hides this from her colleagues. The labels "respectable" or "not-respectable" reference women's actions and, especially, their sexuality, and yet they are curiously divorced from their actual actions and sexual behavior.

In this sense these labels are simulacra. They are copies with no original. They are signs of the real instead of the real. They are thus *more* real than real (Baudrillard 1988). The stories told about women's sexuality construct moral histories that never existed. A woman's respectability is a simulacrum that is produced in negotiation and is constantly being reconfigured, based on a combination of her social network and the way she moves through public space, the narratives established around her activities, and the influence of people, especially kin, in her network (Wynn and Hassanein 2017).

As Jean Baudrillard (1988, 166) notes, "The simulacrum is never that which conceals the truth—it is the truth which conceals that there is none. The simulacrum is true." Baudrillard's analysis is a pseudo-historical account of the signifier being detached from the signified, a way of characterizing the difference between premodernity, modernity, and postmodernity. Here, though, it is productive for thinking about the way a woman's respectability is a social construct, independent of and yet tied to her actions, at once unreal and *really* real. A woman's respectability is a representation that circulates, divorced from the original referent (Wynn and Hassanein 2017).

This can be a terrible burden. An Egyptian woman has to worry all the time about her reputation. Even when she conforms perfectly to cultural ideals proscribing sexual expression outside heterosexual marriage, she still has to worry about what others are saying about her. But this isn't just some exotic phenomenon of the Arab world. Kathleen Stewart (1996, 53) described the phenomenon in a small West Virginian coal-mining town in a way that could equally apply to the North African megalopolis: "Imagine a vigilant scanning become automatic, relentless, compulsive. Picture people . . . how they stare as you pass, keeping track. Imagine the scanning for signs . . . how everything depends on things overheard, overseen." As Baudrillard (1984, 257) argues, the same social conditions that produce the simulacrum produce this compulsive proliferation of surveillance and signs of authenticity: "When the real no longer is what it used to be, nostalgia assumes its full meaning. There is a proliferation of myths of origin and signs of reality: of secondhand truth, objectivity, and authenticity."

This vigilant scanning for signs of respectability is an oppressive, "all-encompassing force field" of social pressure (Stewart 1996, 53). The women I knew in Egypt were aware that there were eyes everywhere, always watching their behavior, ready to judge and spread rumors. Yet the simulacrum of women's respectability, this disjuncture between action and rumor, between behavior and identity, can also be an opportunity, a powerful tool in the project of creating moral identities of respectable womanhood, as women boldly claim for themselves the label "respectable" even as they defy expectations of proper feminine behavior or quietly hide their loves and desires from relentlessly scanning eyes. Indeed, it is in the space between contradictory collective narratives of female respectability that the possibilities open up for creative maneuvers in the social construction of women's moral identities. That, in a long tradition of feminist ethnography looking at women on the margins of respectability (among many others, Cole 2009; Ortner 1978; Ramberg 2014; Rosaldo and Lamphere 1974; Strathern 1981; Wardlow 2006; and Wilson 2004), is the oppressive and creative space that this book explores.

Love and desire are highly moralized cultural domains. They are at the same time individual feelings that are passionately compelling and the ways that cultural values come into being. They are tied to class habitus and tools of social distinction, in a Bourdieuian sense (Kreil 2016b). They are cultural categories that we use to make moral sense of our world and our social relationships, and thus they are tied to larger political projects (Abu-Lughod 1986, 34). This is what Berlant (2012, 6) means when she says that emotions of love and desire are both inside and outside us. Emotions are the terrain connecting individual subjectivities with cultural value systems and political-economic structures. In this book, therefore, I want to start from that structural framework, which alerts us to the simultaneous interiority and exteriority of emotions like love and desire, and from there go on to examine in close ethnographic detail the way local concepts about love and desire revolve around the themes of mimesis, kinship, and gift and the way these construct and deconstruct ideals of respectable femininity and masculinity.

Men face heavy social pressure and scrutiny as they work to create respectable masculine identities for themselves (Connell 1995), a dynamic that Ghannam (2013) has analyzed in her ethnography of masculinity in Egypt and that I here evoke in my accounts of the pressures Zeid faces to prove himself a worthy fiancé. However, in this book, though I touch on masculine projects of creating moral identities, my primary focus is on stories of women and their moral identities, because, as chapter 1 suggests, it is women who are most scrutinized for signs of behavior related to love and desire, and women who pay the greatest penalties for going against social norms regarding their sexuality (Foster and Wynn 2016).

As I narrate this ethnographic account of turn-of-the-millennium Cairo, I recount intimate, individual stories with the aim of sketching a broader picture of how individuals pursue intimate lives in the context of a cultural and political system that organizes love and desire and the possibilities of, and penalties for, going against normative gender roles. And, just as I did in the narratives in chapter 1, I want to continue to focus on the construction and deconstruction of normative and nonnormative sexualities, on the boundary-work that people do to police the borders between the two, and on tactical (in the de Certeauian sense) disruptions of these boundaries. Thomas Gieryn (1983) coined the term "boundary-work" to talk about the efforts that scientists make to distinguish themselves from nonscientists, particularly in the context of New Age appropriations of science (see also Wynn 2007), but it is a useful framework for thinking about the efforts that people make to set boundaries around sexuality and gender. We can see this boundary-work in the debate among Ayah, Zeid, and Kerim about how to define different relationships, what the difference is between love and desire, and how to identify a respectable woman or man.

This book focuses primarily on heterosexual relationships, an artifact of the organic way this research project emerged out of the interests of the people whom I knew, most of whom happened to be heterosexual. (Academic studies of sexualities in Egypt that address same-sex relationships and nonbinary gender roles include Dunne 1996; Hassan 2010; and Jacob 2011.) Yet even though my focus is on the relationship between normative and nonnormative heterosexualities in Egypt, particularly romantic relationships outside socially sanctioned marriages (or, as one reviewer of an earlier draft of this book described it, relationships at the margins or edges of marriage), I have found it particularly productive to draw on the work of queer theorists such as Berlant and Eve Kosofsky Sedgwick, who have laid valuable groundwork for exploring the possibilities and constraints of nonnormative love and desire. The relevance of queer theory to my ethnographic material about heterosexual relationships illustrates the way different kinds of nonnormative heterosexuality can illuminate each other—and, indeed, the way understanding nonnormative sexualities can also shed light on hegemonic sexualities, as well (Connell and Messerschmidt 2005). By looking at relationships at the margins of social respectability, not only can we understand those who go against social norms, but we can also better understand the social norms that they deviate from. In other words, just as queer theory can help us better understand heterosexuality, so too is an account of premarital and extramarital relationships fundamentally also a story about marriage.

Writing the Anthropologist into the Ethnography

There is a tradition in anthropological writing of starting an ethnography by describing the circumstances of fieldwork and what brought the anthropologist to her field site. Both feminist methodologies and the postmodern turn demand that the anthropologist display a reflexive awareness of her positionality and the ways it shapes the research. Yet the critique of the excesses of postmodern experimental writing simultaneously makes contemporary anthropologists leery of "navel-gazing"—spending so much time reflecting on themselves and the circumstances of their research that they neglect the people they ostensibly went to study.

In this postironic (that is to say, post-postmodern) age, the typical resolution to this dilemma is to carefully tread the middle ground, conscious of "the unusually narrow stylistic demands that hedge about any language that treats one's own" experience (Sedgwick 1987, 110). The safest strategy for an anthropologist to take is to start by revealing something about the fieldwork circumstances and her own positionality. Then, having briefly put the anthropologist center stage, the author must quickly retire this character and press on to show that her real object of academic inquiry is not actually herself.

Yet the anthropologist can never completely retreat from the pages of her ethnography. This is not only a result of the political imperative that requires us to stay reflexively attuned to the structures that generate our research interests, deliver us into a community, shape the kinds of relationships we develop there, and influence what we write. It is also a product of our peculiar methodology—participant observation—which mandates that everything we learn, we learn through our own embodied, subjective experience. (Works exploring this argument include Biddle 1993; Clifford 1997; Coffey 1999; Jackson 1996; Kulick

and Willson 1995; and Okely 2007; among many others.) The process
of subsequently writing up our research results is a process of taking
those complex, confusing, exhilarating, painful, very personal, and intimate embodied experiences and translating them into both a coherent narrative and a theoretical apparatus for interpreting that narrative
(Beatty 2005).

The ethnographic narrative I have presented so far reveals something of the way the anthropologist's knowledge unfolds gradually
through a careful mix of listening and questioning and building trust.
It also makes clear the ways that an anthropologist's knowledge is partial and is revealed through discussions of her or his own relationship: I
learned to publicly express my love for my husband in culturally appropriate ways (vocally enough to convince friends that our long-distance
marriage wasn't just a sham), and when informants commented on his
checking up on me, I used this as a starting point for launching into a
discussion about the relationship between jealousy and love.

Clearly and unambiguously writing the anthropologist into the ethnography is both a philosophical position and a political strategy. Writing culture through the explicit lens of the anthropologist's subjectivity
reminds the reader that everything we know is mediated by the informants' interaction with the anthropologist, and what our informants
choose to reveal or conceal is shaped by the anthropologist's national
origin and the way she looks, acts, presents herself, and engages with
people around her. In short, personal encounters are always structured
by political economy. Including the anthropologist in our ethnographic
representations at once highlights the limits of ethnographic knowledge
and also demonstrates how ethnographic knowledge is created intersubjectively (Jackson 1996, 44).

Mimesis, kinship, gift, love, and desire—all these things I learned
through physical and emotional immersion during three and a half
years of living in Cairo and four years of a marriage that fell apart during the final year of my field work. As Andrew Beatty (2005, 23) notes,
"The learning of an emotional vocabulary is one of the essential skills
of an ethnographer. To survive as a competent social being, the field-
worker must learn how to interpret, if not actually feel, the finer shades
of anger, pity, or whatever the host population specializes in." When
I basked in my Arab husband's praise for being "respectable" because
I came home early at night, or when we later had bitter fights and he
called me a "prostitute" for socializing with belly dancers, I was being
disciplined into incorporating into my own subjectivity the very cul-

tural logics I analyze. When I listened to Ayah describe Ahmed's lack of controlling jealousy as a worrying sign that he didn't really love Nellie, I could appreciate this logic and this form of expressing love in deeply embodied ways that related to my own emotional experiences of marriage and jealousy.

"The anthropologist is not immune," João Biehl (1995, 97) tells us. He means, I think, that anthropologists are just as susceptible to complex emotion as our informants are. The anthropologist does not stand above the action, observing and analyzing dispassionately. We are intimately embedded in the lives of the people whom we write about, and we construct knowledge together through our interactions. My Cairo informants—their lives, their advice, the friendship and personal confidences they offered me—were a prism through which I interpreted my own fieldwork encounters in Cairo and my marriage back in the United States. My own experiences were a filter for understanding the stories told to me by my informants, the questions I thought to ask, and the way I understood their answers. This is the nature of ethnography, and it is this experience that I have tried to convey through the extended passages of ethnographic narrative that constitute half this book. These passages of ethnographic description alternate with more conventional theoretical essays that read these stories of love and desire through the prism of classic anthropological theories.

Cultural and Disciplinary Taboos on Writing about Love and Desire

Desire is an increasingly popular catchphrase and concept in anthropological writing (e.g., Rofel 2007; Hasso 2010), and of course anthropologists have been writing about sex since the earliest years of the discipline, with Margaret Mead's famous *Coming of Age in Samoa* (1928) or Bronislaw Malinowski's more explicit *The Sexual Life of Savages* (1929), replete with descriptions of exotic sexual positions and the erotic possibilities of teeth and eyelashes. Yet for all the attention anthropologists pay to sex and desire, love was until quite recently curiously rare as a subject for anthropological analysis. Perhaps this is partly because love has often been seen as too culturally and historically specific—a modern or Western concept (Jankowiak and Fischer 1992). Love is frequently subsumed under the concept of kinship, which is, in contrast to love, seen as a cultural universal. For decades, when anthropologists addressed romantic love at all, it was often relegated to the corners of their ethnographies as irrelevant or embarrassing—particularly, as Don Kulick and Margaret Willson (1995) point out, when it concerned the love of the anthropologist.

Alternatively, love has been treated as an epiphenomenon, the surface manifestation of deeper structural forces like political economy (Abu-Lughod 1990; Bourdieu 1977) or kinship (Lévi-Strauss 1969). Or it may be described as more than the surface of underlying political economic structures, as a powerful political force in its own right, driving individuals to defy sociocultural norms and political taboos, as anthropologists have done for Iran (Mahdavi 2008), Saudi Arabia (Wynn 1997), Egypt (Abu-Lughod 1990), or Mao-era China (Zhang 2005). Yet this literature rarely treats love and desire as interior emotions.

In the applied anthropology literature, love and desire have often been subsumed under the rubric of sex and intimate relations of power and gender. This literature often reduces love and desire to a public-health puzzle (as in the type of research that asks, How can we get people to use condoms so they don't get HIV?; see, e.g., Hirsch and Wardlow, 2006; Smith 2006; Warr and Pyett 1999).

Only in the past two decades have anthropologists and sociologists begun to take up love as a subject for anthropological enquiry in its own right. (See, e.g., Giddens 1992; Lindholm 1998; Rebhun 1999; Hirsch and Wardlow 2006; Faier 2007; Padilla 2007; Jankowiak 2008; Cole 2009; Hunter 2009; Lepani 2012; Kreil 2016b; and the 2006 special issue on romantic love of the Dutch anthropology journal *Etnofoor*.)

The ethnographic narrative in chapter 1 follows much of the patterns of this short history of anthropological writing on love and desire. We gain partial insight into the relationship between love and political economy, with hints that Ayah and Zeid's relationship is shaped by money problems as Zeid is trying to save up to buy an apartment and pay for the wedding. The presence of foreign women—from the anthropologist to the Pomodoro waitress—is a marker of the liberalization of the Egyptian economy, and in the debate over whether a Pomodoro waitress constitutes marriage material or not, we see different Egyptians' perspectives on how these new arrivals fit into local social worlds. We catch a glimpse of the way that appearing at this expensive nightclub-restaurant enables upper-class and upwardly mobile middle-class Cairenes to assert and perform their social status.

In sum, this ethnographic material conveys the way love and desire in Cairo operate within a moral economy of gender and kin roles, within cultural norms about male and female respectability and shame, and

How does arranged marriage fit into Cairo? Past and present?

Mimesis, Kinship, Gift **43**

within a political-economic framework that structures how and when and whom one can date and marry.

But there is much that this ethnographic vignette does *not* tell us about love in turn-of-the-millennium Cairo. We have very little sense of Ayah and Zeid's intimate life, either their physical intimacy (which we only glimpse when they hold hands under the table) or their emotional intimacy. The public performance of their relationship is one of bickering: Zeid teases Ayah about her weight; Ayah chastises him for his late nights with friends. We see few intimate expressions of affection and love. All their friends knew that theirs was a love match, but they avoided demonstrating that intimate relationship in gestures or words in front of other people. Similarly, Sara's love for Ali is rendered through the alienating perspective of the appalled anthropologist. There is little attempt to describe Sara's embodied experience of how thrilling it felt to be slapped and have her clothes ripped by a boyfriend demonstrating his possessive jealousy and thus his love.

We also don't see much of the anthropologist's relationship with her own absent husband. In this vignette and elsewhere in the ethnography, my husband appears primarily as a topic of conversation through which my informants interpret my behavior and try to explain others' behavior to me. In this scene he is a scolding figure, trying to teach me culturally appropriate ways of being an Arab wife. The more intimate aspects of our relationship, emotional and sexual, remain firmly offscreen.

In short, this portrayal of love in Cairo reflects the key characteristics—and limitations—of most anthropological writing on the topic: love is firmly tied to political economy and to modernity, it skirts around discussion of the anthropologist's own intimate life, and it falls short of representing love and desire as lived, embodied emotions.

This dearth of experiential accounts of romantic love in anthropological writing is the result both of a methodological problem and of cultural and disciplinary taboos. In the cultures of many anthropologists as well as of our informants, there are taboos on talking about love, sex, and other intimate experiences and emotions outside an intimate context.

Consider: when do we talk to our colleagues and friends about love? I talk to colleagues about family in a generic sort of way, and to close friends I may talk or joke about sex, but I do not talk to any of these people about the love I feel for my husband, just as Ayah rarely spoke to me about her love for Zeid, even though we were close friends. We might complain to friends, but we speak of love only to our lovers.

Yet while anthropologists shy away from writing about love, it has enormous currency in popular culture. In songs, it is probably the single most popular lyrical theme. In 2008, Americans spent $1.37 billion on romance novels, and some 64.6 million Americans had read at least one romance novel in the previous year (Wendell and Tan 2009).

In sum, love is both intimately practiced and publicly consumed, both exclusive and awfully banal. We have a voyeuristic longing to view and consume others' love, but this is usually a distant other, the culturally stylized portraits of love in songs, movies, and books. We do not view the love of our friends and family in the same voyeuristic way. We honor their love at particular ceremonies (weddings, anniversaries), but we do not consume our acquaintances' love with pleasure as we do when we go to see a romantic comedy in the cinema. As soon as love is personal and intimate, it becomes off-limits for public consumption.

There are also deep-seated taboos on writing about the anthropologist's own love and sexuality in ethnographic texts (Kulick and Willson 1995; Markowitz and Ashkenazi 1999; Rubenstein 2004). Emotional and physical intimacy, including sexual encounters and romantic love, are common between anthropologists and their informants in the field, and yet they are rarely conveyed in ethnographic writing about the fieldwork encounter (Newton 1993), despite repeated calls in poststructuralist anthropology and feminist writing for the researchers to locate themselves in the field. The dearth of frank and open accounts of anthropologists' experiences of love and desire—except in the context of edited volumes (e.g., Kulick and Willson 1995) and articles (e.g., Rubenstein 2004) that are explicitly framed as defying disciplinary taboos—is all the more striking when we consider the popularity of ethnographies with intimate and emotionally rich accounts of other types of fieldwork experiences, such as Jean Briggs's (1970) famous account of being ostracized by the Inuit community she was studying, Nancy Scheper-Hughes's (1992) wrenching descriptions of how she grappled with infant death in Brazil, or Philippe Bourgois's (1995) depression on learning that his informants had engaged in gang rape and had physically abused a disabled child. These powerful accounts of the ethnographers' own emotions in the field have become classics of the discipline and are frequently assigned in undergraduate anthropology classes, in part because of how emotionally wrenching they are. This disciplinary taboo clearly does not prevent anthropologists from writing about emotion in general or about anthropologists' personal experiences. Contemporary anthropologists locate themselves in their ethnographies in terms of race and ethnicity, gender and sexuality, nationality and privilege. Yet that mandate to locate themselves in their ethnographies and candidly describe their fieldwork experiences comes up against the powerful cultural taboo that specifically discourages them from writing about their own love and desire. Those rare anthropologists who do bring their own affects of love and desire into their ethnographies are at once applauded for their daring and gossiped about behind their backs, as in Paul Rabinow's (Rabinow 1977, 67–69) description of visiting a prostitute in Morocco, which led to much sniggering among anthropology students when I was in grad school.

In short, for most anthropologists, writing about one's own love and desire (as well as one's sexual experiences) is rather like copulating in the corner of one's ethnography. It is at once vulgar and polluting.

[handwritten margin note: love in ethnographic = bad]

Combined, these taboos, disciplinary and cultural, result in a methodological problem: the anthropologist uses his or her own body through extended periods of participant observation to gather data, but cultural taboos on sharing intimate emotions with an outsider mean that it is difficult for the anthropologist to get close enough to informants to actually understand their affective experiences of love and desire. On the other hand, the anthropologist who experiences the cultural meaning of love through his or her own body, that is, through richly affective experiences of loving, desiring, and being loved and desired, has few models in the anthropological canon for how to write about it.

This methodological problem is entangled with a problem of representation: portrayals of love and desire in the ethnographic literature are by and large etic, experience-distant accounts that fail to convey the affective quality of the experience and perception of love and desire.

In some cases this anthropological neglect of love leads to absurdities, as when Claude Lévi-Strauss claimed that kinship was reducible to the exchange of women, writing out an entire realm of subjective experience of courtship, marriage, emotion, and sex. There is much of value in Lévi-Strauss's structural analysis, and we will return to him in chapter 8 on kinship, but as Margaret Trawick (1990) points out in her discussion of love and kinship, it is radically incomplete to try to understand kinship as structure without also taking seriously the subjective experiences of love and desire and other powerful emotions that spring up around them, such as jealousy and anger. Here I follow João Biehl and Peter Locke's (2010, 322) reading of philosopher Gilles Deleuze (2006, 126), who "emphasize[d] the primacy of desire over power." In this ethnography of love and desire, I want to insist on the importance of taking seriously these emotions as potent subjects for ethnographic analysis in their own right, rather than trying to reduce them to the structures and power relations that are often emphasized in the anthropological literature on kinship, mimesis, and gift.

Many academic texts on sex and desire assume that these can be boiled down to structures of power—often economic (as in analyses of sex workers) but also political (as in analyses of gender relations)— within a society. The emotions attached to those relationships of desire are either bracketed off so that more serious analysis can occur or portrayed as mere superstructure. But what if we flipped that around? What if we considered emotion to be base and structure, the fundamental glue linking kin and society, and considered money merely a kind of frosting that decorates and adorns these emotional structures, or a lubricant that greases the mechanisms of affective ties?

My informants argued passionately about the proper behavior of a "respectable woman." I have not written fully about how high emotions ran over such matters, because several of the characters in my book might become recognizable if I told certain stories, and protecting their privacy is an ethical imperative that overrides my desire to tell about the powerful emotions triggered over threats to the respectability of female kin. In a couple of cases that I cannot detail, concerns about female respectability culminated in emotional trauma and, in the case of one man, in a mental breakdown when he feared his wife had been unfaithful. Or consider Sara's love for Ali, which persisted even as he physically abused her. Such intense emotions are not merely *by-products* of cultural norms about gender roles, nor are they simply the superstructure adorning underlying political economic structures. They are *driving forces* compelling people to enact or defy cultural norms.

Of course, neither emotion nor political economy is primarily structure or epiphenomenon. Neither comes first or has primacy over the other. Love and desire and affection impel people to purchase commodities and give gifts; gifting and receiving bind people together in social relations that engender emotion. Both economy and affect are interrelated and mutually constitutive, and they cannot be studied in isolation from each other (Kreil 2016b; Schielke 2015). But the emotions of love and desire have been strikingly absent from many discussions of affect-rich domains such as kinship and gift economies, including marriage, dating, and courtship. This book attempts to take those emotions and subjectivities as fundamentally important for an anthropological understanding of how people move through social fields and navigate cultural norms.

So, for example, we can interpret Sara's talk about her love for Ali in terms of class, gender roles, and cultural expectations about extramarital relationships in Egypt. But it is also something much more: it is Sara's experience of love; it is her reveling in Ali's violent display of jealousy, possession, and attachment; it is her passionate attachment to him—and without understanding that, we cannot fully understand why she puts her respectability at risk by talking at work about her passion for a married man, or why she refuses a respectable marriage to engage in an illicit romance.

Similarly, Ayah and Zeid's relationship is a good illustration of love's power to unseat social expectations. At the level of social class, they were an unlikely pair. Ayah's father was a remnant of the pre-Nasser landed aristocracy who led a life of leisure while dabbling in conservative politics, and she lived in an exclusive apartment in a posh area of town, furnished with antiques and overlooking the Nile. Zeid's father was a middle-class army officer who had benefited from Nasser's socialist policies and elevation of the military, but ultimately they were still middle class and resided in a modest, kitschy flat in the inexpensive outskirts of the city near the pyramids, which constantly irritated Ayah's aesthetic sensibilities. Without love binding the two together, Ayah would not have dated Zeid for years while he saved up enough money to be able to ask for her hand in marriage, and she would not have gone to the effort that she did to convince her upper-class father to permit her to marry a middle-class nobody. If there was not a deep emotional intimacy between Ayah and Zeid, then there would be no way to explain her willingness to submit to his constant teasing about her weight, his insults to her friends and mother, and his very unsatisfactory (to her) evening excursions. On Zeid's part, though Ayah was perhaps an avenue for his upward social mobility, she was also a demanding girlfriend. And since men pay a bride price (*mahr*) and supply the marital residence in Egypt, she brought little to the marriage financially, while her social class ensured that her expectations were quite high, making her a clear financial liability. Yet despite their bickering about excursions and the financial pressure that being engaged to Ayah placed on Zeid, he was fanatically devoted to her. They might bicker in front of me, but he loved her deeply. He once confided in me that he could not imagine having sex with any other woman, and when he married Ayah he was a virgin, which was quite unusual for a man of his social class and charisma.

In short, without taking into account the love between Ayah and Zeid—a love that is only barely glimpsed in the portrait I have so far drawn of them—it becomes practically impossible to explain their relationship and its success.

To appropriate anthropologist Michael Jackson's (1996, 22) critique of Pierre Bourdieu and Michel Foucault, if we do not take love and desire seriously as primary phenomena that drive and create structure, rather than simply masking or decorating it, then we fail to understand "the very site where life is lived, meanings are made, will is exercised, reflection takes place, consciousness finds expression, determinations take effect, and habits are formed or broken."

Limitations: Reading Love in the Traces

Yet as my analysis of chapter 1's narrative demonstrates, my attempts to write about love and desire are hedged about with limitations. When I describe Sara's brief account of having her clothes torn up and her face slapped by a jealous lover, I do very little to convey the interiority of emotion that she felt in that moment or the embodied desire she felt for Ali. Unlike a romance novelist, as an anthropologist I do not have the scope for imaginatively describing what it might have felt like to Sara to be kissed roughly and passionately by her lover. If I did, her continuing love for Ali might make more sense to the reader. Here we also come up against the limits of my own empathetic imagination. As much as I want to take love and desire seriously, I find it quite difficult to imagine my way into someone else's head and describe those feelings from their perspective. My own affect also gets in the way of such creative imagining. In the case of Sara's romance, for example, I frankly did not like her "beloved," Ali. Here I recount how Sara described her feelings, but my own feelings of revulsion constrain my ability to fill in the blanks of what Sara does not tell us about her relationship with Ali.

Other informants were even more circumspect than Sara about revealing their love and desire. This is a key limitation to writing about love, a limitation that goes beyond one ethnographer's failure of imagination or empathy. Anthropologists seek to understand the lived experiences of our informants, but we can only know those experiences through a combination of discourse—asking people what they think and feel, and listening to how they narrate those thoughts and feelings, which means that any experience is necessarily mediated by narrative styles, the limitations of language, and what people do and don't, will and won't say—and participant observation, which allows us to describe how we think and feel when experiencing the same things that our informants are experiencing but is no guarantee that our experience is the same as our informants'.

The discussions about love and desire narrated in chapter 1 show the importance of *talk* in Cairene perceptions of love—not only the talk we *hear* (gossip, rumor, scrutiny of others' reputations) but also the talk we *imagine* (people talking about one's own reputation)—and show how this simultaneous *memory-imagination* of talk about love mediates and tames a person's experience of desire. Rumor and talk shape ideas about feminine comportment. Rumors about unrespectable women circulate in a way that defines group boundaries and solidarity (as men in the group declare that women who are not part of their group are not respectable, but nevertheless deem respectable the women within their group, even though their public behavior is not significantly different from that of the unrespectable women). At the same time, rumors teach women that they are being watched and judged by others (Wikan 1996). What woman could abandon herself to unbridled passion while remembering what men say about women who are too "hot"?

This talk about love, desire, gender, and normative and nonnormative sexuality is not just a taming force, as functionalist accounts of gossip point out (e.g., Gluckman 1963); this talk can also be generative (Besnier 2009), equipping women, for example, with an ability to generate love and respect in men by mimetically enacting cultural norms of womanhood that render them respectable and thus desirable in marriage. Discourses about desire are not the same as desire as a lived feeling, but those discourses about desire nevertheless do shape people's narratives and subjectivities around affect (Abu-Lughod 1986).

Yet talk, though important to understanding Egyptian theories about love, is incomplete and partial. The difficulties of understanding intimate experiences through narrative are compounded when approaching sensitive topics such as love and desire and sex and money. I had an intimate friendship with both Ayah and Zeid, so they were willing to argue in front of me (which I appreciated), but they rarely told me any details about their physical sexual relationship. It took a decade for Sara to trust me enough to tell me about her sexual relationships with men. Because talking about love and desire is hedged about by taboo in Egypt, I had to seek people's experiences of love and desire in the traces of their speech, in gesture and glance, and in the popular culture they consume. What is *not said* about intimate relations can be just as important as what *is said*.

In chapter 1, for example, we see the "interweaving of the visible and invisible" (Lawlor 2002, xvi), the "reflections, the shadows, the levels, the horizons between the things" (ibid., xii), the said and the hints of the unsaid, as my informants sought evidence of love (or its lack) and respectability (or its lack) in the traces of people's behavior: male jealousy and controlling behavior reveals love and concern for a women or kin; female "heat" betrays not only desire and a woman's inability to control it but also the history of her physical contact with other men; patterns of residence reveal a women's respectability and thus marriageability. And just as my informants read love in the traces, so too did the anthropologist. I knew it would be a huge faux pas to ask an unmarried couple about their physical intimacy, so I found hints of it in the way they held hands under the table after their argument; I knew Zeid couldn't talk about money woes without lowering his social status, but I interpreted his and Ayah's arguments about going out at night as a displaced language for dealing with the financial tensions entailed in their shift from a secret romance to a public engagement.

Our discussions about the nature of love in a posh Cairo nightclub and a run-down antiques shop thus illustrate more than culture as the "organization of diversity" (Wallace 2009). Such talk also constitutes— to use one of Maurice Merleau-Ponty's concepts—the pivot, hinge, or juncture (Lawlor 2002, xxiv) between people who cannot access the interiority of the other and who are thus—like the anthropologist—continually engaged in an interpretive and generative exercise, trying to work out what they, and others, believe about love and desire.

Beyond failures of empathy and imagination and cultural taboos on talking about love and desire, the final type of major limitation to writing on this subject is ethical. As Steven Rubenstein (2004, 1043) notes, in the libidinal economy of fieldwork, where the anthropologist desires to capture the intimate knowledge of others and our informants seek to capture the exoticness and power of the anthropologist, the secrets that our informants keep are part of their power: "Agency and voice often present themselves as secrets and silences that resist representation." Often the anthropologist's task is "not to uncover the truths behind a secret but to understand the power *of* the secret" (ibid., 1058). Respecting others' silences and privacy in writing about their intimate lives is as much an ethics of research and representation as it is a methodological limitation. Topics that are as hedged about with taboo as love, desire, and sex can be dangerous and must be written about with great caution to protect one's informants. I have already mentioned one of the things

I cannot write about without betraying the identity and the confidence of both a friend and an informant: one informant's mental breakdown, triggered by fear that a spouse had been unfaithful. There were numerous other events that informants did not wish me to write about—extramarital affairs, premarital sex, abortions, and sexually transmitted infections—or that I myself decided not to write about because I worried that I might reveal identities.

Separating out those events from the ones I did have permission to write about was a complex process, but the guiding ethical principle was simple enough: when it comes to my research participants, I don't have the right to tell someone else's story unless they give me permission *and* no harm will come to them through the telling. I shared a draft of this book with my key informants, both in English and in an Arabic translation expertly rendered by Tarek Ghanem of Metalingual Translation and proofed by Saffaa Hassanein, and I invited them to tell me if they wanted me to omit anything or to make changes to better protect their privacy. I took extra steps for one informant: in the case of Sara, whose personal life I have recounted in the most intimate detail, I discussed with her at length what I could and could not include and what steps I would take to obscure her identity in the text. This process of translating and sharing drafts with informants made for a slow production process but was ethically necessary for writing about such intimate and taboo topics.

Even more complicated was figuring out how to write about my own experiences. If few anthropologists write about their own love and desire, it is not only out of respect for their own cultural taboos. It is also because it is difficult to write about one's own sexual partners and protect their privacy.

A basic assumption about most ethnographic writing is that we will use pseudonyms and change identifying details in order to disguise our informants, as a matter of anthropological ethics. But it is nearly impossible to disguise the identity of the partner of an anthropologist who publishes under her own name. And yet if the anthropologist learns another culture through her own body and social position—if, for example, she learns about Arab cultural ideals of respectable womanhood partly through instruction from her Arab husband—then it is also nearly impossible to separate the anthropologist's own experiences from her partner's. (While there is a long-standing disciplinary tradition of the male anthropologist taking his wife into the field and writing about that—a tradition that I invert as the female anthropologist who brings her husband into the field as a concept and an influence rather than a physical presence—this husbandly presence becomes all the more fraught when the anthropologist's failure to live up to his ideal of respectable womanhood eventually resulted in divorce. Claiming those experiences as stories that I have a right to tell thus became hard to disentangle from the kind of claiming of property that surround the dissolution of a relationship. "You take this, I'll take that, and I'm keeping my own stories, dammit!")

In writing myself into this ethnography, I have had to walk an incredibly fine line, describing my own experiences while acknowledging that there are other narratives that could be told about my intimate relationships, and avoiding writing about my husband except where his story was inextricable from mine and my story was in turn inextricable from the process of gaining anthropological knowledge.

Narrative before Theory

The rest of this book follows the pattern set so far, alternating between ethnographic narrative and theoretical analysis. Rather than seeking a seamless fit between ethnographic description and theoretical frame, in this text the two weave in and out of each other in discrete, distinct passages. Chapters of ethnographic narrative describe the temporality, uncertainty, ambiguity, and instability of everyday life (Desjarlais and Throop 2011). Interspersed with these chapters of ethnographic narrative are essays that explore how well classic anthropological theories—on mimesis, kinship, and gift—work when applied to decidedly nontraditional ethnographic subjects. My interlocutors include not only born-and-bred Egyptians but also expatriates and tourists. This is a book, therefore, not only about love and desire and female respectability in urban Egypt, but also about Western social science theories that have been used to write about the Middle East and about what happens when we combine classic theories with unconventional ethnographic material.

In chapter 4, "Mimesis, Genre, Gender, and Sexuality in Middle East Tourism," I ask how cultural mimicry is gendered in the context of a transnational tourist economy by examining interactions among tourists, hustlers, and shopkeepers in Cairo's famous Khan el-Khalili tourist market. In the context of the transnational circulation of representations of Arab men's sexuality and the jokes by shopkeepers that parody these stereotypes (by, for example, offering camels in exchange for a female tourist's hand in marriage), I argue that any anthropological analysis of mimesis must take into account not only the structures of inequality that impel one group to perform culture for another but also the particular genre of that performance. This chapter also shows that it is impossible for an American-Australian anthropologist to describe Arab culture without staying attuned to the dialectical interplay between that culture and the transnational circulation of representations of Arab sexuality.

I begin chapter 6, "Gift, Prostitute: Money and Intimacy," with a paradox. During the first part of my fieldwork, people used the term "prostitute" in perplexing ways. Even Egyptians who didn't speak more than a handful of words of English would often say the word "prostitute" in English (since the Arabic equivalent sounds too rude), yet the word was rarely used to refer to the exchange of sex for money, and, surprisingly, it did not even necessarily refer to sex at all. Grounding my analysis in anthropological and sociological theories about gift exchange in intimate relationships, I examine the way the label "prostitute" is used to discipline women's behavior, and the way that it also works to comment on the moral circulation of sex in the gift economy. This chapter rejects the simplifications of terms like "prostitute" to define what women do—morally, sexually, economically—but at the same time recognizes how powerful the term is for both describing and also shaping idealized female behavior.

In chapter 8, "Kinship, Honor, and Shame," I examine relationships between married men and their mistresses and other women who circulate in the alter social spaces of Cairo's demimonde, looking at the way women maneuver through masculine spaces through both the lens of Lévi-Strauss's theory of kinship as the exchange of women (linking this chapter with that on gifts) and that of anthropological writing on honor and shame. This chapter brings together key recurring themes in this ethnography, including love, sex, and female respectability, while considering how these work in a realm of very *un*idealized female sociality. Instead of seeing mistresses and dancers and "prostitutes" as inhabiting a different moral realm from that of the "respectable" women whose sexuality is more contained, this ethnographic account pushes us to see continuities between respectable women and not-respectable women, the similar ways that both are disciplined and self-disciplined, and the similar ways that both defy ideals of female behavior while still demanding the label "respectable."

These theoretical concerns are picked up again and again in the narrative chapters between the essay chapters, where they appear and reappear as intertwining variations on themes. Mimesis is not only the camel jokes of Egyptian shopkeepers, mimicking and mocking European tourists' stereotypes, but also the American anthropologist's mimicry and mockery of Arab ideals of female respectability. The relationship between gift economies and sexuality are a concern for young men hoping to marry and to get laid, for belly dancers angling for luxury items that their wages couldn't pay for but that a wealthy patron might provide, and for an anthropologist trying to figure out just how much of her sexuality she would have to offer up in order to work on the periphery of the dancers' social world. Kinship is a courtship, a secret marriage, a scandalous pregnancy, an engagement, an extramarital affair, the exchange of respectable sisters and loose women to strengthen the ties between businessmen, and husbandly and brotherly advice and remonstrations. Across all these domains is continual debate over moral codes and stigma and, above all, the meaning of love, which is at once a moral horizon, an attribute that "naturally" inheres in particular social relations, a social phenomenon created and strengthened through cultural concepts of gift and kinship, and an emotion deeply felt by individuals.

Threading through each of these essays on anthropological theory, we see Cairenes' concerns with female respectability as well as its ambiguous, oppressive, opportunistic, and simulacral nature. We see, in other words, continual processes of making and challenging cultural meaning, and the relationship between dominant social norms and subversive practices.

Finally, the concluding chapter, "Love, Revolution, and Intimate Violence," revisits core themes of the book through the lens of a discussion on revolution and the international political economy of representations of the Arab world, starting with Western fantasies about honor killings, the violent zenith and nadir of the so-called Mediterranean complex of honor and shame (Peristiany 1965) that has so long fascinated anthropologists. As Marcia Inhorn (2012) has argued in her study of Arab masculinity, it is not possible to write about sexuality and gender in the Arab world without actively grappling with these Western stereotypes about male oppressors and their corollary: the oppressed, agentless Arab woman (see also Naguib 2015; Ghannam 2013; Abu-Lughod 2013; Malmström 2016). And in a world where such stereotypes inform (or at least retroactively justify) military interventions into countries like Afghanistan, fueling a neocolonial zeal to "protect" Muslim women from Muslim men, we must remember that these politics of representation can be not merely academic debate but a matter of life and death. Like Inhorn, I am interested in exploring the difficulties, and also the imperative, of describing romantic relationships and love within and against the context of Western stereotypes about Arab men as oppressive and domineering and Arab women as oppressed. It is important to write about loving Arab husbands and powerful Arab women in the context of normative heterosexual married relationships in pursuit of that most normative of heterosexual married relationship goals, having a biological family (Inhorn 2012). And it is even more important, and even more of a challenge, to convey the love between Arab men and women in nonnormative relationships: people in extramarital affairs, for example, or women who are so firmly in the category of "not-respectable" that they are not sure if they can ever get married and have children but who still love and desire, and who are loved and desired.

A final epilogue tells the reader what happened to the main characters in the ethnography over a fifteen-year period.

In chapter 3, we will revisit some of the issues raised in chapter 1 about female sexuality, respectability, and the question of "prostitution" from the perspective of a real, live belly dancer, that fabled creature so often labeled a prostitute herself (whether in condemnation, as by my husband, or cheerfully, as by Kerim, who always begged me to introduce him to "a pretty prostitute"). But before we meet our first belly dancer, a few words of context to set the scene.

Belly Dancers, Sex, and Female Respectability

In Egypt, belly dancers are hired to perform at weddings and the festivals that mark the birthdays of popular saints. The same dancers who are hired at weddings also dance at nightclubs and cabarets. Depending on the venue, the audience in these nightclubs may be made up mostly of men who watch from their seats and occasionally shower the dancer with paper money to pay her a compliment, or it may include families and children.

Dancers perform to a mix of popular music and more classical tunes, songs whose lyrics were written by some of the most famous poets of the last century. I still vividly remember an evening when I saw the belly dancer Dina performing at the nightclub of the Semiramis Hotel. Her closing number was danced to a song about lost love originally sung by

Umm Kulthum, and she was accompanied by a live orchestra but no singer. As she danced on the stage, wearing one of her famously revealing costumes but with a grave look on her beautiful face, a chill ran down my spine as the room filled with a kind of eerie chorus. I looked around me and saw that at every table, people were softly singing the words to the song, their eyes locked on the dancer who interpreted the sadness of the song with her body. I still shiver to remember the shared reverence of dancer and audience for that song, the emotion that hummed through the room.

Dancers are often actresses as well. For example, Nesma (one of the employees of the antiques shop) commented to me once that her favorite dancer was Fifi Abdou because "she plays roles similar to her own life. She is uneducated and she acts uneducated in her films. She doesn't act cultured and put on airs. And in real life, she has married 'urfi several times, I think five or seven 'urfi [unregistered] marriages and two shari'a [Islamic] marriages, and she plays characters who get married 'urfi in her films too."

Yet dancers were also stigmatized for the very things that Nesma admired about Fifi Abdou. On one television show, Nesma told me, "Fifi said that she has a daughter at university, and on campus the students shout, 'Hey, you daughter of a dancer' as an insult."

When I asked George to explain why he thought dancing wasn't a respectable profession, he said, "Aren't you going to interview some belly dancers and see them dance? You can find out about this from the dancers you are going to meet by asking them certain questions which will indirectly lead them to address these issues." He gave me a list of questions, ticking off each one with a finger and waiting as I wrote each down. "What is your opinion about dancing? Did dancing alienate you from your family? And what are the negative consequences that occurred as a result of your dancing?" Finally, he suggested that I ask the question, "Do you dance because of your love for the dance or to make money?"

Nesma sighed. "I love dancing."

"Okay everyone, Nesma is going to dance for us!" I said, grinning. Everyone else laughed but she looked scandalized.

"Of course I can't dance for people here!"

"Why not?" I asked her.

"'Ayb. Shameful. I can't dance in front of men, and in the store."

"Who can you dance in front of?" I asked her.

"In front of women, or in front of my family, or in a wedding in the street. But if my brother was at the wedding, I couldn't dance in front of him. It's shameful ['ayb]. You know brothers look after their sisters; they are jealous and they don't like anyone to look at them at all."

All of this is important for understanding what dance means to Egyptians. Whatever stereotypes may circulate about belly dancers being seductresses and femmes fatales, in Egypt, they perform just as much for women as they do for men. Their performance both reflects and brings joy to a celebration. It also occasionally rises to the level of great art, and Egyptians hold the great dancers—Taheyya Kariokka, Nagwa Fouad, Fifi Abdou, Lucy, and Dina—in high regard (Said 2001). Many of these famous dancers were and are also movie and television stars, playing roles that, as we saw in Nesma and George's discussion of the career of Fifi Abdou, sometimes closely echo their own glamorous and troubled lives.

Yet despite the fact that this is family-friendly entertainment and even though belly dancers' performances bring joy to festive occasions and they may even become international celebrities, most dancers are socially stigmatized. We can see this in George's sly questions designed to reveal the dancers' alienation from their families.

Anthropologist Karin van Nieuwkerk has written an entire ethnography puzzling out this apparent paradox. She tells us that Egyptian dancers and musicians are well aware of the stigma associated with their trade, but they insist that it is just "a trade like any other," not scandalous and not a front for sex work, just a job (Van Nieuwkerk 2005).

The colloquial term for belly dancer in Arabic can be used as an insult, nearly a synonym for prostitute. (Susan Seizer [2005] describes a parallel in the way the term "actress" is used in Tamil popular theater.) There have been attempts by Egyptian intellectuals to recapture belly dance as a respectable, high art form, as Walter Armbrust (1996) has described in his analysis of the popular Egyptian film *Khalli Balak Min Zuzu* (Mind Zuzu), in which a beautiful belly dancer who is stigmatized for her profession by her classist schoolmates is redeemed by an upper-class intellectual man who persuades his family and peers at university that belly dance, like ballet, is an art form. Some of the most successful dancers have gained wide respect as great artists, even becoming national icons, as Edward Said describes in his 2001 essay "Homage to a Belly Dancer." Yet belly dance and those who perform it remain stigmatized even as they are celebrated.

Although the dancers that Van Nieuwkerk describes are Egyptian (almost akin to a caste of musicians and performers who are born into performing families), when I went to do my fieldwork in Cairo in the late 1990s, I found something that at first seemed quite strange: around half the belly dancers performing in nightclubs, on Nile cruises, and even at weddings (but not at saint-day festivals) were not Egyptian, nor even Arab. I met dancers who were American, Australian, Argentinian, Belarussan, British, French, German, Japanese, Kazakh, Russian, Spanish, Swedish, and Ukrainian. They performed with bands of local Egyptian musicians and singers, and some, like the Swedish dancer Semasem, with her famous mane of thick, waist-length blond hair, were quite well known, even to Egyptians who didn't follow the nightclub-cabaret scene at all, because of their appearances at weddings. Yet these dancers are scarcely mentioned by Van Nieuwkerk in her ethnography; Van Nieuwkerk's focus is on the dancers who perform at *sha'abi* (working-class) weddings and saint-day festivals, while the foreign belly dancers I encountered mainly performed at middle- to upper-class weddings and at nightclubs. In fact, very little of the academic literature—with a few exceptions, such as several of the contributions to the volume edited by Anthony Shay and Barbara Sellers-Young (2005)—discusses the prevalence of foreign (non-Arab) belly dancers in the Middle East. As I planned my research agenda in the late 1990s, I was inspired by anthropologists such as James Boon (1999) who were calling for anthropologists to avoid looking for stereotypically authentic-looking informants, and in light of the relative lack of scholarship on this phenomenon of foreign belly dancers, as well as of the fact that they were an important part of the tourist scene that I was studying, I decided to focus my research on foreign dancers.

The questions Van Nieuwkerk asks about how dancers fit into Egyptian society are important ones to contemplate in this ethnography: if dancers bring joy to festive occasions and couples want a dancer at their wedding, why, then, are dancers generally seen as disreputable women? Or perhaps the reverse question makes more sense: if dancers are seen as disreputable women, not far from whores, then why are they wanted at weddings? We can distill Van Nieuwkerk's formulation to the heart of her question and apply it more broadly to women other than just dancers: How and why do respectability and its lack mingle so comfortably in Cairo? If Egyptian women are so concerned with how to behave as proper, respectable women, and if the so-called honor-and-shame complex is as culturally central in the Arab world as anthropologists have historically argued it is, then why do we see behavior that many would clearly mark as "not respectable"? And how is it that women who behave in ways that would scandalize many still claim the label of, and are accepted as, respectable women in certain contexts? Yet at the same time, and somewhat paradoxically, others who may appear to be completely innocent—sexual naïfs like Ayah's friend Rasha, who at age thirty had never even kissed a man—may be crudely labeled a "prostitute" or, to use the phrase that people more polite than Zeid use, "not a good woman" (*mish sitt kwayyisa*).

In short, how do women in Cairo inhabit—and also reject—the labels that simultaneously describe and police their behavior?

As a first step toward answering that question, let us resume our narrative with an account from my field notes about the first belly dancer I ever met, Malak.

CHAPTER 3

"Why Can't You Study Respectable Women?"

Each of us knew that we were experiencing an immensely exotic—because endlessly deferred—erotic experience, the likes of which we could never hope to match in real life. And that was precisely the point: this was sexuality as a public event, brilliantly planned and executed, yet totally unconsummated and unrealizable. (Said 2001, 349)

After a couple of months of asking around, I finally got an introduction to a belly dancer. Malak was from Spain but had settled in Cairo ten years earlier, and now she gave private and group belly-dance lessons. She knew about my research project, and after a few weeks of attending her dance classes, she invited me to her downtown apartment for an interview.

Her story started, "I was a dancer, an Oriental dancer, long ago." She had worked all over Europe, she said, at parties and dance demonstrations and stage performances, sometimes flying to London or Rome for a party, but mostly performing in restaurants. While performing at one Lebanese restaurant in Europe, an agent approached her and asked her if she would like to work in Dubai. She was excited but nervous. It was a scary thing back then for a woman to travel alone to Dubai to dance, she said. This was in 1985, the beginning of the oil boom, and Dubai, long before it gained its reputation as a tourist mecca in the Arabian Peninsula, was known as a conservative Gulf country. Few Europeans ventured there. The agent arranged the visa.

In Dubai she mostly performed at hotels and nightclubs, and only once did she dance at a wedding. That was a surprise for her, because she hadn't realized that weddings there were sex segregated until she was actually on stage, dancing, and started to look around at the audience. She thought to herself, "There is something strange about this audience," before eventually realizing that there were no men in it. Like many weddings in the Gulf, it was sex segregated, and she was performing only for other women.

As I wrote furiously in my own invented (and therefore not very effective) shorthand, she lit a cigarette, then said, "In Dubai, I also sometimes performed at private parties."

I looked up from my notes. "Private parties?"

"These are parties that were very special. Where I was not dancing."

When pressed to explain, she said, "People come from Saudi Arabia and Kuwait. Their cultures are restrictive, and those who were very, very rich, they would have their own suite of rooms in a hotel, and they would want their own entertainment." I asked her if she was just speaking about men. "Both men and women would want to be entertained in their hotel suites, but speaking of the men, these people come to Dubai principally to look for alcohol and women. Often they expected to spend the night with me, according to payment." Sometimes, she said dryly, they would respect the dancer's desire whether to sleep with them or not. She said that among the dancers, there were plenty of girls who entertained "both on the stage and in the rooms." Others refused; "they say that they are professionals, performers, and not prostitutes." Dancers "who are not very classy work as both." *prostitution fr*

I asked how she felt about sleeping with these men. She shrugged.

"I have done it from time to time. In principle, I wouldn't mind if some nice man wanted me to sleep with him and then wanted to give me money for it. The problem," she continued, laughing, "is that it's almost never the nice men who want you—it's always the old, ugly, and disgusting men."

She described one time when she was asked out by a customer at the nightclub where she performed. They went out to dinner and then returned to his hotel, where they had sex. Afterward, when she had to leave for work, he gave her the equivalent of $3,000, an amount that was even vaster then than it would be now. "I was very confused," she told me: at once happy to have such a large sum and disgusted by it. She hadn't gone to his room expecting money. She didn't consider herself a prostitute. She had gone because she wanted to sleep with the man, and the money made her suddenly rethink the entire experience.

She told another story. Once when she was dancing on stage, a man caught her hand, took the ring off her finger, and didn't put it back. After her dance, he vanished. She told the manager, "He took my ring!"

The manager calmed her, saying, "Don't worry, he is a very good customer of ours; I'm sure he will give it back." He came back five days later, and while she was dancing, he took her hand and replaced the ring that he had taken and then put another ring on her other hand. He had taken the first ring to get the correct ring size. The gold ring he gave her had a one-karat diamond in it. She said the man was very nice and extremely rich. He drove a Rolls-Royce. Not long after that he was shot in the head. She shrugged. "Must have been Mafia."

She said she had no moral objection to sex work. "The only kind of prostitution I cannot stand," she declared, "is when you are in competition with other people to perform somewhere, and a dancer sleeps with a guy, the manager or person booking the shows at a nightclub, to get the job." But, she said, "Personally I don't like prostitution for myself. I like men too much for that. It is a very strange thing to be obliged to touch and kiss someone and feel absolutely nothing for him—you must either hate men or be incredibly materialistic." She said she sees two types of "call girls": those who hate men, and those who are materialistic. Some, she said, are "so sweet and superficial": they do it because they just want nice clothes. "I think these women have a very strange relationship with their body."

She came to Cairo because succeeding as an "Oriental dancer" in Egypt, where the dance originated, was "consecration" for Western dancers. She settled in Cairo, where she danced for a year. After that, "the market was very bad," and after so many years of life on stage every day, three or four performances a night, she was tired and wanted to stop, so she decided to teach dancing. Now she performs only occasionally, at private parties.

She stood and wandered to a bookshelf, where she rifled through folders of papers, finding and passing to me a flyer announcing a dance seminar she gave. At first I didn't recognize the picture on the cover as Malak. She was wearing garish stage makeup that made her eyes look long and flat, pharaonically elongated, rather than beautifully deep set and round as they actually were. The dark lipsticked smile in the picture was not the subtle, hinting smile that she usually wore.

She couldn't find some other paper she was looking for, so she returned to the couch. She was wearing a net-like short-sleeved shirt and leopard-print pants that suited her wild hair, and her small belly bulged when she sat down. "When you dance on the stage," she continued, "everyone is looking at you, and not just at your body, also at your face. For the Oriental dancer, the face is very important. You must know the

keeping your way ahead

words to every song and pay close attention to the relationship between the words and the expression on your face. Some foreign dancers have no understanding of the words to the song they are performing to. They are absurd. They will put a ridiculous grin on their face while dancing to some mournful line like 'I have cried so much for you.' If you don't understand the music, you cannot communicate with people at all.

"Communication is a critical part of the performance. The Oriental dancer is famous for talking to her clients while on stage and making jokes with them. The dancer must have a great sense of humor and know how to joke around. But," she continued, "Westerners often imagine the dancer as the fatal woman. But the dancer is not a fatal women. She is a mother."

"Fatal woman?" We looked at each other uncertainly, and suddenly I realized what she meant. "Do you mean femme fatale? In English, we don't translate this, we say it in French."

"Yes, femme fatale. She is not a femme fatale. She is a big Mother." I could actually hear the capital *M* when she said that, I thought, as I quickly scribbled my notes.

"The dancer must be able to deal with every situation: a drunk man, a jealous woman, a veiled woman, an unhappy bride, a child. Both men and women are watching the dancer. Some might imagine that it's mostly the men, but in fact the women are looking at her just as much as the men, maybe more." Malak thought this all went back to the idea of the mother. "There is a French psychoanalyst, a Moroccan Jew, a Lacanian. Daniel Sibony." She went to the bookshelf again and pulled out a book entitled *Le corps et sa danse*. She handed it to me. "He has written about the symbolization of the Oriental dancer. Sibony is the one who says the dancer is the mother. He says that all men, when watching the dancer, feel that she is both *umm* and *umma*, mother and motherland. The two main parts of the body of the dancer, the breasts and the hips, these symbolize motherhood.

"I don't entirely agree," she continued. "There is a dimension Sibony has forgotten, although perhaps this is included in the concept of mother too. When the dancer makes jokes, there is always sexual connotation in the jokes and songs." Then she raised her eyebrows and cocked her head, as the smoke trickled up from her joint. "But again, maybe this is part of the mother."

She took the book from me and flipped through the heavily underlined pages. "Here," she said, "I will translate. 'The dance is a ceremony in which emotion goes to the breasts and hips of a woman, symbolizing the mother. This belly is her belly and the belly of the Other, and the Common Belly.'" She pointed to a line in the book. "Here, copy in French." I wrote, fumbling to get all the accent marks right, "*Ce ventre est á la fois le sien et celui de l'Autres ventre commun aussi de la oumma—de la Matrie—jouissant d'elle-même*." While I copied, she stubbed out the rest of her joint.

I handed back the book. "The idea that is most important," she continued, "is that the dancer is enjoying the movement of her body itself. She takes sensual pleasure in the movement. All the men are brothers, the mother feeds them from her body, like the Arabic language carries and cradles those who use it." She flipped through the book and handed it to me again. "Copy this." I hunched over my notebook and wrote, "*Elle vibre et chante dans leur corps. Que réveille danseuse dans ces corps d'hommes? L'image—mère assoupie qui se dresse en même temps qu'elle?*"

She asked if I had read the work of Karin van Nieuwkerk, a Dutch anthropologist who wrote an ethnography of dancers and singers in Egypt. "According to Van Nieuwkerk, the Oriental dancer is transgressing social rules, since as an entertainer, she is using her body to make money. But in Egypt," Malak continued, "some dancers are married; they have children. They do the job to make money. Maybe they don't even really like the job. It's not such a flashy, showy life as people imagine. It's just a job that the dancer leaves at the end of the day to come home to her family."

I thought of Kerim. If he was so insistent that he would never marry a Pomodoro waitress, then how much worse would he consider marriage to a belly dancer? "Most Egyptian men I know say they would never marry a dancer since she is not respectable," I commented.

Malak nodded knowingly. "Yes, there are many like this. But the great thing about Egyptian society is that you can always find people who are not so obsessed over traditional norms. Also, dancers often marry singers or musicians. They are in the same community, they know how the dancers live, and they don't have fantasies about the glamorous life and sex with clients. They recognize that it's a hard job. You get cheated by the manager; you have arguments over pay; you struggle to find work."

She lit a cigarette and stroked her Persian cat. "There is a kind of man in society who loves to look at women. He looks absolutely like a character from a book of Naguib Mahfouz. He likes drinking, dance, women. He likes life. He goes out every night to see women dancing.

"You know," she added, "the beautiful thing about this dance in Egypt is that it is not class exclusive. You can find every type of venue. From the most expensive, three hundred pounds an evening, to the cheapest twenty-pound evening. Even a taxi driver can enjoy a dancer. It is no more expensive than a movie and popcorn. There are men from every class who love seeing dancers, who love women. And maybe these," she said finally, "are the ones who marry a dancer."

Malak had become restless, constantly moving around and rearranging papers. I thanked her for her time and told her she was an anthropologist's dream: an informant who knows all the key theorists in the field.

She walked me to the elevator, then stopped the doors from closing. "By the way, would you like to come with me some time to see a dancer perform?" My eyes went wide with excitement. "Good. You see, I have a friend who likes dancers and he knows all the places; he can take us out sometime." I asked if it was expensive, wondering how I could afford it on my meager research stipend. She smiled her subtle smile and said, "Oh, I think he will pay. This is not something for you to worry about."

As I stepped out of the building into the light, the doorman bowed to me. I nodded to him, then stepped into the street to wave for a taxi. The taxi that pulled over already had someone sitting in the front passenger seat. I slid into the back seat of the Fiat.

The driver was an old Nubian man with dark skin wearing long robes and a turban. He was talking amiably with his other passenger, an elderly man dressed in a suit. I listened quietly in the back as they reminisced together about how much things had changed in Cairo and how different everything was from the days of King Farouk. "Everything changes but the cars!" the driver exclaimed. "They're still the same as in the days of King Farouk." He pointed to a decrepit old Mercedes. "Look, that one is definitely from the era of the kings."

The banker laughed and pointed to another car. "Look, that one predates King Farouk!"

I thought about the interview with Malak. Lacan, Sibony, Van Nieuwkerk; "the big Mother"—I could actually hear the capital *M* when she said that—the womb, the common belly. I should just ask her to compile a reading list for me and make her one of my dissertation advisers. It didn't bother me so much. Graduate school had inured me to feeling bad about having my ignorance revealed, since it happened so often. Anyway, Malak had been gentle; she hadn't tried to show up my stupidity.

The taxi driver was taking me to al-Hussein so I could visit Sara and Nesma and George. He dropped me off just before al-Azhar Mosque. When I handed him ten pounds, he said politely, "No, keep it!" I had to insist several times before he would accept cab fare.

When I got to the antiques shop, I greeted Sara and Nesma with four kisses each. George smiled and raised his hand in greeting. The air conditioner was sputtering uncertainly. I sat down on a little wooden stool and was telling them about my first interview with a belly dancer when a couple came into the shop, an Egyptian man with a fair woman who spoke with an Australian accent. He translated for her, and they kept touching affectionately. Sara watched them move around the store. The tourist asked questions in English, and the man translated her questions and George's answers. I wondered why George didn't just speak to her in English. Nesma spoke only a smattering of English, and Sara almost none at all, but George was nearly fluent. Yet he only spoke Arabic with the couple, leaving the man to translate.

When they had left, Sara commented, "You know, there are a lot of Egyptian men who marry foreign women, usually tourists they meet here, and whenever Egyptians see that, they always assume that he married the foreigner to travel and live outside of Egypt because of economic circumstances. Everyone assumes that it's self interest, not true love. But the stereotype isn't always true. I know one foreign woman, I think she was German, she fell in love with the son of the owner of a small grocery near where I live. He's an educated young man but they're not rich or anything, and it was really a story of true love. The man never wanted to leave the country, he was happy where he was, and it was the girl who wanted to leave, and that was their problem together, that they each wanted to live in a different place."

"But how do you decide if the man loves her or he's only marrying her out of self-interest?" I asked.

"First of all, you can tell he loves her if he tries to get her to convert to Islam, if he's Muslim; and second, if he wants to have kids with her. The two go together, because if he really wants to build a life and family with her then he'll try to convert her so that they can raise the children together as Muslims. Even if she remains unconvinced and doesn't become a Muslim, the important thing is that the man tries to convert her and at least introduces her to his religion."

Nesma spoke up from where she was arranging a display of Turkish silver boxes. "I know of one guy, he's the son of my maternal aunt, and he's one who married a foreigner just out of self-interest. I don't like to say this about a relative but unfortunately it's true. First he was engaged to a foreigner, an English woman, and he had a carpet store, so this girl used to bring her foreign friends to the shop and drum up business for him. Then he met an older German woman who was rich. She came to Egypt as a tourist, and she was a lot older than my cousin; she already had grown children of her own. So you know what he did? He broke off his engagement with the first and married the second because of what she could do for him financially."

She locked the display case with a key she wore around her neck. "Probably the woman knew that he was interested in her for her money and that she'd have to spend money on him, but maybe she just considered this part of the cost of vacation. You pay for what you get, and the guy was handsome in the way that foreigners find attractive. It was like part of her travel expenses.

"Anyway, so they married and the woman spent a lot of money on him, buying an expensive apartment and furnishing it really nicely, and they got a car and he was always driving it around, of course. Then he met another woman. She was also a foreigner but a lot younger, and so he broke it off with the older German woman. He told her that he loved her but he was desperate to have a family and he couldn't do it with her because she was so old. He said that if he could have children with her he would have stayed with her, but he couldn't, so he needed to find someone young to have kids with.

"And then he stayed friends with his German ex-wife and he encouraged her to become friends with his new wife, and if you can believe it, the first wife actually visited him and the second wife in Holland! That's why I say that she was just doing it as part of her vacation, because she didn't even care that much when the relationship ended. I mean, who goes to visit their ex-husband with his new wife? The woman must be crazy.

"So finally he left the country with his second wife, because he'd already gotten all he could out of Egypt with the first wife, and he had kids with the second wife, but I don't think he really cared about them. He didn't try to convert the wife and didn't worry about her religion at all. Some people are like that. They just have kids but they don't give a damn about them and they don't worry about raising them in their religion. When the relationship with the foreign woman goes bad, they just leave the woman with the kids and don't give a second thought about them."

George had been listening, and now he said to me, "So you see, Lisa? It's not just Egyptian men who are trying to sleep with foreign women. It's also foreign women who come here to sleep with Egyptian men. It's well known that no foreigner can compete with Egyptians in bed."

"Oh, please!" Sara sneered at him.

When I stood to leave, Nesma said, "You're not going, are you?"

I kissed her on the cheek. "Yes, I have to go write my notes about the belly dancer."

"Why don't you come to my house for lunch sometime? My mother wants to meet you."

"Of course I'd love to meet your mother," I said.

"How about tomorrow? I'm only working a half day." I was startled to see the vague invitation become concrete so quickly. But I didn't have anything scheduled before my evening dance class with Malak, so I figured I might as well keep myself busy. Besides, my husband was always urging me to spend more time with "respectable women," so maybe lunch with a woman and her mother would morally counteract the time I was planning on spending with belly dancers and their men, who would, it seemed, mysteriously pay for me to see other dancers perform. So I agreed to meet Nesma the next day.

Sara stood up and said, "I'll walk you out." She grabbed her cane and followed me down the rickety steps, then hooked her arm in mine. "I'm going to the hospital for surgery soon," she said casually.

"What?" I exclaimed, stopping to look at her. "Why didn't you tell me about this before?"

"I tried to call you last night to tell you, but there was no answer." She patted my arm and urged me to keep walking.

"I was out with some friends."

"Thank God for your safe return." Sara winced as she stepped in a pothole.

"And may He keep you safe. Now what's this about the hospital?"

"I told you before that I had to have surgery."

"What kind of surgery? What's wrong?"

She explained in Arabic, but I didn't have the vocabulary to understand. All I could make out was that there was something that they had to cut out of Sara's leg.

"Oh, that sounds serious," I said. We turned down an alley. "How long will you be in the hospital?"

"Maybe a few weeks, a month. After I recover from surgery, I have to go through physical therapy."

"How soon after the operation can you have visitors?"

"Anytime. Are you going to visit me?"

"Of course, I will! May God keep you well."

"And you."

"You must be scared."

"A little. Not too much." We stopped in a café at the edge of al-

Hussein Square so that Sara could rest her leg. She waved away a waiter, who looked at her cane with sympathy. Nearby, a group of Americans were buying beaded scarves from a shop that specialized in belly-dance costumes for tourists. I eavesdropped.

"And who is this?" the shopkeeper asked in English, smiling broadly at the young lady in the group.

"This is our daughter," said her mother proudly.

"What a beauty! Does she have a husband? Would you like to marry her in Egypt? I can offer you many camels for her!" he said, joking. The mother smiled nervously but did not respond.

After their transaction was concluded, they walked away, and as they passed by me and Sara, the woman said to her husband in a shocked tone of voice, "Can you believe it? He actually wants to buy her with camels!"

I translated for Sara, who laughed with me. The comedy in this exchange revolved around the tourists' credulity. Egyptian men don't pay for wives. What's more, the scarf vendor from Khan el-Khalili would probably never in his life buy, sell, or barter a camel, in exchange for a bride or for anything else. In fact, tourists were far more likely to come in contact with camels than urban Egyptians. Tourists often take rides around the pyramids on the camels stabled in the neighboring village of Nazlet el-Semman, but few urban Egyptians ever go near a camel.

We rose and started walking again. "So," Sara said, "do you have male friends here?"

"Yes, I have male friends."

"Do they come over to your house?"

"The men? No, I see them outside. Why should they come to my house?" I didn't count Zeid, who only visited accompanied by his fiancée, Ayah.

Sara said, "You know, if there is a man and a woman alone together in a room . . ."

I completed the phrase, ". . . the third one in the room is the devil."

"How did you know that?" Sara asked with surprise. "It's a religious saying."

"Everyone says it," I shrugged.

Sara nodded. "You know, it's true. If a man and a woman are alone, the devil really is there, whispering to them, trying to convince them to hold hands, to kiss . . . and then you know what comes after kissing, don't you, Lisa?" she said, giggling.

me + you + the devil

I raised my eyebrows. "And will Ali come visit you in the hospital?"

"God willing."

"And will you have a private room?"

Sara grinned. "Are you joking? Do you think I have enough money for a private room? Just buying the blood for the operation will leave me broke."

A taxi honked to get our attention, and Sara put out her hand to flag it. I kissed her on both cheeks. "I'll come see you in the hospital next week."

That night I talked to my husband on the phone. I told him about all the places Malak had danced. I didn't mention anything about her description of dabbling in prostitution. He already thought little enough of dancers.

"She invited me to come see a dancer perform with her one night," I told him.

He sighed, sounding exasperated. "Now you're not just taking classes with them and interviewing them, you have to go out with them at night?"

"I can't understand belly dancers without seeing them perform. You can't just understand someone's life by interviewing them."

"Why can't you study respectable women? I never hear you talk about your neighbors. Why don't you get to know the women in your building? Go and drink tea with them in the afternoon."

"I'm not doing research on women drinking tea."

"That's right," he said. "You're not doing your research on anything respectable. You're an Orientalist, doing your research on dancers and things that are exotic and have to do with sex."

I was suddenly intrigued. My husband had never studied the social sciences, the Americans he hung out with were not intellectuals, and I didn't recall ever talking about Edward Said with him, so where had he learned the term "Orientalism"? He had said it in Arabic, *mustashriqiyya*. I had only learned the word in Arabic the previous year when I was studying at the American University in Cairo.

"What do you mean, where did I learn *mustashriqiyya?*" he said, exasperated. "It's well known."

"It's known in Saudi Arabia?"

"Of course! Don't be stupid, *ya* Lisa." He sounded extremely irritated at the insinuation that people in Saudi Arabia might not know the concept of Orientalism.

"Anyway, tomorrow I'm invited to Nesma's house to have lunch with her mother, and I'm sure that lunch will involve drinking *tea*. Doesn't that sound respectable?"

Now I was the one who felt irritated as he praised me and said that visiting Egyptian families at home was what I should be doing all the time.

The next day I arrived at the antiques shop at one o'clock. Nesma seemed almost surprised, and then she asked me if I was going to eat lunch with her. I wondered if the invitation hadn't been serious, or if she had forgotten issuing it, so I politely declined several times, but she insisted, cajoling and pleading, until I was convinced that she really wanted me to come over.

Her family lived in a small apartment in a *sha'abi* (lower class) area on the outskirts of Cairo. It took an hour and two microbuses to get there, and by the time we did, I had no idea where we were geographically. Exposed brick apartment buildings lined dirt streets next to a small field with oxen and burning trash and sludgy-looking canals full of rubbish. Plastic bags were spinning in the small whirlwinds of air between buildings. We climbed up some stairs to her apartment, and she gave me a tour. There were only two bedrooms, and with three children and only two beds in one room, that meant that all three children, including grown-up Nesma, shared two beds in one room. Yet despite these modest circumstances, there were three televisions, one for every room of the house except the kitchen and bathroom, and Nesma's father carried a cell phone, which even I couldn't afford.

We all sat there, staring at each other and making difficult conversation. Nesma was cloyingly polite, in a way that she had never been in the shop. There, I could always count on her to tell me interesting things and joke with me, but here, everything seemed desperately serious. Her mother just sat in a chair, staring at me with a little smile on her face. She didn't speak; any questions I posed were answered with a minimum of words, and then she would fall silent again and continue to stare at me.

Over the couple of hours that we sat there awkwardly alternating between my questions and long bouts of silence, I pieced together the information that Nesma's father worked all day and went to his sporting club after work to hang out with his friends, but his wife never went out alone and didn't let her fourteen-year-old daughter go out alone. If Nesma came home from work late, her mother would beat her with a slipper. Nesma told me this, not her mother. Her mother just stared.

Eventually Nesma's mother roused herself enough to offer me some little seashells that she found on the beach. She advised me to arrange them on top of my television. "Nothing looks so nice as a little piece of nature on top of the television set."

I politely declined. "I don't have a television, actually."

Nesma looked aghast. "But what do you *do* with yourself in the evenings?"

"I write notes on my computer." She stared at me like she had just discovered that I lived with pigs or something. After that, we lapsed into awkward silence again.

I thought to myself, Why am I here? What is the point? So I'm hanging out with some Egyptians in their home. How is this relevant to my research and my life? I had thought it would make me both a virtuous wife and a virtuous anthropologist to spend the day with a Real, Authentic Egyptian Family. But, I thought, this excursion could only be relevant to my research if I were to change my research topic to "really boring stories about really boring people." Then I would have been sitting on the research mother lode.

Yet, as is always the way with ethnographic research, boredom and doubts about the value of participating in long, painful rituals of everyday sociability can instantly transform into revelational moments.

After lunch, the children's English tutor came over, so Nesma's mother called me to come "help out with their lesson." But the tutor didn't want to give a lesson; he just wanted to chatter away at me in Arabic and give me a lecture on the Islamic conquest of Egypt and on religious harmony in Egypt, a lecture that was later repeated by Nesma and her mother, all for my benefit: How Christians and Muslims Live Together in Harmony in Egypt. When the tutor appeared to be getting overly friendly, batting his long, pretty eyelashes at me and completely ignoring the children, I mentioned my Arab husband. "Oh, so you're married," he said, and then, after a pause, he asked, "And is your husband *mutashaddid wa mutamassik* [strict and holding tight] to his religion?"

"What exactly do you mean?" I asked him, feeling increasingly annoyed at his personal questions and wondering if Nesma found me and my questions annoying in the same way.

He said, "You know, strict and moral. For example, my morals are such that I can't let my sister do just anything or go out alone; I have to keep a close eye on her and everything she does."

I said, skeptically, "That's by way of morals?"

"Yes of course," he replied in a pedantic tone of voice. "The older brother's word in the house is stronger than anyone except the father's, and he's the one who watches over his sister and what she does and makes sure that she doesn't go out alone and doesn't have any relationships with men."

He continued to chatter on. I could barely stand to listen to him; I was still seething over his suggestion that my husband should be strict and controlling with me to prove his moral standards. Meanwhile, Nesma's mother continued to stare at me as if I came from another planet.

When I finally declared that I needed to go home to catch my dance class with Malak, Nesma said, "Next time, you have to make yourself free for the whole day, and you can't have any appointments that make you have to leave early."

The thought of a whole day of this made my stomach turn, but I knew it was just a polite formula; they were probably just as tired of me as I was of them, so I only said, "I would love that, of course." It was only later when I was typing up notes about the day that I even realized what I had learned, that surprising gem of cultural insight into the logic of masculinity revealed in my conversation with the annoying English tutor who claimed that controlling the women in his life was how he proved his own moral worth as a brother and as a man.

All these conversations with and about very different kinds of women—from a foreign belly dancer who casually admitted to receiving money for sex, to the shop employees who were as fascinated by belly dancers as they were eager to condemn their lifestyle, to the piously respectable family of one of those shop employees—illustrate different ways that men and women in Cairo engage with hegemonic ideals of respectable womanhood. When the tourist and her Egyptian boyfriend entered the shop, provoking a flurry of debate over how to discern true love from mercenary economic interest in a relationship between a poor Egyptian man and a tourist woman, we saw the complexities of understanding love and desire when these are also inflected by not only cultural but also class differences. In short, despite the hegemony of a fairly narrow ideal of feminine sexuality, there were in practice many different ways that women pursued love and desire in Cairo, shaped by class, family, culture, and individual inclination. In chapter 4, I discuss this complex interweaving of gender, culture, and economic difference in the context of a transnational tourist economy, putting this ethnographic data in dialogue with the theory of mimesis.

Mimesis, Genre, Gender, and Sexuality in Middle East Tourism

Fast forward several years. My marriage had collapsed years earlier under the weight of my refusal to be the respectable woman that my husband wanted me to be, a decision born in large part out of my growing certainty that I couldn't make the organizing principle of my ethnographic research methodology determining whether people were respectable enough for me to want to learn about their lives. We divorced. After the bitterness came cordiality. We started to occasionally share news with each other. We both remarried. A tentative, remote friendship had resumed.

I was working on this book when my ex-husband sent me an email. It said, "Here is my recent picture after I quit smoking last year. please don't laugh at me because i lost some of my teeth." I opened the attachment and burst out laughing. The attachment was a picture of a white camel with long eyelashes whose mouth was wide open. Its tongue was green, suggesting that it had eaten grass recently, and it was missing several teeth.

My ex-husband's email gag provoked me to think about genres of joking, and in particular, about jokes about camels told by Arabs. As we saw in chapter 3, vendors in Cairo's tourist market often joke with tourists about exchanging camels for one of the women in their group. The joke I described wasn't unusual. I heard it again and again. What is more, it is a staple in the tourism industry across the region. Friends and colleagues have told me that the same joke is told in the tourist markets of Amman, Damascus, and Jerusalem.

Now *there* is a fact that is completely fascinating to an anthropologist. The *same joke* is told across the entire Middle East by people who don't know each other, who have never met. What prompts Arabs to make jokes with Westerners about camels? These jokes link tourism with a broader national and regional history of mimetic engagement with Western representations of Arab otherness and constitute a regional genre. In other words, Arabs in Cairo and Amman and Damascus and Jerusalem don't have to know each other to know that Westerners imagine them in relation to camels. And they deal with this bizarre fact—because, just to be clear, the vast majority of Arabs don't actually interact with camels—with jokes. For Egyptians in the tourist market, joking about exchanging camels for a tourist wife is a humorous way of addressing Western tourists' stereotypes about Arabs and their primitiveness. Such jokes slyly elicit Western representations of Egyptian otherness, simultaneously fulfilling those stereotypes and mocking those who believe them.

But there are also interesting things that this camel joke can tell us about the performance of love, desire, and female respectability, because these jokes are highly gendered exchanges that not only mimetically recapitulate European imaginations of Arab sexuality but also parallel local genres of gendered play, flirtatiousness, and courtship. By exploring these jokes and the gendered logic of exchanges with tourists more generally, we can gain insight into a variety of Egyptian theories about love, sex, and gender roles.

Recall the incident I related at the beginning of chapter 3: I was sitting in the antiques shop near Khan el-Khalili, Cairo's main tourist bazaar, and an Egyptian man entered the shop with a woman speaking English. Their appearance in the shop silenced the employees, who curiously watched the couple and then, after they were gone, got into a lively discussion about how to read and interpret romances between Egyptian men and foreign women. I later learned that the man was what the shop employees called a *khirty* (plural: *khurateyya*), a slang term that might be roughly glossed as "tourist hustler." Both the Arabic and English terms carry the same pejorative connotations of someone who is aggressive and possibly dishonest in pursuit of money.

Egyptians who didn't work in tourism often told me that they had never heard the term *khirty*, though they *had* heard the word *turkoman*, which means the same thing. Whereas the former term has only a marginal presence in popular culture (appearing, for example, in an Egyptian film about a man working in Sinai who has a relationship with a foreigner), the latter term has appeared in several classic Egyptian films. Jumana Bayeh (personal communication) has pointed out to me that in Arabic, *kharrat* means both "fibber" and "mapmaker" (see also Hout

2012, 212n5). The etymological connections among "fibbing," "story-telling," and "mapmaking" in the context of tourism (informal guides at once fibbing and making maps for tourists) is intriguing. The more widely known (and somewhat less pejorative) term *turkoman* probably derives from the Arabic root word *targama*, meaning "translation"; the multilingual *turkoman* is the ultimate translator, both linguistic and cultural.

In this chapter, I want to describe the cultural scripts for gendered and sexualized banter that inform interactions between tourists and *khurateyya*, drawing parallels with flirting and courtship in Egypt. I want to examine Egyptian theories about the morals of women and men who work in tourism, which will help us begin to understand the relationship among love, money, and morals—a nexus we will return to in more detail in chapter 6, when we will look at rules about gift giving and theories about prostitution in Cairo.

After examining the "rules" of picking up tourists, I will circle back to the camel-bridewealth joke and show how it indexes inequalities in the global economy and a cultural genre of gendered role-playing that both characterize tourism in Egypt. Finally, I will show how this ethnographic material from Cairo links up to a broader regional economy of signs and representations of Arab sexuality.

The intertwined sexual play and economic critique implied by the camel joke offers insight into theories of mimesis in touristic encounters. Anthropologists have used the concept of mimesis to map out histories of imagination, moments of first contact between Europeans and Indigenous peoples, economies of signs, colonial terrains of power, and their continuities in postcolonial tourism. Here, though, I explore how the concept of mimesis can be used to describe jokes and sexual harassment in the international tourist economy. I will draw parallels between Egyptian interpretations of the tourist hustler (*khirty*) and anthropologists' use of the term "mimesis" to denote a mimicry that somehow fails to achieve what is perceived as the "normal" levels of intersubjective mimicry in human interactions and that thus appears absurd or parodic. Following Erich Auerbach's (1953) analysis, I argue that any discussion of mimesis must take into account not only the political economy in tourism but also genre. The mimesis of tourism in Egypt is more than subversive parody (Bhabha 1994) and more than earnest entreaty (Ferguson 2002): it offers itself for both readings, depending on the inclinations of the audience. The genre of mimesis in tourist encounters in Egypt entails partially concealed meanings that are only selectively available for tourists to read. This hidden level of meaning is linked to ways that the broader tourist economy is shaped by strategic revelations and an economy of secrets, as well as to the gendered and often sexualized role-playing between Egyptian male tourist hustlers and female tourists.

Tourist "Hustling" and Stereotypology

In 1999, I obtained permission from the owner of an antiques shop (which I will call by the fictitious name Ammoula) in Khan el-Khalili to use the shop as a research base. I had already been hanging out there with Sara, Nesma, and George, so it was just a matter of formalizing this arrangement with the mostly absent shop owner, who kindly agreed to let me sit in the shop as often as I wanted. Khan el-Khalili, Cairo's most famous tourist market, is a maze of shops selling silver, gold, gemstones, inlaid mother-of-pearl chests, rugs and tapestries, hand-blown glass, scented oils, incense and spices, papyrus, beaded belly-dancing costumes, musical instruments, antiques, T-shirts, and cheap replicas of pharaonic statues. Ammoula is frequented by both tourists and Egyptians, and its central location enabled me to observe customers, the salespeople's interactions with customers, and the salespeople's commentary on tourists; it also facilitated my admission to neighboring shops. While my research at the time mainly focused on the perspectives of those in the tourist industry, I also conducted informal interviews with tourists—often at the instigation of tourists, who were curious to know what I was doing and eager to share their own experiences. For over two years I spent two or three days a week at Ammoula; in the intervening decade, I have made regular return visits to the shop and to Sara, a key figure in this ethnography.

All anthropologists yearn to become insiders. This is particularly true when their topic of research is tourism and there is an imperative to display a deeper, superior, more authentic knowledge so that they won't be mistaken for tourists (Crick 1985). Yet even after a year of fieldwork, I realized that I still could not pass for or be recognized as any sort of local in Khan el-Khalili, and probably never would. Like many other anthropologists who have studied tourism, I was continually confronted with my own relationship to tourists and to the wider global economy that produces both anthropologists and tourists (see also Brennan 2004, 49). As often as I walked through the narrow, winding alley that ran from al-Hussein Mosque to the *sagha* (the metalsmiths' district), none of the shopkeepers along the route ever seemed to recognize me. Every trip to and from Ammoula was a gauntlet of aggressively friendly hails by shop employees who addressed me (and anyone else who looked like a foreigner) with "Hello, my friend!" or called out with a genial and ironic "How can I take your money today?" Other, more mobile characters, always men, would follow me on my walk, using catchy lines and gimmicks to get my attention: "Hey, you dropped something!" If I looked back, he would say, "Your smile. You've dropped your smile." If that elicited so much as a smirk, the man would immediately start walking in step and turn on the charm, inviting me to accompany him shopping or to the pyramids. Some men would pursue me for blocks, only abandoning their quarry when I reached Ammoula.

Side by side with these clever men who win over tourists with their charm and multilingual gifts are other men, possessed of somewhat less charm, who work the same territory. "Downtown is the *worst* for foreign women," declared Marita, a Swedish belly dancer. "I don't know why Egyptian men feel they have to make a comment to every passing foreign woman." Marita told me that with the influx of Russian tourists and dancers in Cairo, the men in the downtown streets started calling out "Can I fuck you?" in Russian, assuming that she must be Russian with her pale skin and long blond hair. "Unfortunately my Russian is not really good enough to talk to them and embarrass them. They used to say the same thing in English and I would say to them, 'What have you got to fuck me with? Show me, what have you got?'" She laughed. "Then the guy gets really embarrassed in front of his friends." The unofficial guides who work downtown Cairo and Khan el-Khalili to pick up foreigners—often foreign women, but also couples or male tourists—thus shade into sexual harassers, and foreign women often find it difficult to distinguish between them.

The *khurateyya* were occasional visitors to Ammoula. In chapter 3 I described a visit by an Egyptian man and an Australian tourist; the man translated for her while his hands continually petted her. I assumed she was his girlfriend, but the shop employees immediately put him in the category of *khirty*. What about this interaction between the couple led the shop employees to deduce that he was someone who picks up strangers on the street and then uses them to earn a commission on their touristic souvenirs? To answer this question requires an explanation, first, of the role of the *khirty* in the tourist economy and, second—as the shop employees' long discussion of the ratio of affect to mercenary self-interest in Egyptian men's liaisons with foreign women suggests—an analysis of local ideologies around gender roles in romantic relationships.

There is a relationship both symbiotic and antagonistic between *khurateyya* and shopkeepers. *Khurateyya* have informal agreements with certain stores, in both Khan al-Khalili and around the pyramids, to bring them customers. The tourists are reassured by their "guides" that they are getting a bargain. "I know this guy," they tell tourists, "and I can get him to give you a good price." The guides then circle back afterward to take a commission on what the tourists have bought. *Khurateyya* show the tourists around the shop and act as translators. Shopkeepers I spoke to claimed that *khurateyya* sometimes pretend to bargain the prices down for the tourists, while actually hiking them up so that they can take a higher commission. As translators they facilitate cultural interactions, but they also control them; pretending merely to translate, they can manipulate prices. Tour guides and shop owners all build up their overall wealth of linguistic capital, social capital (whom they know and what favors they can pull, such as knowing an antiquities inspector who can get people into a site after hours), and, most important, cultural capital: knowing how to interact appropriately with tourists to put them at ease, fire their imaginations, fulfill their fantasies, and encourage them to spend.

It is important to understand this secret commission system because friendship (or at least friendly social interactions that mimic friendship, which is why shopkeepers so often call out to tourists, referring to them as "my friend") becomes a means to economic profit for tour guides. But in order to profit, the economic motive must be hidden and the friendship emphasized. This is what lies behind my shopkeeper friends' skepticism about the authenticity of the intimacy between tourist and guide when the guide is taking the tourist shopping. It also explains tour guides' drive to understand tourists' desires, so that the guides can produce themselves as the object of those desires.

Part of this mimetic engagement with touristic imagination involves building up a personal inventory of stereotypes about what tourists are and what they want, in order that the hustler or salesperson might be what the tourist wants him or her to be: an entrepreneurial enactment of otherness (Comaroff and Comaroff 2009, 50). For example, here is how Osama, a gem merchant in Khan el-Khalili, described his method for sizing up tourists and what they want. I was asking him about how he interacted with the range of tourists who visited his shop. He explained to me that he judged tourists as individuals from their appear-

ance, and after determining their national origin and individual characteristics based on their clothing and their facial features, he tailored his
interactions with them accordingly. Curious to try to better understand
his gift of discernment, I asked him what it was in tourists' clothing
or face or manner that told him where they came from and what they
wanted. "I can't explain it," he told me. "It's just a feeling or intuition,"
he claimed, and he said that everyone who worked in that market, dealing with customers from so many different cultures, needed to have this
instinct for how to size up a customer and know how he or she wanted to
be treated, or else they would never succeed in tourism.

It was a two-part process, he explained. First, he must figure out
where the tourist is from. Then, he has to be what the tourist wants him
to be. He offered a couple of examples to illustrate how he discerns and
fulfills tourist imaginations. Some female tourists come in and, he said,
he could tell that they are very religious. They might be wearing *hijab*
(a head covering), even *niqab* (a veil for the face); often they are Muslims from Malaysia or Indonesia who are studying at nearby al-Azhar
University. He must act religious with these types of tourists, he said,
to avoid offending them and to make them feel comfortable. He must
not touch them, not even graze a hand while passing them stones to
examine.

On the other end of the spectrum, he said, are Russian tourists. Russian women like to be flirted with, he claimed, so he smiles at them,
laughs with them, and compliments them. They might offer a price for
something they want to buy, and he might agree with the price, but if
he shows that right away, they might doubt they are getting a good deal.
So he will say to them, "Well, I don't want to sell it for so little, but I'll
agree if you'll give me a kiss." Then, he says, he kisses them and they
feel happy that they have gotten a bargain because of their charm or
beauty.

Yet as Marita's comments suggest, Russian women don't see themselves as longing to be flirted with. Several Russian dancers told me that
going shopping in Khan el-Khalili was like being in a zoo, where they
were the animals being teased and taunted by Egyptian men.

Like Osama, nearly every merchant, shop owner, and salesman that
I interviewed in Khan el-Khalili had a list of national stereotypes that
they operated from when dealing with people. The stereotypes often
varied radically—one would say that Italians were ornery and paranoid
about being cheated, while another would say that Italians were open
and friendly just like Egyptians—but what was consistent was that each

shopkeeper had a mental list of characteristics he associated with the different nationalities of tourists visiting.

Osama invoked this capacity for stereotypology and mimesis as an essential instinct that was necessary to be successful in the tourist market. It is reminiscent of Michael Taussig's (1993) *Mimesis and Alterity*, in which he marvels at the way Charles Darwin and other early colonial travelers repeatedly commented on the natives' uncanny intuitive capacity for mimicry. Osama's claim, however, is more modest than Taussig's: not *all* "natives" are intuitively mimetic, only the ones who work in tourism. Nor are all "natives" very good at intuiting the desires of tourists and mimicking these back at them, as the case of the Russian belly dancers illustrates.

Camel Jokes and an Economy of Representations

Intense competition for tourist dollars means that bazaar merchants and informal guides are constantly calculating the best strategy for capturing tourists' attention, and they experience constant rejection. They have various mechanisms for navigating the complex terrain of economic and cross-cultural personal interactions as they attempt to earn a living and maintain their dignity, and coping with rejection may entail both humor and aggression. A compliment can quickly transform into a lewd remark. At one place I regularly passed in Khan el-Khalili, the shopkeeper's preadolescent brother would hang out in the alleyway. When I was approaching the shop, he would say, "Nice eyes!" When I passed without entering, he would call out, "nice ass!" at my retreating figure.

Eve Kosofsky Sedgwick (1987, 129) analyzes the "(pseudo)metonymy" by which women are "described as 'ass,' as in 'a piece of.'" It is a form of male homosocial bonding with other men; the phrase, she notes, "is never addressed to a woman, but only 'used behind her back' to another man." In the bazaar encounter just described, even if the comment wasn't addressed to me, it was clearly said (loudly and in English) for the (foreign) woman to hear, and this is part of the homosocial bonding that Sedgwick describes, as it makes sure that the woman hears her own objectification, whether complimentary (to her face) or vulgar (to her back[side]), without being able to respond to it.

But in the context of tourism, this comment is more than just homosocial bonding and objectifying or harassing women. In this and similar jokes made with and about tourists, there is often an element of something hidden that is a sort of invitation to the tourist to either join in the joke or become the butt of it (pun intended). If I had stepped into the shop, a casual compliment ("nice eyes") would have segued seamlessly into courteous attention. It was only when I refused his advance—in the context of a tourist economy where shopkeepers are constantly, discouragingly, refused—that the complimentary approach transformed into homosocial masculine objectification.

The camel joke is a good example to illustrate how jokes and comments in the tourist bazaar ambiguously shift registers from laughing with to laughing at, depending on the reaction of the tourist. The shopkeeper simultaneously complimented the tourists' daughter and invited them to laugh with him at his joke about camels. When they didn't—when they, instead, took it as serious evidence that he wanted to buy their daughter with camels, despite his laugh and joking manner—the joke turned on them, highlighting for the Egyptian vendor and his friends the tourists' ignorance about modern Egyptian marriage customs. The camel joke uses humor to slyly address Western tourists' stereotypes about Arabs and their primitiveness.

In fact, camels exist in Cairo and its outskirts only *because* of tourists, not because Egyptians need them for marriage transactions. This point was driven home for me one day in late 2009 when I was talking with a friend, Anwar, a doctor. We were talking about poverty and class structures in Egypt, and he was telling me about the house calls he makes in a village near the Giza pyramids. "It's so depressing. When I go to these people's houses and see how poor some of these people are. . . . And you know, these are people who, when you see them, they look normal, they don't look that poor. But then you get to their houses and you see how bad it is. . . . You know, I don't want to take their money, I want to say, 'No, keep your money.' They're so poor that sometimes they even have a camel in the house with them. And the camel is like a family member, you know. More valuable than the family members, because that camel is their bread and butter; it's what helps all of them survive."

Perplexed, I asked how they could get enough milk from a camel to support a family. Wouldn't it be more trouble than it was worth to feed the camel?

Anwar laughed. "They don't keep camels for milk! I mean, sure, if they get some milk out of the camels, then that's a bonus, but that's not why they have them. They have the camels because of the tourists, because tourists like to ride camels around the pyramids! That's how they make their living."

In short, the camel joke works with tourists only because camels loom so large in the touristic imagination of Egyptian life, to the extent that it is only *because of tourists* that Egyptians on the outskirts of Cairo keep camels. When tourists take the joke seriously as an expression of bridewealth tradition in Egypt, they reveal not only their ignorance about Egyptian culture but also their ignorance about how the tourism industry revolves mimetically around their own imaginations of Arabs and their camels.

The camel-bridewealth joke is one of many jokes about camels that are told across the Middle East, often in response to Arab perceptions of Western stereotypes. When I lived in Saudi Arabia, for example, a Saudi woman who had visited the United States complained about being asked by Americans whether Saudis rode around on camels or not. She would respond dryly, "Yes, and my camel's name is Mercedes."

Camels are an enduring theme in Western representations of the Middle East. Edward Said (1978), for example, criticized Bernard Lewis's interpretation of the etymological origin of the Arabic word *thawra* (revolution) as having its root in the "rising up" action of an excited camel. Often Western portrayals of Middle Eastern men and their camels carry sexual overtones. Consider, for example, the children's T-shirt that I picked up in the Cairo airport in 2008: an image of a camel like the one on cigarette packages is paired with the text "9 out of 10 men who try camels prfer [*sic*] women." Or a March 16, 2008, article in the *New York Times* by Katherine Zoepf on camel breeding in Saudi Arabia, which insinuates that Arab camel breeders harbor a thinly veiled sexual love for camels:

> "She isn't married yet, this one," Shammari said. "She's still a virgin. Look at the black eyes, the soft fur. The fur is trimmed so it's short and clean, just like a girl going to a party." Suddenly, Shammari grabbed the white camel's chin and kissed her square on the mouth. "When you get to know the camels, you feel love for them."

The stereotype about Arabs' supposed attachment to camels tells a story about an exotic nomadic other. This imagery has been romanticized in the photography of the twentieth-century English travel writer Wilfred Thesiger and the writings of Western travelers to Arabia over the past couple of centuries. But it also can allude to an imagined perverse Arab sexuality, sexual repression leading to sexual perversion. This is an enduring theme in Orientalist representations of the Middle

East, as Edward Said (1978), Rana Kabbani (1986), Malek Alloula (1986), and Joseph Massad (2007) have shown.

Thus the depiction of Arabs as camel lovers, with all the double entendre that "lover" implies, is a stereotype with a long pedigree, one that Arabs are acutely aware of. (And Orientalism is certainly not, as I naïvely thought back at the turn of the millennium before my Arab husband taught me otherwise, only a Western academic frame of analysis for the history of European study of the Middle East. As my Moroccan dissertation supervisor Abdellah Hammoudi taught me [personal communication], Said's critique was preceded by those of a number of Arab intellectuals who wrote about decolonizing the social sciences, including Anouar Abdel-Malek [1963] and Abdallah Laroui. And Ridwan al-Sayyid [2004] documents how "nationalists and Islamists were criticizing orientalism long before Abdallah Laroui, Anwar Abd al-Malek or Edward Said." What is more, the critique of Orientalism is not just the domain of Arab intellectuals; see Transfeld 2014 for a translation of a Jordanian rapper's song about Orientalism in the contemporary Middle East, suggesting that Orientalism shapes not only the way academics and our audiences shape Western views of the Middle East, but also Middle Easterners' self-representations.)

In short, the Arab camel lover is such a well-known stereotype that it has become a genre for Middle Easterners to talk about Western representations of themselves. But I want to push this a little further and argue that we can use the camel-bridewealth joke and gender in the Egyptian tourism industry as a lens to examine theories of mimesis, and vice versa.

The Gendering of Tourism: Courtship Scripts

In Osama's description of how to interact strategically with female tourists, in the "nice eyes, nice ass" comments from the boy in the Khan el-Khalili, and in the various camel jokes, it is clear that sexuality and gender are important aspects in the tourist encounter and in the imaginations of both the tourists and the touristed. As my account of the antiques shop employees' discussion suggests, there is a common perception that for many tour guides, the economy of commissions on souvenirs flows almost seamlessly into an economy of sexual conquest (c.f. Bowman 1989). The informal tour guide, the *khirty*, does not go to school to learn his trade (unlike the licensed official guides, who must complete four years of university studying tourism or antiquities); he learns on the street, through his interactions with foreigners. Each interaction builds up his stock of linguistic, social, and cultural capital, which is parlayed back into his business as cultural translator. Even when he makes no money out of an interaction, the *khirty* gains other kinds of capital through friendships with foreigners, up to and including sexual encounters with foreign women, which not only give him prestige among his friends but also represent the most intimate kind of privileged access to a foreign culture. He accumulates cultural capital as he learns some new words or expressions, information about a foreign country, or even more ephemeral insights about how to convey reliability, sociability, and trust. He is a cultural *bricoleur*, to use Lévi-Strauss's concept: perpetually improvising and cobbling together the insights gained through an idiosyncratic history of interactions and fashioning these into a unique approach, a sell, and possibly a score.

The older *khurateyya* whom I interviewed scorned the practice of combining guide work with sexual conquests and said that it gives the trade a bad name. Yet nearly all the tourist women I interviewed described the sexually aggressive pickup lines used on them by informal guides, and said there was a thin line between friendliness and sexual advances after contact was established. For example, two Australian tourists whom I interviewed described a day of touring with two men they had met who made constant advances in physical proximity coupled with innuendo. One girl laughed and said, "I even got the 'cinema stretch'!"—mimicking someone pretending to yawn and stretch his arm and then casually laying it across the shoulders of another person—"I haven't seen that since I was twelve!" Her companion laughed and said to the other, "A little chocolate in the milk!" before turning to me and explaining that this was one of the lines the men had used on her.

This pattern of advance reproduces on a sexual level the pattern of social assertiveness that characterizes the dogged persistence of informal tourist guides, who recruit tourists off the street in heavy competition with other would-be guides. And the masculine role of the *khirty* in pursuit of tourists has its parallel in cultural scripts for dating and courtship in Cairo. Recall Nesma's claim in chapter 1: "Man is naturally a hunter. He loves the chase." The shop employees in Ammoula believed that the cause of Sara's lack of success in obtaining commitment from Ali boiled down to her aggressive pursuit of him and her failure to act sufficiently feminine and coy. While a man hunts, women are expected to be reactive, playing the role of sexual gatekeeper to the man's sexual advances (though, as Nesma's advice to Sara suggested, a woman may indirectly pursue a man by placing herself in a man's path and then firing his interest by adopting this coy role). And just as it is the man who is expected to make the overt effort in courting a woman in Egyptian culture, so the *khirty* must court strangers, both figuratively and even literally.

An Egyptian television commercial circa 2000 exemplifies this cultural courtship script: a young man sees an attractive fair-skinned woman on the street and follows her into a grocery store. While staring at her, he asks the grocer about *halawa*. *Halawa* is a dessert made of sweetened dry sesame paste that is sold in tubs. But *halawa* also means "sweetness." Asking about the tub of *halawa* while looking at the woman is clearly meant as a reference to her attractiveness, and the grocer immediately understands the young man's meaning. "Yes, look how white it is, and how sweet!" he says, raising his eyebrows up and down comically. "White" refers to the purity of the *halawa*, but fairness of skin is also considered beautiful by many Egyptians. (A popular skin-lightening cream on the market in Egypt is called Fair and Lovely.) "Is that imported *halawa*, or Egyptian?" asks the young man, glancing at the woman and implicitly wondering if she's Egyptian or a foreigner. The woman, who has been listening with a small smile on her face, tosses her head coyly to indicate that she understands his Arabic. The grocer winks and says, "It's local *halawa*, all right." The commercial ends with the smiling young woman leaving the store and the young man hot in pursuit. She is pleased because of his clever way of complimenting her. However, she does not respond to the compliments, nor does he expect her to. She is supposed to be coy until he has found just the right approach to win her over, and he will persist until he does.

The *khirty*'s paradigmatic pursuit of tourists mimics this advertisement's idealized portrait of a man pursuing a woman. *Khurateyya* approach strangers and try to come up with witty, complimentary things to say that will win them over. They do not expect it to be easy to win over the tourists; in fact, they expect rejection. But they hope that if they persist and turn on the charm, they may succeed. Egyptian friends constantly warned me to not give the slightest notice or response to any man who flirted with (*'akisni*) or harassed me in the street because any response, even an insult or verbal rejection, would be seen as an opening, an invitation for him to carry on. Similarly, tourist hustlers hope to elicit any kind of notice from the tourists they are pursuing. If they are completely ignored, they become discouraged and might even hurl insults, with flirtation seamlessly transforming into harassment (as in the nice-eyes-nice-ass routine), but as long as they get some sort of response, even a polite rejection, they persist. They persist because this is part of the culturally scripted role they are playing: to pursue relentlessly until they find the right way to win over their target, ignoring rejection and looking for any opening that might offer an opportunity to win the tourist over. This script for the pursuit of tourists clearly parallels the script for the masculine pursuit of women portrayed paradigmatically in the *halawa* television commercial.

Striking evidence of the masculine nature of the *khirty*'s role is the fact that I never encountered a female *khirtiyya* (feminine for *khirty*), nor did any woman ever call out to me or follow me on the street—in spite of the fact that many women work as official (licensed) tour guides and in shops frequented by tourists (as Sara's and Nesma's jobs attest). One *khirty* once told me that he knew of one woman working at the trade; she was fluent in English and spoke bits of several other European languages, but, according to my informant, she found it hard to approach tourists on the street, so she usually paired with a man, letting him make the initial approach. Local cultural scripts for gendered romantic pursuit—the genre of courtship in Cairo—thus informs the workings of the tourism industry, locally inflecting a global trade (Brennan 2004).

The literature on gender and the service industry under contemporary capitalism points out that women are channeled into this industry with great success because the gendered cultural roles that they internalize mesh so neatly with the demands of service jobs (Hochschild 1983). In Egypt, however, gender roles map out unevenly on service jobs in the tourism industry, and what determines the gendering of a tourism job is not who is culturally conditioned to smile and to please but, rather, who makes the initial approach and whether they recruit in public spaces (the street) or private spaces (a travel agency). The aggressive pursuit of tourists is such a culturally masculine role that this lone female *khirtiyya* reportedly could not herself approach tourists. In contrast, many Egyptian women work as official tour guides, and this is seen by most Egyptians as a job that is not at all incompatible with female respectability. This is not just because it is a "real" (state-sanctioned) job, whereas the *khirty* is part of the informal economy. It is also because, working for a travel agency, the licensed guide doesn't make the initial approach and hard sell on the street. Instead, the tour guide plays the role of host. The tour guide who welcomes tourists to his or her country behaves like an Egyptian who invites guests into his or her home, and generosity and hospitality are gender-neutral traits that Egyptians universally admire.

This analysis of the cultural scripts informing both romantic encounters and informal tour guides' pursuit of tourists partially explains why shop employees assumed that the Egyptian man entering the store with an English-speaking woman must be pursuing a mix of sexual conquest and economic self-interest. The negativity implied in that judgment is not only a merchant's resentment toward a middleman who takes a cut of the profits, nor does it (necessarily) derive from the fact that in the slippage between guide and boyfriend, the presumed *khirty* crosses boundaries of religion or ethnicity. It is also because in the (assumed) act of earning money from the purchases of a woman with whom he is intimate, he violates norms of idealized masculinity by failing to economically provide for his (would-be) girlfriend. Even as the *khirty* enacts a cultural script of masculine pursuit of a tourist/woman, he undermines it by profiting from her.

After labeling an unknown customer "*khirty*," the antiques shop employees followed up with a long discussion of the complicated calculus one could use to discern the "true" motivations behind a poor Egyptian man's liaison with a wealthier foreign woman, even while acknowledging the difficulties in finding the cultural sense in some of these relationships, with their extraordinarily complex blending of affect and economic incentive. But here I want to examine their labeling not only as a way of understanding the complexity of subjectivities and forms of autonomy, agency, and contestation that characterize the tourism arena, but also as a way of shedding light on the concept of mimesis in anthropological and postcolonial theory.

Defining Mimesis in Terms of Desire, Power, and Performance

Egyptians are acutely conscious that many Western tourists think that they are some sort of primitives or, at best, exotic other. Sometimes they handle this with humor, as in the camels-for-a-bride joke. Sometimes they express frustration or disgust at tourist ignorance (Wynn 2007). Other times they exploit it mimetically. You want exotic? We'll give you exotic! It is a performative response to tourist imaginations of self, and it is also internalized into their identities of what it means to be Egyptian (Adams 1996). For example, Timothy Mitchell (1995), writing about Luxor, reports that Egyptian tour guides had come to say "we" when talking about the ancient Egyptians, and he argues that this identification with pharaonic Egypt came about as a result of monuments-oriented tourism in the Nile Valley.

The word "mimesis" has an ancient pedigree. In the works of Plato and Aristotle, it referred to the representation of nature in art. Plato and Aristotle disagreed, however, over its moral implications; in Plato's *Republic*, mimesis was depicted as false, inauthentic, and, in literature and drama, emotionally destabilizing because of the intense emotions it aroused. For Aristotle (1917), imitation was human nature and fostered moral learning through the cathartic power of emotionally experiencing the other. Frankfurt School theorists such as Theodor Adorno and Walter Benjamin pushed this early philosophical interest in the relationship between nature and culture by exploring the connections between the "primitive" mimesis of magic and more "modern" forms of mimesis, from language (Benjamin 1978) to art that could mobilize the masses, whether to revolutionary (Benjamin 1968) or fascist ends (Huhn 2004, 160).

In the anthropological literature, mimesis has been used to refer to the process of taking elements from a foreign culture and imitating them, incorporating them into one's own culture, but with different meanings that make the act more than mimicry; mimesis is also creation, interpretation, and sometimes parody. Taussig (1993, xiii) famously defined mimesis as "the nature that culture uses to create second nature, the faculty to copy, imitate, make models, explore difference, yield into and become Other." Mimesis in this definition is a different order than mimicry. It is more than copying; the thing is not only copied but interpreted, put into a new context and given new meaning, even as it draws on the power of the original. As Taussig (1993, 1997) argues in his reading of Benjamin, in making a copy, mimesis takes for itself the cultural power of original, but the copy ends up imbued with more power than the original itself; mimesis flows into simulacra: copies with no original (Baudrillard 1988). As Osama sought to align his desire for commerce with his imagination of Russian tourists' desire to be flirted with, that imagination of Russian women's desire was a kind of simulacrum, a reality that existed in his mind and informed his interaction with tourists yet had no basis in the desires of any of the dozen Russian-speaking women I spoke to. Yet regardless of whether it has any basis in reality, this simulacrum of Russian tourists' sexual identity is incredibly powerful—more real than real, as Jean Baudrillard argues—because it powerfully shapes the way tourists and shopkeepers interact.

Whereas Taussig explored mimesis in first contact and colonial contexts, Vincanne Adams has taken the concept of mimesis and applied it to think through relationships of power and the circulation of representations in the postcolonial context of Nepalese mountaineering tourism. In *Tigers of the Snow and Other Virtual Sherpas*, Adams (1996) uses mimesis to refer to the act of imitating not others but what others think you are (or should be). For Adams, mimesis is "the imitation of what is taken to be one's 'natural' self by way of the Other, through whom one's constructed identity is made visible to oneself" (ibid., 17). With echoes of Baudrillard, she argues that these "virtual Sherpas" that are created out of the engagement between Nepalese Sherpas and the Western imagination of them are "more 'real' than reality itself" (ibid., 20).

> Sherpa mimesis reflects not simply what the Western Other is and does, but also what the Western Other seems to want and desire in the form of cultural differences between Westerners and Sherpas. . . . Sherpas do not just become like the West or that which the West desires; the West becomes part of them as Sherpas find their place as persons and icons in the Western imagination. (Adams 1996, 74–75)

Similarly, Egyptian imaginations of what tourists want take on the force of reality as they inform interactions in the tourist bazaar, even as they are divorced from the reality of what tourists may actually want. Driving the cross-cultural encounters, these imaginations of tourist desires become "more 'real' than reality itself."

This mimetic engagement with others' imaginations of self is one way of understanding the camel-bridewealth joke. Such mimesis is an essential aspect of the tourism industry and, indeed, of the service sector of any economy, which involves the commoditization of pleasantries and emotions (Hochschild 1983), configuring one's affective performance to meet another's expectations. And as with the camel joke, this version of mimesis retains that element of absurdity that Taussig (1993) and Homi Bhabha (1994) have identified as a byproduct of the mimetic faculty.

When I teach the concept of mimesis to anthropology students, the most common reaction I encounter is polite, sometimes irritated, befuddlement. What, they ask, is the difference between mimesis and mimicry? Taussig and Adams have somewhat different interpretations of the concept of mimesis, while postcolonial theorist Bhabha (1994) uses both words, "mimesis" and "mimicry," sometimes interchangeably, in his essay on colonial mimicry. Students—and even some of my colleagues—

find the lack of academic consensus over the definitions of the terms to be frustrating.

Other students have pointed out that mimicry and mimesis, variously defined, are everywhere and in every human interaction. The performance of masculinity and femininity in a romantic relationship, for example, is a mimetic engagement with cultural expectations of gender and aesthetics. The way students interact in a seminar is a mimetic engagement with the teacher's expectations of how students should behave and their own notions of what constitutes academic thought and comportment. What is the utility of a term that is so all-encompassing?

When we boil the concept down to its basics, finding what is shared among the multiple modern (I am excluding Plato and Aristotle) definitions of mimesis, we can see that there are two unifying factors behind every anthropological and critical-theory reading of mimesis: desire and power. Both are necessary components, and looking at the interaction between the two can offer critical insights into the nature of society and culture.

A power differential between two people(s) compels one to perform mimetically for the other or compels an external observer to read that performance as mimesis, regardless of how authentic the performers themselves view it. For example, both Adams's Sherpa guides and Western mountain climbers see Sherpas as "naturally" hardy mountain guides, even though historically Sherpa culture saw mountaintops as the realm of powerful spiritual forces and therefore off-limits; the power differential inherent in the global tourism economy that brings Westerners to Nepal to hire mountain-climbing guides compels the historian to read Sherpa mountain-climber identity as mimetically produced by Western imaginations. Or, to use the example of the Egyptian man who the shop employees automatically assumed was a *khirty* and not the foreigner's boyfriend, the (assumed) economic disparity between the two led my Egyptian informants to interpret the man's affectionate intimacy as economically motivated and thus a false performance of boyfriendness. Looking at this interplay between socioeconomic difference (the wealth of the tourist and the tour guide's need for a job) and desire (the Nepalese tour guide's wish to live up to the Western fantasy of Sherpaness; the Western mountain climber's desire to find the authentic Sherpa guide of his or her imagination; the tourist's or guide's desire to have a sexual encounter with an exotic other or to gain economic benefit from the relationship) illuminates the relationship between the political economy and culture, the ways that political power, economic difference, and a colonial history mold both cultural forms of behavior and constructions of gendered cultural identity (Jacob 2011; Kozma 2013). Economic difference intersects with fantasies of exotic otherness to shape affective and sexual subjectivities for both tourists and hosts (Frohlick 2013).

One must desire the approbation of others to be willing to make the effort to engage in mimesis. That desire, of course, is sometimes compelled by inequality or by a clear power difference, as when a tour guide desires the business of a wealthy tourist. Or the desire can exist in moments where there is no clear imbalance of socioeconomic power, as when a man or a woman performs a gender role in order to attract the regard of a social equal, or even when one partner in a romantic relationship is wealthier and more successful than the other but still works to make him- or herself appealing because he or she desires the love and regard of the other.

We could read mimesis into, for example, the relationship between Ayah and Zeid: Zeid's family had less socioeconomic power than Ayah's, and so he constantly felt compelled to perform his masculine ability to financially support his fiancée, even as he chafed against the requirements of this performance. On the other hand, Ayah, who was from a wealthier and more socially powerful family than Zeid's, also felt compelled to live up to his ideas of feminine respectability, even as she chafed against his conservative notions of appropriate female behavior and smoked cigarettes behind his back.

Why did wealthy Ayah submit to the demands of her socioeconomically less powerful boyfriend? In part, we could attribute this to the fact that Zeid's status as a man gave him power vis-à-vis Ayah, which counteracted the socioeconomic power of her high-status family. Or we could say that Ayah was bowing to the dominance of gender-role expectations in Cairene culture, which were powerful enough that even her family's status didn't give her enough power to defy Zeid's demands that she conform to his definition of appropriate behavior for a modest, respectable Egyptian fiancée.

And yet neither of these explanations is sufficient to explain why either of them bothered. Why make all that effort, when Zeid could have found a girlfriend who demanded less of him or forgone a romantic relationship altogether and focused on his "hectic" job and enjoyed going out late at night to eat at roadside eateries with his male friends, or when Ayah could have given Zeid the boot and stayed out until three in the morning clubbing and smoking with her school friends? Aside from the desire that both of them felt to improve their social status (Zeid to marry into a powerful family, and Ayah to get married and leave her natal home to become mistress of her own household), they both desired and loved each other, and that desire for the affection and approbation of the other, the love that each felt for the other, was the glue that bound them together, despite the tensions and conflicts generated by their different goals and opinions. A concept of mimesis that dwells on power cannot capture the emotional intensity and even the erotic charge (as we saw in Sara's wistful recollection of being slapped by Ali) that can emerge out of making oneself vulnerable to the desires and demands of a beloved. To return to Lauren Berlant's definition of desire (2012, 6–7), their struggles to live up to each other's idealized gender roles were constituted in their attachments formed in that space between the other person that each was attached to and their aspirations: for social advancement, for sexual intimacy. It was both something that each felt as a powerful internal emotion and something that was constituted in the society around them, including class and gender normativity and cultural rules around sexuality. This space of desire generated a willingness to engage with the other person's ideal gender roles, even when they conflicted with the way each wished to live. Socially appropriate dating behavior was negotiated intersubjectively, between Ayah and Zeid and with reference to—and sometimes in defiance of—dominant social norms about respectable femininity and masculinity.

Turning now from romance to the tourist economy in Egypt, how do desire and power interact with culture?

In my reading of Taussig, Bhabha, Adams, and Arlie Hochschild, mimesis appears as a kind of interaction and a way of imagining the other that inheres in a particular structural or historical moment of power relations, whether it is the uncanny mimic at imperial moments of first contact between Indigenous people and Western explorers/colonizers (Taussig 1993), the colonized manners of Indian civil servants (Bhabha 1994), the economy of signs in Nepalese mountaineering tourism (Adams 1996), or emotional performances in the service sector of late capitalism (Hochschild 1983). What are the political and economic structures conditioning mimetic touristic exchanges in Middle Eastern tourism? As Susan Frohlick (2013, 1) notes, "heterosexual sexualities"—of the sort visible both in my informants' relationships and in the flirting and sexual harassment that characterize the tourism market in Cairo—"don't just happen." They are given shape by political, economic, and historical forces, which coalesce into individual subjectivities and affect.

As we have seen in this analysis of Egyptian jokes with tourists, on the surface of these exchanges is politeness and humor, but there is often a frustrated or aggressive undercurrent that reminds us that the tourism encounter is an unequal one, one that Mitchell (2002), Lila Abu-Lughod (2005, 77–78), and others identify as a site of structural violence in Egypt. Mitchell describes how the vast majority of tourist revenue goes to wealthy Egyptian elites or flows right back out of the country, while poor villagers who live next to touristic sites are forcibly excluded by the state from accessing the tourists and benefiting from the lucrative tourist economy. It is "a system of almost total segregation" in which tourists spend all their time either in enclave hotels or tour buses, and "the few occasions in which organized tourists encountered the local street . . . became frenzied scenes in which local peddlers, merchants, and entrepreneurs tried to secure some small share of the tourist business" (Mitchell 2002, 198). In the case of villagers in Luxor, a popular tourist destination in the south of the country, the Egyptian government under Hosni Mubarak spent tens of millions of dollars trying to work out how to evict the villagers so as to purify Luxor as a world heritage site (ibid., 200), and in 1998 this structural violence turned into deadly physical assault when police opened fire on villagers who were protesting attempts to bulldoze their village, killing four and injuring twenty (ibid., 186).

Yet that violence must be cheerfully borne and superficially denied by tourist merchants and workers in the tourism industry in order that they might gain some small benefit from the tourist encounter. It is in this context that we can understand the nice-eyes-nice-ass types of exchanges in Khan el-Khalili; it is this context of mingled cosmopolitanism and structural violence that informs the complex entwining of desire and hatred in the tourist bazaar in Jerusalem that Glenn Bowman (1989) describes in his article "Fucking Tourists." The polysemy of the title phrase—used both as an expletive expressing frustration and as a crude way of talking about sexual conquests—encapsulates the conflicting desires that the Palestinian male merchants expressed for Western tourist women. The (relatively) wealthy tourists symbolized at the same time the economic oppression of Palestinians and the possibility of escape for those men lucky enough to marry one and emigrate:

> The tourist merchant's obsessive interest in having sex with, and in stories of having sex with, foreign women served a dual purpose: it provided merchants with a field in which to play out scenarios of vengeance against foreigners who, in their eyes, oppressed them both economically and socially while at the same time constructing an arena in which

the merchants, all of whom were similarly at the mercy of economic demands over which they had no real control, could compete for the status of being one of those few able to master the masters. (Bowman 1989, 79)

Relationships of love and desire are deeply felt subjectivities at the same time that they are social, political, economic, and historical (Frohlick 2013, 8). The economic and social contexts of Palestine in the late 1980s and Egypt at the turn of the millennium are not very different from each other in the general strokes—the juxtaposition between tourist wealth and local impoverishment; the metaphorical or literal violence underpinning the tourist economy. But while Bowman focuses on Euro-American women tourists in Palestine, this account of tourism in Khan el-Khalili shows a much wider range of tourists (in part because of its proximity to al-Azhar University and the many Muslim students from around the world who study there) and thus a greater range of opportunities for imagining and performatively engaging with otherness. It is not all about sexual conquest. That is a role that the gem merchant was willing to play when he thought it might help make a sale with Russian tourists, but he was equally happy to play the role of respectful pious Muslim to the al-Azhar students.

Bhabha's key insight into mimicry is that it is in the slippage between the performance one is impelled to give and one's ability or desire to achieve mastery in this performance that we see the limits of power, and the uncanny or the absurdity that we read into these slippages offers up for our reading a critique of structures of inequality that are denied or hidden by the ideologies of the powerful. It is this slippage that shapes the play of humor in merchants' exchanges with tourists in Khan el-Khalili, with a joke about camels that invites the tourist to either laugh with them or laugh at them, depending on how they are so inclined, and if the tourist decides to laugh at them—at the Egyptian's apparent simplicity and ignorance of modern norms of romance and marriage—the tourist automatically and unwittingly becomes the butt of the joke by displaying his or her own abysmal ignorance of Egyptian modernity. As the joke plays on the tourists' knowledge of Egypt, it also indexes the way that knowledge is circulated in the tourist economy and secrets are kept for profit, as we saw in the logic of tour guides' commissions. Recalling the economic stakes and the usually veiled but sometimes naked violence of the tourism industry further reminds us that mimesis is not only parody and play; it is also, as James Ferguson (2002) has argued, an earnest statement about global inequalities.

Mimesis as Genre

But what this reading of the multiple layers of a joke also illustrates is that mimesis is more than just economy and structure, more than the witty interplay of parody and earnest commentary on structural violence. Mimesis is also genre. Indeed, as I have shown, camel jokes are a regional genre. The significance of genre is apparent if we examine the meaning of mimesis a bit more closely.

Though Taussig, Adams, and many other anthropologists use the term "mimesis," Bhabha speaks of "mimicry" as well. As I have noted above, the variety of terminology and the different ways that mimesis is defined in the literature often sparks confusion and frustration among my students. Graham Huggan (1997), Paul Ricoeur (1981, 180), and others have attempted to carefully disambiguate mimicry and mimesis; here I am not concerned with parsing the difference between the two words, particularly since different authors have used different words to examine similar concepts and the same words to describe different phenomena. Instead, I offer a definition of my own: in addition to that interplay between desire and power, the other essential concept that I am interested in exploring under the rubric of mimesis is the *performative engagement with some representation of otherness.* The notion of *performance* captures not only the embodied aspect of mimesis that Michael Jackson (1983) and Malcolm Haddon (2003) have identified but also concerns about subjectivity that were essential to early philosophers theorizing mimesis through theater drama. The idea of performance also evokes genre, which is essential for thinking through mimesis because of the way it binds together the subjective and the historical aspects of representations, which Adams explores in her analysis of the economy of signs and representations of Sherpaness. And in focusing not on otherness but on *representation of otherness*, we see how mimesis is a different order from mimicry (Bhabha's ambiguity of terminology notwithstanding); it is mimicry taken to another level of creativity and representation. It is metamimicry, and that second order of representation allows all kinds of other interesting things to enter the picture, such as aura (Benjamin 1968) and the semiotics of tourism (Culler 1981). It allows us to encompass in our definition of mimesis both the creative, appropriative imitation of other (as in Bhabha's and Taussig's analyses) as well as that imitation of the self that is reflected in the other's imagination (as in Adams's use of the term).

But in this definition of mimesis as the performative engagement with representations of otherness, the concept that I want to particularly dwell on is that of *engagement*. The concept of engagement highlights the fact that mimesis is not monologue. It is created intersubjectively. It is articulated within the context of an epistemic regime of gender norms (Butler 1999), our engagement with those norms, and our cocreation of those norms in interactions with other people. And yet, as we have seen in the camel-bridewealth joke, neither is mimesis straightforward dialogue; there are also aspects of monologue within it, things that one side says that the other side does not hear, and polysemy, readings and interpretations that some audiences perceive and others do not. In his analysis of mimesis in ancient Western literature, Homeric and biblical, Auerbach (1953) points out that there is always something hidden in this literature, something that is available to the audience but not to the characters. But the *way* it is hidden, and *what* is hidden, depends on the genre.

We can apply Auerbach's insights to the camel jokes. The camel jokes are a particular genre of mimesis, and in examining what is hidden or what is partially revealed—namely, the kinds of kinship arrangements and sexual relationships that constitute the culture of urban Egyptians, and the Egyptians' cosmopolitanism or backwardness—we can see echoes of the tourism industry, which itself is predicated on the appeal to stereotypes about the Middle East that have their roots in colonialism and centuries of Orientalist representations and also on an economy of secrets and knowledge. Similarly, the genre of courtship in turn-of-the-millennium Cairo conditions tourist exchanges, casting tourists in the role of the coy, pursued woman and the *khirty* in the role of the pursuing male, simultaneously aggressive and charming. Yet outside observers—such as the Egyptian employees of an antiques shop on the fringe of Cairo's tourist bazaar trying to interpret what it means to see an Egyptian man and a blonde tourist woman holding hands—read Egyptian-tourist intimacy as a parody of courtship, one in which the Egyptian man hides his economic interest in the relationship and the foreign woman takes advantage of her holiday to enjoy a performance of exotic virility from an Egyptian man. Just as anthropologists and postcolonial theorists use "mimesis" to describe the slippage past normal intersubjective human mimicry into parodical excess generated when a power differential compels one person or group to engage with another's fantasy of otherness, so too does the *khirty* (hustler) label signal an Egyptian awareness of the conditions of socioeconomic inequality in the tourism industry that make it impossible for my informants to read

Egyptian-tourist intimacy as simple affect and to instead interpret it in terms of a complex performance of romance generated (and tainted) by economic aspirations.

As we have seen in this analysis of tourist hustling in Egypt, there is more than just money at play. The gender and sexuality of the tourism encounter reminds us that mimesis is a bodily genre, a "putting oneself in the place of another" or "a bodily awareness of the other in oneself" (Jackson 1983, 340, 336). This genre of bodily awareness and cultural scripts for gendered courtship explain Egyptians' interpretations of tourist "hustling" as a fluid yet flawed merging of economic goals and sexual conquest that binds together desire for the other and anger over the global economic disparities that are embodied in the tourist.

Summary of tourism

Similarly, both my ex-husband's joking identification of himself with a toothless camel and the camel jokes told in the tourist markets of the Middle East are witty commentary on Western ignorance and fantasies about the Arab world. Even as the camel-bridewealth exchange potentially makes the tourist the butt of the joke, it invites the tourist to knowingly join in the laughter, recognizing and mocking that Western imagination that they participate in. (And if they don't get the joke, they prove their ignorance.) At the same time that this joke references a global political economy of tourism, it is also part of a regional genre that comments on Orientalist representations of Arab otherness and sexuality while enacting cultural patterns of gendered play.

As I have argued in the case of female respectability, these imaginations of tourist desires may have no basis in reality, but they are *really* real—more real than real, in the words of Baudrillard—in the way that they powerfully organize people's actions and shape the way they interact with each other. This chapter also illustrates the extent to which local imaginations of otherness partake of an international political economy of representations of gender and nation. It is this mix of local cultural genres and winking engagement with Western imaginations of Arab sexuality to which we must remain attuned in the chapters to come.

CHAPTER 5

Demimonde: Belly Dancers, Extramarital Affairs, and the Respectability of Women

Everything I thought I understood about gender roles and sexuality in Egypt was unseated when, several weeks after I had first interviewed Malak about her belly-dancing career, I got to meet her friends and realized that there were lots of different ways of engaging performatively with social expectations about respectable femininity and masculinity. Up until that time, all the Egyptians I had met paid some kind of lip service to bourgeois sensibilities about normative sexual and gender roles. Even those among my friends who defied the social norms did so secretly, thus maintaining the hegemony of dominant norms even as they privately subverted them. (For example, Ayah might smoke with her sisters, but she didn't tell her fiancé, thus reinforcing the idea that respectable women didn't smoke and that she subscribed to this norm.) But Malak's friends showed me that there were many other different ways of living in Cairo that unsettled all my ideas about the imperative of being socially "respectable" while pursuing love and desire. They had carved out a space for themselves to dance and sing bawdy songs, flirt and have extramarital affairs. It was a kind of subcultural realm that for me evoked the demimonde of courtesans of the nineteenth century. Like Cairene belly dancers, they were cultured, artistic women who pursued relationships with men but rejected the respectability of "polite society" (as it was called in the nineteenth century) and the constraints of kinship in favor of independence in residence and action. And yet even as they rejected the dominant standards of respectable womanhood, they insisted on the label "respectable" (though sometimes, also, they embraced the label "prostitute," signaling their awareness of how far they deviated from dominant norms).

My introduction to this demimonde began when Malak called to tell me that she was going out to dinner with a group of friends. Her boyfriend had told her that she could invite anyone she liked. "So I thought of you. Would you like to come? I think you will find it interesting. My friend is an expert on belly dancers. He can tell you some good stories."

I was both thrilled and apprehensive. I didn't know how to dress, so I wore something simple and red lipstick. Apparently I had chosen well, because Malak approved. "You look almost European!" Malak said when she saw me. "Most Americans don't know how to wear a good red lipstick!" I felt like a child playing dress-up.

We took a taxi together to an odd restaurant that I had never seen or heard about before. It was located downtown in an area that had been chic sixty years earlier but was now leaning toward rundown. You had to ring the doorbell to be let inside the restaurant, and it gave you the feeling of being admitted somewhere very private and exclusive.

"This is the kind of place where men bring their mistresses," said Malak conspiratorially as we walked in. "There are two classes of nice restaurants in Cairo," she explained. "One kind is for the family; the other kind is *not* for family. This restaurant is known by men who all come here under the same circumstances—never with their wives—so since they are all in the same boat, nobody gossips about anybody else. It is like a big secret that they are all keeping for each other. The kind of place where you never have to worry about running into your wife's respectable relatives, you understand?" She gave me that charming smile of hers and I felt thrilled to have been let in on a secret. But then, Malak could make you feel that way about anything she told you.

We had reached a table full of people, about eight or ten, who all greeted Malak enthusiastically. They were all Egyptian, and all looked to be between ten and twenty years older than I was. I was seated near the end of the table, with Malak directly across from me. I was reassured to have her nearby, but she immediately launched into conversation with the man sitting next to her, who had been introduced as Farouq. Knowing no one else at the table, I sat quietly and looked around me.

The restaurant held an oblong central platform for the performers, and long tables were arranged around it. The walls and ceiling were painted a midnight blue. Because all the edges of the room were such a dark color, and because of the smoke that filled the air and the dim lighting that radiated out from ceiling spotlights in the center of the restaurant, the room seemed to blur at the edges, fading away into night. At one end of the room was a bar, and at the other a small band was set up on the platform, but they weren't performing yet. The singer was chatting with people at different tables. One of the men she was talking to had a thick moustache and looked like a famous actor, but I couldn't be positive in the darkness.

The man to my left spoke to me. He had been introduced as Haroun, and the woman on his other side was Alia. I presumed that they were a couple since the woman was hanging on his arm affectionately. Haroun said, "So, Miss Lisa—is it Miss or is it Madame?"

"Madame."

"Madame Lisa, then. You are American?"

"Yes."

He looked at me thoughtfully. "What are you doing in Egypt?"

"I'm doing my research for my PhD in anthropology."

"Ah. Very interesting. That's fine." He patted me on the arm and then rested his hand casually on my right shoulder, propping his arm on the back of the chair I was sitting in. I was startled by the physical contact.

Haroun was an attractive man, fit, with neatly cropped hair and even features and honey-colored skin. His most striking feature was his eyes, which were an unusually pale shade of amber. He wore a lightweight blazer and trousers that were elegant but casual in cut. Alia, sitting next to him, was a very beautiful woman in her late thirties. She had large almond-shaped brown eyes and high cheekbones. During this exchange, she leaned around the front of Haroun to see me, one hand resting possessively on his chest, and she watched me curiously with a small, wary smile. She was dressed more formally than Haroun, wearing a cream-colored suit and a gold-and-diamond necklace.

"And you, Mr. Haroun, what do you do? I mean what is your profession?"

"Me?" he looked amused. "Well, I'm a businessman."

"What kind of business?"

"Oh, lots of different things, here and there." His reluctance to talk about it made it sound mysterious and shadowy. Later on I learned more about his business, and it was no more mysterious and shadowy than business in Egypt ever is, and it really did consist of lots of different things, here and there; but at the time, the setting, so exotic to me, and the fact that these were Malak's friends to whom she had so often alluded, always fleetingly and without any specifics, set my imagination on fire.

"And do you speak Arabic, Madame Lisa?" (He had been speaking to me in English.)

"Yes," I responded.

"No!" shouted Farouq from the other side of the table. I jumped in my seat, but Haroun just laughed, patting my shoulder reassuringly. "You shouldn't have told him that!" Farouq complained. "You should have told him that you don't speak any Arabic. Then you could eavesdrop on whatever he says. You might have overheard Haroun paying you a compliment!"

Haroun smiled and shook his finger at Farouq, and then Farouq laughed, his whole body moving up and down with his laughter. He was in his late forties, perhaps, with the sallow skin of a chain-smoker. He had silvery-gray straight hair—which he wore longish on top to show it off, since straight hair is prized by Egyptians—and jowls. His fair skin had liver spots, and perched on his narrow, slightly beaked nose was a pair of rectangular wire-rimmed glasses that were slightly askew. Nothing ever sat quite straight on Farouq's body. There was always something off—glasses not quite right, a button undone, a pocket half-turned inside out, a streak of dirt down his pants leg.

Farouq leaned over to me. "So you are doing your research on belly dancers!" I nodded.

"Eh? What's this?" asked Haroun.

Farouq leaned back and put both his arms around Malak and squeezed her. She protested, laughingly. "This is your best subject. The best dancer in Egypt!"

"Here, here!" said Alia, raising her wine glass. We all toasted Malak.

Farouq set down his glass and said expansively, "I can give you lots of information about belly dancers in Egypt."

"It's true," Malak said. "He is an expert on belly dancers."

Farouq looked pleased. "Do you have a tape recorder with you?"

"No."

"At least a pen and paper?"

"No," I said again, indicating my small purse, which had room for little more than lipstick.

"No? What kind of researcher are you?" he shouted, gesturing wildly with his hand.

I was startled, but everyone else just laughed, and Haroun patted me again. Eccentric outbursts seemed to be Farouq's style.

"Okay, you will just have to rely on your memory. Listen, because I will tell you some good stories about my history with belly dancers."

I soon learned that Farouq, when sober, was moderately reserved but loved to tell stories and make you feel that he was taking you into his confidence, and he loved to laugh at his own jokes and hear other people laugh and feel himself the center of attention. As he got more and more drunk, he was less and less reserved, told more secrets, and repeated himself over and over again, with that habit that drunks have of forgetting what they have told you just a moment ago. He loved to boast of the women he had had and the money he had made and spent.

After I had known him longer, I realized that these "secrets" he was revealing were not secrets at all, but just stories he made up on the spot. Each time he told one about himself, he had a different number of ex-wives and current wives, and each time the mother of his children changed nationality. (He used the expression "mother of my children" to distinguish between his first, primary wife and later, temporary wives who did not procreate.) So little of what he said was true that I never knew which, if any, of his stories were real. But he always told them with a smile, and he never tried for consistency, as a man who is lying in earnest does. If I called him on a contradiction (for example, pointing out that this time the mother of his children was German, but last time she was Egyptian, and the time before that, Iranian), he would just laugh and make up another story to explain the inconsistency ("Well, you see, she is Egyptian, but her parents are of Iranian descent, and she was raised in Germany"; much later Alia told me that the "mother of his children" was "pure Egyptian").

Finally I concluded that Farouq was, simply, a storyteller. He loved to spin long, earnest stories that might be loosely grounded in actual fact but that he twisted, adorned, and embellished to suit his mood. He didn't care if you believed him or not. All that counted was the story.

But I didn't realize that about him until after I had listened to many such stories. This was the first time, so I listened intently, memorizing details, and dutifully wrote it up as field notes later, something that later made me laugh at my own gullibility.

"I love women," he said, giving Malak a squeeze. "And I love dancers. My first girlfriend was a belly dancer. This was at age twelve. Yes, age twelve, and she was much older than me! I'll tell you how it happened.

"It was in Alexandria, and I used to go once a week to a movie with my friend; my mother allowed this. I was going with my friend to a movie, and then he convinced me to go to the second showing of another film. Now when it got out, of course, I was scared of what my mother was going to say about me coming home so late, and I was walking along when I saw a bully from my school, and he said, 'Come here; come up with me,' and so I did what he said. He took me up some stairs, and then we were in a cabaret where women dance, and he made me sit down and asked me what I wanted to drink, and I said I would have Coke, and he said, 'You'll have a beer.' I didn't drink then, but he made me drink.

"And then all of a sudden one of the dancers came over to me. At that place, like at many places, the dancers sit with the different customers before they dance. And she came over and sat with me, and she said that she liked me, and she said for me to meet her in a certain place after the show was over. So I went and met her, and she took me to a room where she slept, and it was very poor. There was something on the floor that she slept on; she took me over to it and lay down with me. Now I never did anything with anyone, but I had an idea from what I'd seen in the movies that you start with kissing and hugging, so I started to try to do what I'd seen in the movies, kissing her, and she pushed me and turned her back to me. So I was confused. I jumped over onto the other side of her, and I started kissing her again. Again she pushed me away and turned over and gave me her back. I jumped over again. This happened about five times, and finally I was tired from jumping over her all the time. Finally she showed me that she wanted it from the back. That was my first time!

"She was called Aida el-Khawal [Aida the Faggot] because she liked to take it from behind. Of course the men she slept with talked about her, and the other women spread the rumors, and so she ended up with this nickname, Aida el-Khawal. After that I became known as Aida el-Khawal's boy. I was like her boyfriend, I was supposed to protect her, can you imagine? I was only twelve, going around Alexandria trying to protect this belly dancer. One day a group of men came to me and said, 'We've taken Aida el-Khawal, and you won't see her again unless you give back what she's stolen. We'll kill her unless you give back the gold.' I didn't know what they were talking about; they said that she'd stolen some gold and then she told them that she'd hidden it with me. So I said, 'Bring her here,' and when they brought her, I said, 'Where is the gold?' And finally she got it and gave it to them. After that I left her. No more Aida el-Khawal after that.

"My next girlfriend was also a belly dancer, and she was called Nadia Tizu [Nadia the Arse]. They called her Nadia Tizu because when she danced, she always showed her back; she never showed her face. You only saw her from behind. So she got the nickname Tizu. My first two girlfriends, when I was only twelve: Aida el-Khawal and Nadia Tizu!" He laughed. "And I have loved belly dancers ever since that time."

Malak interjected, "He is like one of those men I was telling you about in a Naguib Mahfouz novel who loves dancers."

"So you have never married?" I asked. He wore no wedding ring.

Malak laughed at my naïveté. "Oh, he is married!"

"I've been married many times!" he declared. "Thirteen times! And there have been so many others I haven't married."

"Thirteen in a row, one after another?" I asked.

Alia laughed. "No, not in a row! All at once!"

But Farouq said gravely, "Not all at once. My wife is the mother of my children. She is the mother of my children! But I love women. I have married thirteen!

"The first time it happened, it was with my neighbor. My wife went away on a long vacation, and I was alone in the house. The day after she left, my neighbor came over asking to borrow something from the kitchen. I said, 'I don't know what is in the kitchen, but you can take whatever you want from the house, just go and take whatever you want.' After that, I saw her once while I was shopping. And then I ran into her another time and she started telling me about how she was having problems getting her apartment. The Greek who owned the apartment would be back in a couple of days, and he would not rent to her unless she was married, so I said, 'Look, I'll marry you, then you can sign the lease with the Greek, then we'll get divorced. So you'll benefit, you'll get your apartment.'"

I asked him, "She lived alone, not with her family?"

"Yes," he said, "she had problems with her parents. She was a performer and her mother took all her money that she earned and spent it on herself. So she left her mother and had gone to live by herself.

"So we married, and then after two days the Greek didn't come back, so she said he was supposed to come back the next day, and he didn't come. She said he would be back the next week, so I said to her, 'Look, as long as we are married, we can make love.' So we made love. But the Greek didn't come back. After four months, finally I said, 'The Greek hasn't come back—this wasn't part of the arrangement.' My wife had found out, you see, and she was angry, really angry. So I was going to divorce her. I wasn't going to wait around forever for the Greek to show up. She said, 'But I love you!' I said, 'No way, this wasn't part of the arrangement for the Greek to never come back and you to love me!' So I divorced her."

Malak lit another cigarette. Everyone at the table was chain-smoking except for me. "He loves performers, dancers and singers and musicians and actresses. I think everybody he ever married was a performer, with the exception of his wife." She meant, I presumed, the mother of his children.

"I like to throw money to the dancers and musicians," Farouq said. "These musicians, you know, they are so talented and yet so poor. I used to hear a lot of people talking to me about religion; they would tell me that you have to pray, you have to fast, you have to give money for the poor, and I would give them money, but then I don't know where the money is going to. Are they really giving it to the poor? I am just giving money to these religious men. Who knows what they are doing with it? So I decided that I prefer to throw money at the dancers and the musicians. This seems like a better way to give away my money. Those musicians are so poor."

Malak had a way of smirking that started with one laugh, one expulsion of breath, followed by another, then another, one after the other more and more quickly until she would break into laughter outright, with one eyebrow cocked and one corner of her mouth turned up. Now she smirked like this at his pretensions of charitable piety, and Farouq just snorted and waved his hand at her dismissively.

I chatted with Malak and another man for a time while Farouq and Haroun murmured quietly to each other. All of a sudden Farouq smacked a wad of bills down on the table in front of my plate. "We have a bet," he said to me. "What color underwear are you wearing?"

I stared at him, a bit shocked. This was certainly not the polite conversation I had come to expect from Egyptians. Egyptians that I knew didn't discuss sex or, presumably, underwear with someone of the opposite sex unless there was a very close, not to mention intimate, relationship between them. Zeid and Kerim might speculate about the morals of women at a distance, but I knew that they would never bring up the topic of my underwear, much less bet on it. Kerim had looked like he would choke when I mentioned hymenoplasty.

Haroun patted my shoulder reassuringly yet again and said, "Don't worry, we won't ask you to show us your underwear, we just want to know, is it black or white? I say black. Farouq says white. I'm sure it's black, isn't it?"

I looked from one of them to the other. "You say black, and you say white?" They nodded agreement. I hesitated, worrying about what sort of message I would be sending them if I told the truth. Eventually I said, "It's black."

"Oh ho ho!" said Haroun with a leer, as he snatched up the money.

"Black!" Farouq chuckled and didn't look at all bothered about losing the bet.

The rest of the evening passed with more or less standard conversation, except for when Haroun and Alia started discussing the idea of putting chili paste in the vagina to enhance sex. Malak was repulsed. "That would be painful! No, that is too much. That is sadistic, *ya* Haroun!" she said. But Alia said with a coy smile, "It might be nice! I don't mind trying anything once," and she gave Haroun a meaningful glance. He gave her an affectionate squeeze on the shoulder and kissed her on the forehead.

At about three o'clock in the morning, everyone at the table got up to leave. Haroun paid while Farouq pretended to not even see the check. We walked out of the restaurant, the rest of them laughing and a little tipsy, and waited for someone to bring the cars around. I leaned over to Malak and asked in a low voice, "But is that normal for Haroun to talk that way with his wife in front of people? Chili paste and vaginas?"

Malak gave me an amused smile. "Lisa, don't be naïve! Of course Alia is not his wife; she is his mistress!"

Farouq came over and stood between me and Malak and put his arms around the two of us. He was laughing at nothing at all. He was going to drive us home. I wondered how much alcohol he had drunk that evening. Haroun and Alia came to say goodbye before getting in a car together. "We will see you again, Lisa? We must see you again. We want to hear all about your research!" Haroun urged Alia to take my phone number, and she said she was going to call me later.

"I'll call you so that we can really talk. There wasn't much of a chance tonight." She kissed me on both cheeks. "We will see you soon, God willing."

Once Malak's boyfriend Farouq knew that I was interested in belly dancers, he insisted on inviting me out to cabarets with the two of them. Sometimes it was just the three of us, and sometimes Malak invited other belly dancers along, friends of hers. Farouq loved being in a crowd of women. He and Malak would drink wine and chain-smoke steadily until five or six o'clock in the morning, and then he would drive us home with the dawn light, and I would creep upstairs exhausted, hoping none of the neighbors saw me. Farouq drove a surprisingly shabby car, considering how much money he threw around. He literally threw money on belly dancers, just as I had seen in pictures of a *National Geographic* story on Arab oil wealth. He would fan out the bills and then let them rain over the dancer slowly, as she shimmied next to him, and when he was done, she would pirouette away while the waiters ran to pick up every bill from the floor. Once he even let me throw a pile of ten-pound notes, but I was clumsy and half of it ended up falling off the stage. Nervous waiters peered into every crack to make sure they hadn't missed a bill.

I was going out more and more with Malak and becoming closer to her. At least I thought so. I didn't know for sure what Malak thought about me, but she often called for a friendly chat on the phone, and I was particularly encouraged one day when she told me, "You know, Lisa, something I've noticed, a good thing about you, you don't smile all the time like most Americans. I mean you smile, but it's not that big smile and nodding your head around. This is something very disturbing to Europeans. When you see an American smile, you realize that they have no appreciation of subtlety. Those big fat smiles, it is very scary, sometimes you want to jump away from all those teeth." I made a mental note to try to keep my smiles small and subtle, but it wasn't from any innate Europeanness that I smiled small smiles around Malak and her friends. It was mostly because I was often confused about what was going on around me. And I didn't know how to behave properly around people who acted so differently from the other Egyptians I knew, so I stayed quiet and watchful and smiled politely.

What I loved about Malak was that she was so straightforward. She said her opinion, boldly and directly, and didn't mind if others did the same. She loved a good argument, someone to spar with. That was never my style. I was always trying too hard to be agreeable, and if someone said something I didn't like, I was less likely to voice my objection than to simply withdraw and avoid the person in the future. I thought that Malak's approach was much more admirable than mine, but I was too shy and too much of a natural sycophant to imitate the dancer's frankness.

Malak wasn't just honest and straightforward in expressing her opinion about other people and other things; her honesty was also directed toward herself. She could analyze her own actions and motivations with an equally detached and critical eye. I remember how surprised I had been when I first interviewed her and she talked about sex work and the time that someone had unexpectedly paid her after sleeping with her. With time I learned that this openness was typical of Malak, and as I interviewed more dancers, I found that this directness was rare among performers. Maybe it was because Malak was retired from dancing, so she didn't feel the imperative of continual self-promotion. More likely it was just her character.

And the last thing that attracted me to Malak was her sheer exoticness. She lived a lifestyle unlike anything I had seen before starting my research. She knew so many people. Strange people. Wealthy men with famous last names (like Haroun, who was related to a former president of Egypt) and their mistresses. Sculptors and photographers and filmmakers and dancers and musicians and journalists. She took me to art openings and performances. We went to see a jazz band with one of her friends and to the famous cabarets of Pyramids Road, and the men always paid at these outings. When I went to Pomodoro with my friends, Zeid paid for Ayah, and it was a clear indicator that she was his fiancée, but Kerim and I paid our own share of the bill, carefully calculated according to what each person had ordered. Now I was going to expensive places with Malak and her friends, places I could never have afforded myself, and the men were picking up the bill, and everyone acted as if that was the natural order of things.

I wondered if it indebted me in any way. I asked Malak, and she said, "You don't owe anybody anything. You add to *manzar el-tarabeza* [the look of the table]. Haroun wants to go out with Alia, but he's well known and people might recognize them, or he might run into his wife's relatives. But if he's in a group of respectable-looking people, he can always tell his wife that he's out with businessmen friends, and he can blame the women in the group on Farouq, who is known to be always mixed up in a scandal. When you come out with us, then there's an odd number of women to men, and you don't look like a whore, you look presentable, so you're useful." I marveled that all I had to do to earn my expensive dinners was not look "like a whore."

Malak became my point of reference, the cultural translator when the anthropologist didn't understand. I had thought I understood Egyptian life, but Malak made me realize that I only understood three subsections of Egyptian society: young adults of the bourgeoisie represented by Ayah and Zeid and Kerim, middle-class academics like the Egyptologists I got to know working on the Giza Plateau, and working-class women, represented by Sara and Nesma in the antiques store.

Meanwhile, Malak introduced me to ten more subcultures and willingly explained them in detail. She was rapidly supplanting Ayah and Sara as my chief informants. I told Malak that, and she found the idea amusing. Malak liked the role of informant because she was naturally analytical.

But my husband didn't like Malak. He continued to refer to her as "that prostitute." And after I told him about one late-night cabaret excursion with Malak and Farouq, he outright forbade me to go to cabarets any more. We fought over it. He told me that if I wanted to stay married to him, I had to be a respectable wife. That meant no more going out with belly dancers and strange men at night.

I was frustrated. The cabaret trips were for my research. And I needed Farouq to take me out; without him, I would never be able to go see belly dancers perform. Kerim and Zeid wouldn't take me; they considered such places beyond the pale for a self-respecting middle-class man. Nesma and Sara weren't allowed to stay out so late.

My husband didn't distrust me personally, he said, but he worried constantly about my respectability, and even without me telling him about Malak's experiences receiving money for sex, he claimed that all dancers were "prostitutes" and I would be tainted by association. I didn't much care whether people thought I was respectable or not, and I certainly didn't care whether the belly dancers I knew engaged in remunerative sex. If they did, I was interested in knowing about it for my research. If they didn't but people like my husband said they did, then I was interested in that, too. But I was getting tired of having battles with him about the morals of my research informants. I thought about it for a long time and eventually decided to continue to go out with the belly dancers and just not tell my husband so that we could avoid the arguments. I wrote about my decision to hide things from him in my field notes. I continued to go to the cabarets.

I still went out with Ayah and Zeid and Kerim, though never more than once a week now, because Zeid's work was too "hectic" and Ayah had lots of homework and I was going out with Malak and her friends. On the last weekend before I was to go home for Christmas vacation, we went to Pomodoro for an early dinner, arriving at 10:30 p.m. After a blonde waitress with a British accent took our orders, Kerim picked up his fork and pointed it in the direction of two women who were sitting at a table in the corner. "Look Lisa, a case study." Both had short hair and wore lots of makeup.

"You really think they're prostitutes?" "Case study" had become our code phrase because of my claim to having an academic interest in the subject.

Ayah glanced over and agreed with Kerim. "Definitely case studies," she said in her low, husky voice.

"I just don't see it," I said with some frustration. "What is it about them that makes you identify them as prostitutes?" The others couldn't point out any specific marker that defined the look of a prostitute. But they were positive that they saw it in these women.

"Look," I insisted, "there must be something that makes you say, 'That's a prostitute.' There must be something that you all see with your cultural knowledge that I don't see. Try to analyze it. Try to explain it to me so I can see through your eyes."

Zeid just shrugged, but Ayah made an attempt. "It's a lot of things— they way they look, the way they dress, their makeup, their attitude, the expressions on their face, body language . . ."

Kerim added, "And it's a combination of these things, and not one alone—for example, you couldn't say that someone is a prostitute just from the way she's dressed because someone else could expose just as much skin and people would think she looks like a decent, respectable girl."

I was irritated. I always tried to understand the signs that they saw, but I could never pin them down to describe exactly how it was that they saw a prostitute. "So we're making up a story about them for ourselves, but we don't know for sure. Probably lots of people look at us and say the same things about me too."

"No, for sure nobody would ever think you are a prostitute. First of all, you're always with the same people. The worst they might think is that you're the girlfriend of Zeid or me, but we don't sit close together or touch, so they probably wouldn't even think that. Second of all, your makeup isn't like those women's. They're wearing thick black kohl all around their eyes, top and bottom. Third of all, your clothes are more decent—you cover up more than they do."

"Maybe tonight I'm covered up, but sometimes I show more skin."

"Still, it's not like the way they're dressed. And you never wear short skirts."

I laughed. "That's because I have fat legs."

He rolled his eyes. "Anyway, you're American, and Americans aren't usually prostitutes here."

"You know I'm American, but not everyone else does—someone else might look at me without hearing me speak and think I'm Russian." In the preceding decade or so, Russian women in Egypt had gotten a reputation for being dancers and "prostitutes."

"No," Kerim shook his head, "definitely you don't look Russian. You have red hair like a lot of Russians, but your style is too American." He looked back over to the two women. "Okay, look, I found one thing that I can point out about those women. You see that one that's wearing the short sleeveless dress? Look, you can see her bra underneath the arm-holes. And the hem keeps turning up and showing her slip. Put the two things together and you can see that they aren't used to dressing up and looking comfortable in elegant clothes."

So it had something to do with class, I thought. These women didn't look like the upper-class elite who were the only kind of women who could be from "respectable" families and still stay out so late and dress in such clothing. Most women from the lower and middle classes would not be allowed by their families to dress skimpily, go to a place like Po-modoro, and stay out so late; if a woman was doing so, it must mean that her family wasn't maintaining her respectability through curfews and close monitoring of her behavior.

I started thinking guiltily about all the times that my bra might have peeked out from under an armhole. Geez, did I really have to worry about things like that in order to not be thought a whore?

Zeid yawned. "You're obsessed with prostitutes, Lisa."

"Look," I persisted, "everyone likes to talk about everyone else and it's easy to call someone a prostitute, but you don't really know what her story is. There could be a million explanations for her behavior, her ap-pearance, the people she's with, etcetera, that we don't know about."

Kerim shrugged. "If she wants to avoid having people think that she's a prostitute, she should avoid the behavior that will make them think that."

"Maybe," I said, a bit sullenly. "I just don't see how you can tell if someone is a prostitute just by looking at her."

"That's true," Kerim said absently, checking his mobile for messages. "Sometimes a woman might look very respectable and it's only after you get to know her that you realize what she is. I've told you that before."

In December, I went home to visit my family and my husband for a month. I spent the first two weeks watching enough television to make up for all the months that I hadn't seen any. In the third week I had to travel to Princeton to take care of some paperwork and meet with my advisers. While I was gone, I left my laptop behind in my husband's apartment. I didn't think much of it at the time. I didn't want to lug around the extra weight, and I didn't have any field notes to write, for a pleasant change.

When I came back from my short trip, I found that my husband had read my field notes while I was gone. He read about all the men whom I had met through Malak who made passes at me, about Farouq and

Haroun betting on my underwear, about coming home at six o'clock in the morning. He also read what I had written about my decision to deliberately lie to him, to not tell him about all these things. Our marriage nearly ended that week.

I couldn't believe how stupid I had been, to leave my field notes lying around for anyone to read. I had always been so careful. We had had it drilled into us in graduate school that the ethics of the anthropologist entailed always protecting the privacy of our informants, and I had imagined the secret police suspecting I was a spy and reading my files. Zeid was always telling me that I fit the profile of an undercover CIA agent perfectly: foreign researcher, fluent in Arabic, who didn't drink alcohol or use drugs. And I used to retort that his suspicions were a sign of megalomania, since why would the American government possibly be interested in the likes of *him*? But just in case, I always used different names when writing about any belly dancer or man that I met through a belly dancer, and I changed identifying details in my field notes. So it is ironic that while I was being so careful, always imagining cloak-and-dagger spy scenarios (a bit of a megalomaniac myself, since why would the Egyptian government possibly be interested in the likes of *me*?), changing names so that nobody could be identified, I never took into consideration that the person most likely to have access to my writing wouldn't give a fig about names and identities but would be all too interested in other details.

To save our marriage, I promised not to go out with the belly dancers any more. I could see them during the day, and I could see them in their houses—though not if they were having a party—but he absolutely forbade me to go to cabarets or nightclubs with them. "Talk to them on the phone," my husband said. "You can get plenty of information that way. Go drink tea with them in their houses, instead of going out and getting drunk with all their sleazy friends." If I protested, "I never drink with them," he would just say, "Yes, but they get drunk with you." He had absorbed all the little details of what he had read in my field notes—such as about the time that one obnoxious friend of Malak's got drunk when we were out together and kept almost falling over and I had to drive him home in his car, stopping so that he could urinate in the road—and he kept reminding me of them. He kept calling all the dancers prostitutes. He also called me a prostitute. It didn't matter that he hadn't read anything about me having sex with another man, much less doing it in exchange for money. I had, he claimed, prostituted myself for my research, because I had deliberately decided to not behave like a respect-

able woman in order to see things and meet people I couldn't under respectable circumstances.

If I showed irritation at all his restrictions, he would sometimes get
angry, and other times he would try to reason with me. "Don't forget,
Lisa, this is my culture. I know what is culturally appropriate there, and
I understand how people think and how they gossip. I care about you
and I don't want anybody to think badly about you and talk about you
behind your back. Do you understand? You've lived there a long time,
it's true, but it's clear from reading your field notes that you still don't
know how people think, the worst things that they can think about
women. I'm Arab, I know how they think. I love you, and I can't bear
the idea of somebody thinking badly of you. I want everyone to respect
you, do you understand?"

He was persuasive. He asked me to defer to his greater cultural
knowledge. Wasn't I an anthropologist? Wasn't I supposed to practice
cultural relativism? I convinced myself that I was playing the cultural
role of an Arab woman. Ayah told me to take it as a sign that he loved
me. He wouldn't care so much about what I was doing otherwise. Yes,
it drove her crazy when Zeid was controlling in the same way, wanting to know exactly what she was doing, how late she was staying out,
and whom she was talking to, but she knew it meant he loved her. And if
he didn't act like that, she would know that something was wrong with
their relationship. Just look at Nellie, she reminded me. Ahmed never
asked her what she was doing. Obviously he didn't care about her. Yes,
they might be engaged, but she didn't think it would last. How could it?
Ahmed couldn't love Nellie enough to marry her, as uninterested as he
clearly was in her activities and her behavior.

But before I could develop any stereotypes about Arab women accepting—even desiring—controlling men, I talked about it with Sara,
who saw things differently than Ayah did. She saw my "cultural relativism" as bad strategy, plain and simple. It was coming close to the time
when she was to go to the hospital for her operation (which kept being delayed because of a lack of qualified doctors who would perform
the operation for free in a public hospital). Maybe next month, she said,
a foreign doctor would bring some part that they needed to put in her
knee. We were talking about this on the phone, and I told her that my
husband wouldn't let me go out with the belly dancers anymore.

"*Gatu nila*," she said in a droll voice. I smiled. It was a rural slang expression she had taught me that meant "May disaster befall him." *Nila*
is the name of a plant that was traditionally used by Upper Egyptians

to dye cloth dark blue; it was the darkest color they could produce with natural dyes, so the cloth was used for funeral clothes. *Gatu nila* means, literally, "*nila* come to him," that is, some disaster that would force him to wear mourning clothes.

"Well, I lied to him. It's my penance. And he's doing it because he loves me."

"Yes, that's your fault, but that doesn't mean you have to do everything he says now. Sometimes you're so naïve, *ya 'abeeta hanim*." Sara called me *'abeeta hanim* (lady idiot) a lot.

"He told me that I have to talk to him before I go out at night or before I go out in any group with men in it."

"What did you say when he told you that?"

"I agreed."

"*What?!*" She nearly shouted. "You *agreed*? What, do you want to make your life miserable? Now he'll think he can do whatever he wants with you. I never, *ever* let any man tell me what I can do and when I can go out and who I can see."

"Well, it's too late. I promised."

She groaned. "Yes, you really are Lady Idiot. You'll see, he'll just control you more and more. It's just the beginning. If you give men an inch, they take a mile."

I thought about that carefully.

I got sick with a virus that took hold and didn't want to let go. I lay in bed for days, barely moving, watching insects crawl around on the mosquito netting over my head. Reading hurt my eyes. Moving hurt my skin. I ached all over.

On the third day of my illness, the visits started. First Zeid and Ayah came. They brought a carton of mango juice and a bag of peanuts— "heavy food for a sick person," criticized Ayah, which meant that Zeid had bought them (playing the role of the man-as-provider—in this case, for his female friend). We sat in chairs in the sitting room, me with my yellow skin and greasy, matted hair, feverish and wrapped in an ugly orange-and-pink wool blanket, while Ayah and Zeid were dressed in chic black cashmere and sand-colored camel-hair coats, respectively. They were visiting me on their way to Pomodoro for dinner.

We sat and talked, or rather Ayah and Zeid talked and I smiled wanly, and they pretended to bicker for me, to make me laugh. Then Zeid spotted a large cockroach on the floor and shrieked. Ayah was the brave one, killing it with her shoe, and then sliding it onto a piece of paper to carry it to the toilet to flush down. But she found that those fat cockroaches don't flush. They float. We flushed and flushed, or rather Ayah flushed while Zeid and I hung back and watched, laughing and shrieking, and the cockroach spun around on top of the water. Finally Ayah got the clever idea of throwing wads of toilet paper on top of it to weigh it down, and it disappeared down the hole. The cockroach-disposal episode was the most exercise I got in a week.

The next visit was from Malak. I had been talking on the phone with her a lot, more since my husband had banned me from going out with the dancers. Hearing about other people's lives was always my escape, and Malak's life was the best escape of all. She remained the most exotic character in my life, and I was completely fascinated by her. She had a kind of delicate smile that glowed; when she smiled at you, you felt warm, but also you felt scrutinized. Like someone was shining a light on you. I was also fascinated with the way Malak held her body. When she stood talking to someone, she always put her weight on her right foot, the left foot extended in front of her, like a ballerina, and she stuck out her stomach slightly. It was an intriguing pose because it was naïve and childish and a little bit sexy and knowing at the same time.

I liked to watch her hands, too. Malak always wore dainty gold rings covered with pavé diamonds, only one on each hand, and a little gold-and-sapphire bracelet on her left arm, a gift from a former admirer, she said. She chain-smoked slender cigarettes and flicked off the ashes in one fast but deliberate motion. Her fingers were long and delicate but just a bit chubby. In short, all her moves, her gestures, her body language, her way of talking and smiling and laughing, even the structure of her body, fused the adult and the child, the bombshell femme fatale and the little girl ingénue. It was the same when she danced. One moment you would be in rapture watching the grace of her arm as she made it writhe like a snake in one fluid movement from her shoulder to her fingertips; the next moment she would be bouncing up and down in an earthy peasant dance with a delicious smile on her face, like a child jumping rope.

Malak had once told me that a dancer must be a kind of social genius: she should be able to handle any situation and any person with perfect aplomb. She must charm a jealous woman and gently rebuff her leering husband; she should make men long for her from a distance while reminding women of their own sensuality. She must accept a compliment with grace and turn back an insult with humor. With one look, she should be able to draw someone to her and, with another, force someone else to keep at a distance.

My wistful dream, then, was to master but one-tenth of Malak's elegance, self-assurance, wit, and charm. Perhaps it was this dream that kept me in Malak's orbit, a hope that somehow some of her aura would rub off, that I would absorb some of her ability, so I would be able to deal with my husband and the men whom I was interviewing for my research and the teenage boys who harassed me on the street. That, too, was a part of Malak's talent: she did not make the women around her feel threatened or outshone; instead, she made them feel that there was hope for them to become a little more like her.

So every day that I was sick, I would pull the phone under the mosquito netting with me, prop myself up on pillows, cover myself with the orange-and-pink wool blanket, and call Malak. She would tell me about her new boyfriend, about a new student she was teaching, about a jewelry designer she had just discovered, about her history as a dancer—whatever was on her mind, and I would just let her ramble on, enthralled.

The single most interesting thing that came out of these phone conversations was the fact that Malak was actually half Egyptian, not pure Spanish, as everybody thought. "Look, this is a secret, just between me and you, because I don't think that you are the kind to talk, no? But you will find this interesting for your research," she said by way of preface. (Malak never forgot that I was doing research on her.) I loved to feel that somebody was confessing an intimate secret to me. It is one of the cheap thrills of the anthropologist.

But the confession didn't come out of the blue. She was talking about the way the dance market in Egypt had changed because of foreign dancers. "Most foreign dancers come here just because they want to dance, not to make money. Of course Russian dancers are in an entirely different category. But I'm talking about Western dancers. There are some Japanese, too. They will do anything to succeed here because for them it is Egypt, the land of Oriental dance, yes? It is the climax of their whole career to dance here. It is their big phantasm."

"Fantasy?"

"Yes, fantasy. And also it is very useful on their résumés when they go back to their own countries. They say that they have been dancing in Cairo; it is a big deal for them to succeed here.

"You know, foreign dancers used to be in demand here; it was very popular to advertise that a place had a foreign dancer. Something exotic, you know, to see a girl with blond hair doing this dance. But now demand is dropping; now everyone wants an Egyptian dancer, or at least an Arab dancer. But they will have to pay! Foreign dancers will dance for nothing just because they want to dance, but Egyptian dancers, they will not dance for such low sums. It is not the same sort of prestige for them. No, they want money. If only I were still performing, it would be a good chance for me now to tell them that I'm Egyptian! Then I could make a little more money!"

"But you're Spanish," I protested.

That's when she told me that she was half Egyptian, swearing me to secrecy.

"Okay!" I said, excited. "The secret's down the well."

"What?"

"I'm just translating into English that Egyptian expression, *al-sirr fil-bi'r.*"

"Ah, yes. Well you see I am really half-Egyptian, but nobody knows this here. My father is Egyptian, and since it's my father, that means that Egyptians consider me Egyptian, you know? Because the child takes the citizenship of its father. My mother is Spanish, and I was raised in Spain, but I spoke some Arabic with my father when I was young, and that helped me a little when I came here and started to learn the language properly."

"But why do you keep it a secret? It would help you out a lot here, wouldn't it?"

"No! Not at all! On the contrary, it would cause me lots of problems."

"How? I mean, why?"

"Look, Lisa, I was raised Spanish, right? My father and my mother, they divorced early, but even when my father was there, he acted Spanish, you understand? He wasn't religious; he didn't teach us his religion or his culture. You see, he wanted a Spanish wife and Spanish daughters. And then they separated, my parents, and almost I did not see him after that. So you see, when I came here I didn't know anything about how to behave Egyptian. So if I went telling people that I'm Egyptian, even if I tell them that my father is Egyptian, *khalas* [that's it], that means that I'm Egyptian as far as they are concerned. And then I will have to act like an Egyptian woman, and for me, no way! No way can I be like an Egyptian woman! Can you imagine? Always being judged and people watching me and calling me a prostitute if I stay out late or if I have a friend who is a man come back to my apartment. . . . Bad enough for me to be like a foreigner! Then I can do what I like, have my freedom. They might talk about me, but in the end they'll just say, 'Well she's a foreigner, she doesn't know how to behave,' you know? But if I'm Egyptian! No! They'll always be watching what I do and when I come home and who visits me. . . . No, it would be prison."

"Yes, I see your point, actually. They hold Egyptians up to different standards."

"But it's not just that! It is not just the Egyptians I have to worry about! It is also the Europeans. You know, if I am Spanish, I am Spanish. But if I am half-Egyptian, then all of a sudden I am part Arab, I am one of the other, you know. No, better to be Spanish and that's that."

The fifth day I was sick, Malak decided to come and make me some soup that she insisted would make me feel better. She brought a bag of vegetables to my flat to cook with.

"My God!" said Malak as she walked in the door. "You have to walk up these stairs every day?" Despite her complaint, she wasn't even breathing heavily. Dancing kept her extraordinarily fit, and the fact that she never made it look remotely strenuous just proved her fitness and skill.

"It's good exercise."

"And you have no doorman?"

"Sometimes we do, and sometimes we don't. He goes back and forth between here and his village, I think."

She set down a bag of vegetables. "You know, *my* doorman is a real pimp!" she said, laughing. "Or at least he dreams of being a pimp; he definitely thinks I'm a prostitute! And the building itself is for prostitutes, the first two or three floors are, what do you call it, a whorehouse? So he's used to the idea of prostitutes and men coming, and he's ready to do whatever to take his percentage. So when I come back, sometimes I come home at five o'clock in the afternoon with a male friend in a nice car, and I get out, and these are just friends, so of course it is impossible for them to come up, and the doorman says, 'Come in, Bey, come in, Pasha'—using all these honorifics, welcoming them to the building, just as if he's my pimp and he's going to take his fee later! He sees a BMW and thinks that this must be a 'client.' This happened once when Farouq dropped me off. It was only the first or second time the doorman saw him, and he was inviting him upstairs! It is a problem, you know. Because the way he is welcoming people in like that, my guests will think that everyone is welcome in my flat. Then everyone will think I'm a prostitute."

She took her vegetables to the kitchen and called back to me where I was sitting in a chair in the sitting room. "You must come out with us sometime, it would be good for you to meet some new people." She seemed to understand that I was lonely these days, although I hadn't spoken to Malak about the problems with my husband.

"That would be nice," I said from inside my blanket.

"What about in a few days, when you are feeling better?"

"I don't know . . . it feels like I'm never going to get better. And even if I do, then I'll be so behind in my work, I'll have to catch up on all the interviews and writing that I've missed."

I wanted to go out with Malak and see her friends. I wanted to have a normal social life and stop having to follow all the rules, but I kept putting her off to avoid trouble with my husband.

"Lisa, I've invited you out so many times, and you're always making excuses! Now I am going to think that you are avoiding me! Nobody could possibly have such a busy schedule that she is never free to go out. Okay, we will assume that you are sick for one more week—God forbid—and then you can take a week to catch up on work. What about after that? I will make reservations with you, two weeks in advance. I am sure you do not have any plans for two weeks from now!"

I agreed, thinking I could always cancel later, and not to accept would be insulting. I hadn't told her that my husband had banned me from going out with belly dancers. I had mentioned once that he didn't like belly dancers, and she had been offended. I didn't want her to think that I was as judgmental as he was, and I was afraid that she suspected that that was the reason I kept avoiding her invitations. At the same time I was curious to see more of her strange friends.

Now, too, Alia, Haroun's mistress, started calling me on the phone to talk. She had some interesting stories to tell. She told me that her first husband had been a big cheater, a womanizer, and that that was why she eventually left him. The fact that he kicked her in the stomach when they fought while she was pregnant was mentioned as if it were merely tangential to his greater sins. He openly dated other women, left evidence of his affairs all around the house, yet expected her to sit at home quietly, never going out herself, watching their son and preparing an elaborate afternoon meal for him every day, which he might or might not deign to come home for. "Egyptian men are all like this," she said. "Either you learn to be patient and tolerate it, or you don't, in which case you end up divorced, like me."

I asked her if it wasn't hard on her, being Haroun's mistress, having to keep their relationship a secret. "No, not really. We love each other and treat each other like husband and wife, and that's what counts." She said that she had no desire to marry anyone else. She had her children to raise, she had her work and her independence, and she supported herself. Given all those things, she had no need to remarry.

I asked Alia if Haroun's wife knew at all about their relationship, and she said that a couple of years back his wife had found out. She had cried and yelled and wailed and screamed, and Haroun had finally promised her that it was over, that he wouldn't be seeing Alia anymore, and she got over it. Of course Haroun and Alia carried on together after that, and, said Alia, the wife suspects that he is still having a relationship with someone else and thinks that this someone else is probably Alia. "But she doesn't say anything because she knows that Haroun is the type to always have something going on the side, and she'll never be able to control him, and at least I'm a safe enemy, because she knows that I'll never break up his family or try to take him away from his wife and kids, so she lives with the idea," explained Alia. "Better the devil you know than the devil you don't."

After a couple of phone calls just to chat, Alia called me to invite me to Haroun's place for dinner that weekend. Galal, a businessman friend of Haroun's, had bought a fondue set, she said, so they were going to try it out.

"Haroun's house?" I asked, incredulously.

Alia had a low, throaty laugh. "Not where he lives with his family. His *wakr*."

"What? *Wakr*?"

"*Wakr*: it means den, the den of the fox. It's a word used for the place where a man takes his secret lover, away from his family. He keeps a separate apartment for entertaining his friends." I said I would be happy to come and asked if there was anything I should bring. "Just yourself. Galal can drive you and Malak; he lives in your area of town."

I had already accepted Malak's invitation, and now Alia's. I let inertia make the decision for me. I didn't cancel with Malak; I didn't refuse Alia. I didn't ask for permission, and I didn't discuss it with my husband. I just dressed to go out. It was a bid for freedom from the oppressive weight of having to be a respectable wife, and it was another betrayal. My marriage ended not long after that.

When we arrived at Haroun's *wakr*, both Haroun and Alia greeted me with such warmth that I felt like a long-lost relative. I was touched by their friendliness. Soon Farouq arrived with a woman named Lulu, who was introduced as an actress. Another woman entered with them, but she was not introduced; she came in quietly and went over to sit in a chair by herself, apart from the rest of the group, and I was confused about who she was and why the others pretended she didn't exist. The others all gathered around the bar attached to the kitchen area, and Haroun poured wine for his guests. While he was handing around glasses, Farouq said something that I didn't catch, but Haroun's response was to go stand next to Alia. Putting his arm around her, he said to Farouq with mocking belligerence, "I'll have you know that this is my personal property, and I'll consider any attack on my property as a personal attack on me." Alia smiled, pleased.

Suddenly Haroun's telephone rang from the top of the stairs. He had left his phone in a little niche up there since the network coverage didn't reach down into the depths of the room, which was in the basement underneath a building he owned and kept his offices in. He took the steps two or three at a time, and he picked up the phone and looked at the number. "Shhhh! Shhhh!" he hissed, waving his left hand at his guests. "My wife." Everyone went totally silent as Haroun took the call.

"Yes, I'm with Galal and Farouq."

Cued, Galal piped up loud enough for her to hear, "Give her my regards." Haroun gave him a thumbs-up. They were his cover for the evening—a night out with the guys.

Haroun kept talking for a short while, then closed his phone. Loping down the stairs again, he shook his head with a smile, saying, "She calls all the time for any reason, or for no reason at all. Just to show that she is in touch with me or to make sure of where I am." But he didn't look annoyed. If anything, he looked pleased. No emotion registered on Alia's face.

Galal was preparing the food and giving orders to the servant, Sayed. Farouq was flirting with Lulu, and while they were thus engaged, Alia leaned over to me and said in a low voice, "She's very vulgar, isn't she?" The actress wore heavy caked-on makeup with sharp lines penciled in around her mouth, eyes, and eyebrows. She spoke with emphatic nods and intonation, vulgar phrases and exaggerated facial expressions. Alia pointed discreetly over to the mystery woman, who was sitting quietly in the corner, clutching a purse and a mobile phone. "Look, she tries to show how important and rich she is by bringing her own servant, someone to carry her phone around with her!" said Alia with a snort. "Or does she think she needs a chaperone? For God's sake! Is she so pure?" That explained who the socially invisible woman was.

After a short time, we were directed by Galal to sit down at the table in the far corner of the room. Galal sat down and instructed us on how to dip our bread into the cheese without losing it. "If a man loses his bread in the cheese, he has to buy the table a bottle of wine, and if a woman loses her bread, she has to kiss everyone at the table."

"Ah!" said Farouq. "What if a woman is dipping her bread in the cheese, and I put in my stick, and I knock the bread off her stick with my stick? Then she has to kiss just me, right? Not the whole table, just me!"

There was a clattering sound in the kitchen, and Haroun shouted at his servant, "That's enough racket, Sayed!"

"Yes, sir!" came a distant call from the Nubian man, who had been cleaning up some of the mess that Galal had made in the kitchen.

Malak came to sit next to me. She was irritated at Farouq, her boyfriend, who had brought Lulu. She leaned over to me and said in a low voice in my ear, "You know, I am thinking about changing my boyfriend."

"Changing your boyfriend? Why?"

"I don't love him; I never loved him. And now he's being a bastard. At least before, there was some sort of agreement and I felt like he was taking care of me; we enjoyed our time together. It wasn't love, but it was a kind of pleasant arrangement. But now he's not treating me right."

"Why? What's he doing?" I glanced over at Lulu, who was smiling widely with her painted mouth at something Farouq was saying. Even from across the table I could see that Farouq's eyeglasses were completely covered with fingerprints. He had cheese on his shirt.

"First of all, he called me the other day, and we were planning to do something later on, but the problem was that I had to go out and meet someone first, so we were trying to work out how we could get hold of each other later, and he said, 'Oh, that's right, you don't have a mobile.' As if he just then remembered that I don't have a mobile!" Malak paused for emphasis and gave me a meaningful look. "But, you see, just a couple of weeks ago he was telling me that he was going to get me a mobile, but of course he hasn't produced anything. I didn't ask him to get it for me—he's the one who brought it up first—and now he acts like he just forgot about it. It's not like he can't afford it."

I murmured sympathetically.

"But there's something worse. He persuaded me to move to a larger apartment because he didn't think my small little apartment was suitable. I told him I didn't have enough money, but he insisted that he would help with the rent. He kept saying, 'We'll consider it a shared apartment, and we can both entertain our friends there.' So finally he convinced me, and I started looking around. It isn't easy finding apartments in Cairo, you know. You have to go from one agent to another and look at so much crap. But anyway, finally I found this place; it's quite nice, but it's double the rent of my previous place. But, no problem, I said to myself, he's going to split the rent with me. So I moved into the new place, but now he doesn't talk about the rent at all. Before, he was encouraging me to move, insulting my old place, saying it's too small. And he admires the new place. But no money, nothing, not even for the deposit I had to pay."

"But you have to ask him for the money," I said. "You have to be direct. As long as he said he's going to pay for part, this is his responsibility."

"Yes, right? You are right." She sat thinking for a moment. "But I don't know how I'm going to ask him for it, if he doesn't offer me the money." She narrowed her eyes. "I'm so pissed at him"—she said it more like "peesssssst," with a very long, hissing *s*—"and I am so pissed at myself for listening to him and moving. I should never have trusted him. He's not straightforward. Not honest. He's a liar, you know; he's a very good liar. But he doesn't show it.

"Anyway, it's not just material things, although those matter, *tab'an* [of course] they matter. It's not like I want money from him. But just like you said, he shouldn't say one thing one day and then change his mind the next day or forget, or pretend to forget. I don't think he's really forgetting.

"But it is other things too. For example, he disappears. One day I call him, and we have a nice conversation, we go out, and so on. Then he'll disappear for a week, two weeks. Just disappear. No calls, nothing. And he doesn't return my calls. Then he comes back and acts like nothing happened. And when we talk on the phone, all he talks about is himself. Himself and his stupid work. He never listens to me; he never wants to know about anything going on in my life. Okay, I don't have to love him, he doesn't have to love me, but at least we should be friends and be able to talk. I should have somebody to talk to about the things that are going on in my life, about my problems. Instead I just have to sit there listening to him." Malak folded her arms.

Just then, Farouq came over to Malak and put an arm around her shoulder, perching on the edge of her chair. "Lovely Malak. What's wrong?" She gave him a half smile and shook her head. "My dear, would you care to dance with me?" She smiled a little wider and agreed, so they got up from the table and went over to the center of the room and slow danced.

CHAPTER 6

Gift, Prostitute: Money and Intimacy

Imagine a vigilant scanning become automatic, relentless, compulsive. Picture people sitting on porches, standing behind fences, clumps of men gathered around benches at the gas station or the stand, how they stare as you pass, keeping track. Imagine that passing trucks can be recognized by their distinctive sounds, that people track and time their comings and goings to figure where they have been and how long they have lingered there. Imagine the scanning for signs . . . how everything depends on things overheard, overseen, on the effort to make somethin' of thangs. Imagine how, in such a heavily occupied place, sociality is not a distanced "social context" but a pressing, all-encompassing force field. . . .

They say women out walking on the side of the road are either in need of help or looking for sex. Yet the women do walk, in pairs and for exercise, and as they walk they dare the others to talk. Eva Mae pushes the always already challenged limits of the normal by dressing in a shimmering red dress, huge rhinestone necklace and earrings, and a red wig sitting askew on her head.

"That'll give 'm somethin' to talk about. They say I prostitutes! Hah! I don't want no old man sweatin' over me, honey." (Stewart 1996, 53–54)

The discussions I had with Zeid and Ayah and Kerim in a Cairo restaurant reveal a compulsive, vigilant, relentless scanning for signs of a woman's respectability. I was fascinated, and I was determined to try to understand my Egyptian friends' faculty of discernment. How did they parse a nightclub full of women—wearing equally (to me) revealing costumes, dancing and drinking alcohol with men—to determine that one woman was a "prostitute" and another was a "respectable" woman? The questions I asked were not only that of an anthropologist, trying to learn to see through a new cultural lens, but also that of a woman trying to understand how to craft an identity, caught between sometimes conflicting desires: to please a husband, to minimize sexual harassment, to collect ethnographic data, and to find diversion from my loneliness, far from home and family.

Sometimes my friends were able to explain their interpretations in a way that made some sense to me; other times I was frankly at a loss. How was one woman's lacy bra peeking out from under her sleeveless top anything different from my camisole? How was a wealthy Egyptian woman's living in her own apartment any different from my decision to spend more than three years living in Cairo away from my husband? Why were Russian women "prostitutes" but American women not? Their interpretations were a complex logarithm of class, nationality, gender, and idiosyncrasy, and at times I despaired of being able to train my eye to see what they saw.

I was slow on the uptake partly because for a long time I took people's use of the word "prostitute" to mean someone who performs sexual services for money. But if we look closely at the ethnographic data, we see that my Egyptian and expatriate informants in Cairo used "prostitute" in ways that did not necessarily have anything to do with money—or even with sex.

What is a prostitute?[1]

Intimacy and Money

I went through a half dozen interpretations for my Egyptian informants' use of the English word "prostitute." When I pressed my friends to explain why the two women across the restaurant were "case studies" in prostitution (as Kerim put it), their explanations often revolved around class, which initially appeared to confirm my definition of prostitution as the exchange of sex for money. They would call a scantily dressed woman a "prostitute" if she didn't look at ease in her fancy clothing, whereas other women whose dress was just as revealing but who looked at ease didn't get the label. The link between prostitution and class was, I thought, obvious: a wealthy woman didn't need to sell her body like a poorer woman might. That also, I thought, explained the association made by many Egyptians between "prostitution" and Gulf tourism or Russian expatriates. Gulf Arabs were thought to be fabulously wealthy with oil money. By comparison, most Egyptians were poor. Thus my friends assumed that any Egyptian women who associated with Gulf tourists must be prostitutes. Similarly, if Russians came to a poor country like Egypt to work (rather than to spend), they must be very poor indeed and thus willing to sell their bodies.

But this interpretation doesn't hold up to Kerim's use of the word to refer to an Egyptian woman who was independently wealthy and lived alone. She had no need to sell her sexuality. So what was it that made her a "prostitute"?

I decided that the code-switching used by Egyptians in order to be polite—using the English term "prostitute" instead of the ruder-sounding Cairene slang term *sharmuta*—was a kind of mistranslation. "Whore" is a better translation of *sharmuta* than "prostitute" since it impugns a woman's moral status without necessarily referring to an exchange of money. Yet a poor translation can become local convention. (There are plenty of instances where this happens. For example, most English-language restaurant menus in Egypt describe crustaceans as "shrimps" and "crabs," as in "shrimps soup," even though the former is not grammatically conventional in English-speaking countries and the latter evokes a sexually transmitted parasite.)

But why would this "mistranslation"—if that is what it is—occur? Could it be that Egyptians don't worry about trying to distinguish between "whore" and "prostitute" because, for them, there is no very important distinction to find? The fact that my Egyptian informants didn't bother to distinguish between "whore" and "prostitute"—a distinction that was, for me, important and the slippage bothersome—might suggest something important about different ways that people think about the relationship between sex and money. If Egyptians fail to distinguish between these two possible translations, that is because in Egypt, taking money for sex does not carry any greater stigma than sex without the monetary exchange.

To test this theory, let us consider Egyptian ideologies about the relationship between money and intimacy.

The economic arrangements in intimate relationships have been an underlying but not always explicit theme in this ethnography. For example, I have interpreted Zeid and Ayah's arguments about going out at night as struggles over Zeid's ability to prove his worth as a future husband by paying for Ayah's evening socializing. What I haven't mentioned is that even unengaged couples shared an expectation that the man would pay for the woman's social excursions, meals, doctor visits, and luxury items such as jewelry and perfume. The closer their relationship, the more he was expected to pay for. When a couple married, the ideal was that men would pay women a bride-price (*mahr*), a sum of money that was hers to spend as she liked (usually on furnishing their apartment), as well as a gift of gold jewelry (*shabka*). Middle-class married men with jobs usually gave their wives stipends, even if the wives had their own jobs. Men who could afford it took pride in insisting that their wives did not contribute to the household finances, even if they worked and earned a salary. For upper- and middle-class Egyptians, women's money was usually conceptualized not as being added to a communal household budget but, rather, as something that paid for luxuries: children's private-school fees or redecorating the house. (Poor Egyptians could not afford to indulge such ideals, a fact that Big Belly drew our attention to when he claimed that women would forgo *mahr* or *shabka* for the social respectability of marriage.)

The dominant expectation among my informants was that men pay for women (whether kin, such as daughters and wives and mothers, or pseudo- or proto-kin, such as mistresses and fiancées); failure to do so was read as a lack of intimacy, a lack of honor (in the man), and a lack of respect for the woman. Many people commented that a man who wasn't willing to spend on a woman with whom he was intimate was clearly taking advantage of her to no good purpose. For example, one woman who worked as a hotel receptionist told me that she had paid the down payment on an apartment for herself and her fiancé since she had a better-paying job than he did. A year into their engagement, she found him in this apartment in bed with another woman. In retrospect, she commented, she should have seen that coming. It should have been obvious that if he was letting her pay for things, it was a sign he didn't really value her. Or for another example: one Australian belly dancer had an Egyptian boyfriend whom, other dancers claimed, she supported with her income. All the other foreign belly dancers in her network talked about how pathetic that was. Instead of reading it as evidence of the strength of their relationship—love conquering money—they believed it was proof that the man was "using her." While these examples don't mean that there aren't people in Egypt who believe that a woman can pay for a man and still be loved, they do show that the dominant ideal holds that men should pay for women; if they don't, the relationship is read as lacking in respect and exploitative.

In many English-speaking countries there are a range of sayings that overtly deny the link between intimacy and money: prenuptial agreements are portrayed as the awful injection of cold calculation into love, the Beatles sang "Money can't buy me love," and numerous other aphorisms suggest that intimate relationships and money are separate and incommensurable domains. Viviana Zelizer (1994) shows that this isn't actually true through a careful analysis of court cases that show that money and intimacy are and have historically been legally linked in the United States, but the ideology that money corrupts intimacy persists as a powerful cultural norm.

In contrast, in the Arab world not only is the relationship between money and intimacy culturally acknowledged, but it is explicitly spelled out in Islamic theology. Marriage contracts, *mahr*, and *shabka* are typically required of men to marry and are said to protect women's rights in marriage, and many interpretations of *shari'a* law hold that a man must financially support his wife. When Zeid's sister was married, I was invited to the *katib al-kitab* ("signing of the book," that is, the registry and marriage contract ceremony) the day before the wedding. (Prenuptial contracts in the United States and Australia—my own points of reference—are a practice of the wealthy, but in Egypt every marriage entails a contract that carefully lays out all financial details of the union; see Quraishi and Vogel 2009.) After the bride and groom signed the marriage contract, the presiding sheikh offered a sermon that railed against *'urfi* marriages (informal, unregistered marriages) for not protecting women's rights in marriage. In part, he said, that was because these marriages weren't socially recognized, leading a woman into exploitative relationships in which her kin could not protect her, especially if pregnancy resulted, but also it was because *'urfi* marriages did not involve *mahr* and the financial support to which she was entitled under Islamic law.[2]

In short, in Egypt we see a culture that does not deny the link between money and intimacy—except when the money flows from a woman to a man. For a woman to expect to be financially supported by a man is seen as completely unexceptional and indeed as the natural (social) order of things. But a man being supported by a woman is often portrayed as an abnormal and exploitative relationship where love was only an inauthentic performance. That is not to say it doesn't happen; I knew of cases of Egyptian women who supported their husbands or lovers. But in those cases, both the man and the woman kept the arrangement hidden, because it shamed them both when people gossiped about how he was shirking his masculine responsibilities and she was being taken advantage of by someone who must not really love her. Even foreign belly dancers internalized this cultural ideal and critiqued the Australian belly dancer's relationship with the Egyptian man who allowed his girlfriend to spend on him.

But not all money is the same within intimate relationships. After all, even in cultures that define prostitution (or sex work, to use the term preferred by many activists and academics) in terms of an exchange of money for sex, a person who receives money from someone with whom they have sexual relations is not automatically called a prostitute or sex worker. Money can be a gift, too, in the Maussian sense: a tool for building and marking social relationships. The theoretical difference between a sex worker and a woman with whom one has an intimate relationship is not just money. The difference between the money one pays to a sex worker and the money one pays within an intimate relationship is like the difference between a commodity exchange and a gift exchange: in both, there is intimacy and money, but in the former the money is exchanged immediately and no larger, ongoing social relationship is established.

This logic—Egyptian acceptance of the place of (masculine) money in a sexually intimate relationship, so long as there is an ongoing social relationship—can be seen in the operational definition of prostitution used by Egyptian prosecutors. I interviewed Mabrouk, a prosecuting attorney, in April 2013 to ask him how police decided that a woman was a prostitute and what evidence was used to build a court case against her. He told me that the definition of a prostitute in Egyptian legal terms was a woman who has sex with men "without distinguishing" or discriminating among them (*duna tamyeez*). (An unmarried woman who has a relationship with only one man, whether or not she receives money from him, might be harassed by the police but is unlikely to be prosecuted.) Evidence of "indiscriminate" sexual relations may include finding money that the women could not plausibly claim to have earned through other means, but this is not necessary and money is not intrinsic to the definition of prostitute. Other evidence is a woman being found in a *sha"a mafrusha*, a rented apartment (that is, not living with her kin), which is considered evidence whether or not she is actually caught engaging in the act of sex. The fact that there is an expectation of male economic contributions toward women in the context of family and sexual intimacy, and that this financial payment is seen as a sign of respect and evidence of the man's ability to provide for dependents, probably contributes to the fact that prostitution is not primarily defined in terms of the exchange of money for sex.

This is true in other cultural and historical contexts as well: Zatz (1997, 279n5) says that in the United States, women were historically defined as prostitutes based not on an exchange of money for sex but on the number of their sexual partners, and contemporary American enforcement of laws against prostitution that focus on street walkers but not on escort services shows that what is in play in condemning "prostitution" is more than just the exchange of sex for money (ibid., 284).

What seems clear in Mabrouk's account is that prostitution is defined for legal purposes in terms of a lack of an ongoing relationship between the "prostitute" and the men with whom she is involved. When prosecuting a woman who has been arrested for prostitution, Mabrouk told me, legal testimony of alleged "indiscriminate" sexual relations was usually obtained by pressuring the men who have sex with such women to make statements against them. The men themselves were never prosecuted (even though, Mabrouk said, the police might try to make them believe that they would be in order to coerce their testimony). A man who refuses to testify against a woman, protecting her from prosecution, thus proves that their relationship approaches cultural norms of the protectiveness expected of a man in a kin or quasi-kin relationship with a woman.

Defining prostitution not in terms of the exchange of money for sexual intimacy but, rather, in terms of a woman's connection with male protectors, usually kin, and in terms of the social status of those men is a principle that can be glimpsed in historical accounts of sex work in Egypt. Prostitution was legal, regulated, and taxed throughout the Ottoman Empire since the sixteenth century and remained legal in Egypt through Muhammad Ali's reign (starting in 1803) and the British occupation of Egypt (starting in 1882); it was not outlawed until 1951 (Kholoussy 2010b, 679). Though prostitution remained legal under Muhammad Ali, he banished it to Upper Egypt in 1834 in an effort, Khaled Fahmy (2002) argues, to gain control over the public health and discipline of his armies and schools. During the British occupation, the Capitulations granted special status to European prostitutes just as they did to European merchants; Egyptian prostitutes were governed by local law. Two historians who have written on the history of prostitution in Egypt, Khaled Fahmy and Judith Tucker, note that women moved in and out of this category in part based on their connections to men who could both protect them from external male predation and vouch for their respectability. In an account that was later echoed in both Suad Joseph's (2000) and Sarah Pinto's (2014) analysis of kinship as a dialectic of care and constraint, Tucker writes:

> The status of women without families shaded into that of prostitutes, whose legal rights were nonexistent. They, and other women of ill-reputed trades, were exempt from the obligations of obedience and lived free of familial control; the absence of obligations also meant the ab-

sence of rights and protections, so that their freedom, the freedom of the outlaw, could be trespassed at will and they were easy prey for official harassment and underworld exploitation. (Tucker 1985, 197)

Fahmy (2002) describes French claims that corrupt Ottoman officials would occasionally threaten to register a woman as a prostitute if she didn't pay a bribe. Once thus registered, it was difficult to be unregistered; to do so required that the woman be vouched for by a respectable (male) guarantor, a man of established social status.

Through these brief glimpses into the history of sex work in Egypt we can infer that women shifted in and out of this category (though it was harder to shift out than in) and that what determined their classification as a "prostitute" was not only an exchange of sex for money but also their kin connections and broader social networks that could enable them to find a powerful representative to speak on their behalf.

What is also clear is that the label "prostitute" is applied based on the way women move through public space, which is linked to their connection with kin. Women who go out in public late at night are criticized as not respectable women, as we saw when Zeid called his fiancée's friend Rasha a prostitute, because they are stepping out of the domain of kin protection and surveillance. Women who are respectable are called *beity* (literally, "homey"), a compliment to a woman who prefers to stay at home in the company of kin rather than venturing out into public space. Women who live alone in rented apartments (*shu'a' mafrusha*), rather than living with kin, are associated with prostitution, as we saw both in Kerim's label given to the woman who didn't live with her mother and the prosecutor's description of how prostitutes are identified and prosecuted. The economic housing crisis in Egypt (Ghannam 2013; Singerman 1995; Singerman and Ibrahim 2003), which has made it so expensive to find accommodation that young couples usually only manage to acquire an apartment with considerable financial assistance from their parents (Kholoussy 2010a), only contributes to and reinforces these norms around residence and gendered moral identities, just as it organizes the older generation's control over the younger generation's sexuality.

Labels Discipline and Generate

My determination to understand Zeid and Ayah and Kerim's ability to spot the "prostitutes" in a crowd in order to index a cultural catalogue of signs of female respectability probably delayed my appreciation of one crucial fact: their talk was not simply a transparent lens on culturally informed observational skills. Their talk was also disciplining and generative. Talk about *other* women serves to discipline women in one's own group ("Be careful how you act and dress, because people are watching"). At the same time it reinforces group boundaries and validates women's status within the group ("You're not like them, no matter how much you appear to be; we don't respect them, but we respect you"), generating both group feeling and a desire to mimetically enact norms of respectable femininity—or to resist them.

As we can see, money and gift exchanges between men and women are associated with love, affection, and masculine care (epitomized in the cultural institution of *mahr*—bride-price—in which the man's family gives money and gold jewelry to the bride at the time of marriage), not with the concept of prostitution. The ethnographic data make clear that not only was the term "prostitute" not about a monetary transaction, it wasn't even necessarily about sex, since a woman could be called "prostitute" when there was no proof that she was sexually active at all. Recall Zeid and Ayah's dispute over Ayah's neighbor Rasha. Zeid claimed that she was a "prostitute" because she drove around alone after midnight, even though Ayah claimed she had never kissed a man, never mind had sex with one. My husband, when he was angry over what he saw as my disregard for the norms of respectable femininity, called me a "prostitute," though he didn't actually believe I was having sex with my informants, much less taking money for it.

What is involved in defining a "prostitute," then, is a complex moral judgment about a woman's social behavior, the number of her sexual partners, the timing of her movement through public space, and the extent to which she submits to kin control over her social life. The judgment operates at the intersection of female sexuality and kinship. *Sharmuta*, the term that my Egyptian friends from all different classes tended to translate as "prostitute" (but which might be better rendered as "whore"), is a highly pejorative term and is sharply contested. When Ayah resisted Zeid's use of the term for Rasha, perhaps it was not only because she was defending her friend but also because she understood how easily the term can be used to criticize any woman who defies social codes of female respectability in one way or another—how easily, in other words, the word can be turned back on oneself.

On the other hand, women sometimes called each other "prostitutes" to mark social boundaries and discipline the behavior of others in their group. When belly dancers accuse other dancers of being prostitutes (as I often heard them do), it is a kind of moral policing, a statement about the ideals of professionalism, a way to talk about the difficulty of getting jobs, a commentary on the way bribes work to secure a dancer's place on a dance roster, and an expression of a fear that competing dancers will edge those who refuse to sell their bodies out of the job market. Malak condemned not "prostitution" in general but only the "prostitution" of exchanging sex for a slot on a nightclub's roster of dancers, which increased the pressure on other dancers to transact in sex in order to work.

The terms "sex work" and "sex worker" are increasingly used by academics and activists because they avoid the stigmatizing connotations of "prostitution" and "prostitute" while simultaneously making explicit that sex work is a form of labor (Jeffreys 2004; Weitzer 2009). Yet Elaine Jeffreys (2004) argues that these terms are not very useful for describing prostitution in many historical and cultural contexts. With the exception of my brief digression into the history of prostitution in Egypt, when prostitutes worked out of brothels and were formally licensed and taxed, I have resisted using the term "sex work" for three reasons.

First, as we have seen, the word "prostitute"—or *sharmuta* (whore), *sitt mish kwayyisa* (not a good woman), *sitt mish muhtarima* (not a respectable woman), or any of the other local terms or euphemisms—encompasses far more than women who exchange sex for money or gifts. It is a term that labels and stigmatizes and that is applied regardless of whether a financial transaction occurs and independent, even, of women's actual sexual activity. Using terminology that takes away the stigma of the word "prostitute" would thus miss a key ethnographic point (Bernstein 2013, 18).

Second, focusing on sex *work* obscures the role of affect in mediating the human relations that structure sexual exchanges. Even when studies of sex work take into account private spaces and domestic relationships, something that the literature has often failed to do (Fassin, Le Marcis, and Lethata 2008), emotions—particularly feelings of love and the romance of falling in love—typically remain outside the scope of such works or appear only in the margins. Even the literature on sex workers who transition to long-term romantic relationships and marriage with former clients (Brennan 2004; Ratliff 1999; Padilla 2007) often focuses on risk paradigms or economic calculations (for example, the goals of upward mobility for sex workers) rather than affect. Yet as this ethnographic account has demonstrated, all sexual relationships are a complex mix of both economic exchange and affect, whether that affect is desperation or loathing or mercenary calculation or desire or affection or confusion over the way all these emotions intersect, as we saw in Malak's deteriorating relationship with Farouq.

Finally, these labels (and the literature on sex work more broadly) draw too-clear lines around complex lives and practices. Words like "whore" and "prostitute" and "respectable" are unstable, their usage shifting in different individual and political contexts, but so are women's sexual lives unstable and shifting in different individual and political contexts. Apart from their stigmatizing effect, labels—whether "sex worker" or "prostitute"—reify the role and draw our attention away from the extent to which women move in and out of different kinds of sexual relationships. Even the literature that attempts to distinguish between types and motivations of sex workers—for example, distinguishing between those who exchange sex for subsistence (that is, extremely vulnerable women who transact in sex for basic needs such as food) and those who exchange sex for consumption (those who transact in sex to consume fashion, cell phones, and cash) (Hunter 2002)—creates typologies at the expense of our understanding of how they lie on a continuum (Fassin, Le Marcis, and Lethata 2008). Even studies of sex work that explicate the enormous range of reasons and ways that women sell sex in different economic contexts (e.g., Bernstein 2013) still draw fundamental lines around sex workers, demarcating their ways of organizing the relationship between intimacy and money as distinct from other ways.

My account of Malak shows how difficult classifying women as a sex worker or not can be and how complex emotions around sex and money are. Malak said that she had dabbled in prostitution, but she never asked men for money to have sex. She occasionally danced at places where she knew she would make a lot of money and where she knew the patrons expected to have sex with her. Other times, she had sex with a man for pleasure and then was surprised to be paid. She didn't love her boyfriend and was annoyed when he didn't pay for certain things. Yet what bothered her as much as his failure to pay half her rent or buy her a cell phone was the fact that he was stingy in sharing a life with her. Malak is perhaps what Ronald Weitzer (2009, 217) would call a "borderline case" (into which he groups lap dancers, "kept" men and women, and geishas).

But what if we thought about *all women* as "borderline cases"?

Focusing on particular categories of women whom we call "sex workers" or "prostitutes" or "not respectable women" (or even "borderline cases") as if they were a different genus from "respectable women" (who do not trade in sex for money or have multiple sexual partners) draws our attention away from the similarities between and overlap of these different typologies of women. The problem with typologies is not just that they don't capture the complex, lived experiences of the prostitute, sex worker, or borderline case; they also obfuscate the relevance of the category "prostitute" for *all women*. No social scientist would ever put me or Rasha in the category of "sex worker." And yet we both at different points in time were labeled "prostitutes," and this label not only defined but also molded our behavior. The women in Egypt whom I write about in this ethnography exist both as sexualized, disreputable women and as respectable ones; the two imaginations of female sexuality—expressed as private pleasure, or harnessed to socially acceptable modes of reproduction—coexist as potential within the same people. These "two apparently contradictory modes of representation: the sensual female-as-body on the one hand, and on the other hand, the woman as a social being, a potential mother of nation-builders . . . must be understood in relation to each other" (Ryzova 2004–2005, 82). They exist in a fluid "relationship of mutual definition" (ibid.), both frames—woman as mother/daughter/sister, woman as whore—mutually constituting each other as ways of understanding women's potential. These frames offer themselves as narrative frames that observers draw on and that women performatively engage with as they construct socially acceptable moral identities.

As we saw when Zeid called Rasha a "prostitute" or when my husband and Kerim called belly dancers "prostitutes" without having any actual idea what kinds of sexual activities they engaged in, a woman's moral status is a *simulacrum* (Baudrillard 1988), a copy that has no original. It is more real than real. It is a representation that circulates, divorced from the original referent, independent of her actions.

Respectable women get called prostitutes; "prostitutes" also call themselves respectable women. Sometimes this appears paradoxical (or maddening, as it did when my husband called me and my friends prostitutes). Yet the mutually constituting fluidity of these feminine archetypes also offer opportunities for creative maneuvering. As Kathleen Stewart (1996, 189) argues, "Ideals stand as material signs not of positive objects and finished facts but of latent possibilities," yet they "bog down in a logic of exceptions, transgressions, and eccentricities." As we will see in chapter 7, my Egyptian informants' relentless scanning for signs and elaboration of feminine and masculine ideals at once judged, accommodated, and reconfigured around exceptions, transgressions, and eccentricities. Mistresses, unmarried women with their lovers, and belly dancers claimed respectability for themselves, even as, like Eva Mae in Stewart's (1996, 61–62) ethnography, they flaunted their transgressions in "mimetic excess."

CHAPTER 7

"Honor Killing": On Anthropological Writing in an International Political Economy of Representations

It was January, and a group of men and women were sitting around a dinner table in Haroun's *wakr*, picking over the cheeses and sardines and caviar and arugula that his Nubian servant Sayed had laid out. Haroun had a gift for pulling together strange and interesting selections of the Cairo demimonde for his dinner parties: businessmen and politicians, actors and actresses, belly dancers and musicians, and one American anthropologist.

The latest addition to the group, an aging actor, was telling jokes and snorting. "A law is issued in Saudi Arabia whereby families that have five children or more will get a gift from the government of 100,000 riyals and a new car. So there's a family with four kids. The guy comes home and says to his wife, 'We need to have just one more child so that we can get the money and the new car.' She says, 'But there's not enough time to have another kid. The law goes into effect next month and you have to have five kids before then.' He says, 'Well, look, there's this woman I know, see, I had a kid with her, unofficially . . . uh, before I married you, of course. So maybe I can go to her and get the kid back.' The wife says okay and he goes off to bring home the other child. When he comes back, the house is empty, except for his wife. 'What happened to the children?' The wife says, 'Their fathers all came to get them.'"

"Ha, ha!" He laughed hard at his own joke, snorting loudly.

Directly across the table, Malak leaned over to me and spoke in a disapproving voice. "He is a very vulgar man. Listen to him snort! It is not a polite sound. He is masturbating when he tells those jokes. He masturbates with his mouth. He is too old and fat and he can't get it up, so the only thing left for him is to talk about sex." She leaned closer to me as if to whisper a secret, but she kept her eyes on Snorter and spoke loud enough for anyone to hear, "Look at him! He's really excited! My God! I think he's going to start drooling in a moment!" Malak never worried about offending anyone, but almost nobody ever got offended when she spoke so charmingly, with her lisping Spanish accent and flirtatious mannerisms. Haroun smiled at her.

"What a coquette you are, Malak! So cute!" He leaned across Alia to caress Malak's arm for a moment, and Alia, his mistress, smiled gamely.

Malak was a paradox: a coquette who was not a threat to other women. Alia was suspicious of every other woman there, but not of Malak, despite all Haroun's compliments and caresses. Malak had the kind of face that belonged to a Madonna, always relaxed and smiling, and shining a little bit. It was a sweet face, the kind of face that made you want to know her. There often seemed to be a shimmering golden halo around her head, though there was nothing about her that was particularly innocent.

Snorter had joined the group for the first time that night with Abdallah, a judge. The judge's poker-faced reserve belied a lewd streak that rivaled that of his friend. Right now he was sitting next to Zizi, another retired belly dancer who had become an entrepreneur, operating a chain of very successful seafood restaurants. The judge leaned over in her direction and spoke in a soft voice. At the same time, he was staring very obviously down her blouse at her ample bosom. She was turned slightly toward him, her shoulders pressed a little forward to exaggerate the cleavage. Haroun saw Abdallah and called out to him, "What are you occupied with, brother? You haven't noticed any of the food in front of you!" The judge looked up with a leering smile. Zizi straightened up and looked away.

Alia caught Zizi's eye and smiled. "Zizi, sing us a song! We want to hear the Sasa song!" Zizi was famous for her songs. She didn't have a strong voice, but it was a sweet and true voice, and her songs were unique. Some were famously dirty. Other songs were more suggestive than shocking. In one, an unmarried woman demurely protests her lack of wifely prowess with the mortar and pestle. "I don't know how to grind, to grind . . ."

The other women were fascinated by Zizi, and a little afraid of her. One minute she would hoot with laughter, and then the next affect haughty detachment. She could get away with saying things that no other Egyptian woman could say in polite company. This was partly because she was so sweet about it, singing with an engaging smile and a twinkle in her eyes that was more flirtatious than lewd, and it was partly because people were afraid of her. If you laughed with her, she was sweet and smooth as honey; if you didn't pay her homage, she would treat you with icy disdain.

Everyone chimed in after Alia, asking for the Sasa song. The judge shushed people. When there was complete silence, Zizi started singing in her sweet, soft voice.

Make me Sultan, crown me King,
and give it to me in the ass, O Sasa.

Everyone cheered and sang along with her when she repeated this refrain. Then she launched into the full version of the song, full of Alexandrian slang.

I'm cold, warm me in your arms. I'm naked, and don't you dare cover me up!
Take your time, but don't hold back. Slowly, slowly, don't hurt me now!

It was the first time that Snorter heard the song, and he was fascinated. He listened closely, laughing and clapping for a particularly clever phrase, and he kept squeezing the knee of the girl sitting next to him. The girl had come with Zizi, and it was also her first time at one of Haroun's gatherings. She had large oval eyes thickly lined with black kohl and a wide mouth painted a pale salmon color. As soon as the girl had been introduced around, Malak looked her up and down skeptically, and now she said to me, "She's a prostitute. Look, obviously that vulgar man thinks so too, because he wouldn't dare put his hands all over a woman unless he was sure she was a whore."

Zizi finished the song and everyone clapped and cheered. Then she settled back into conversation with the people sitting near her. Next to Malak was Sameen. Sameen was examining the hand of Farouq's new girlfriend, a large woman sitting on the other side of him. He opened her hand wide and traced the lines with the pad of his thumb. "Very peculiar," he declared. She squealed with anticipation.

"What do you see, Sameen Bey? Tell me, what do you see?" He continued to caress her hand, as if absorbed in the analysis.

"Do you see this line? It is short and broken. It is your life line. You will live a short but tempestuous life." He looked earnestly at her, but she just scowled back at him. His smile faltered.

Alia, clutching Haroun's arm proprietarily, was watching with amusement. "He reads palms so that he will have an excuse to hold women's hands. Have you ever," she said, now addressing the group in general, "seen him tell a man's fortune?" Sameen ignored her and continued to examine the woman's hand gently pinching the plump flesh of her wrist as if it too might reveal secrets and signs.

Malak said to him in English, so that the other woman wouldn't understand, "You two are very cute together, like a couple of big bears!"

With a sigh, Sameen closed the woman's palm in his hand and patted it gently. He turned to Malak and, with a smile, replied, "Fuck you."

Malak smiled back, switching to Arabic. "So tell us, Sameen Bey, what is it like to be in politics now, after all these years as a businessman?"

He had just been appointed to a political post. "What I've learned," he said, leaning back and pressing his hands into a steeple, with a vaguely gloating expression on his face, "is that women who are attracted to power are different from women who are attracted to money, and sex with the two is different."

"Money is power, Sameen," Alia commented.

"No—okay, yes, but some women are attracted specifically to political power. And they like to be dominated more than spoiled. They like to feel connected more than they like to be spent on." He sat up straight again. "By the way, Haroun, don't you know Mohammed Hussein?"

"What about him?"

"I wish you could get that bastard to leave me alone." He scowled. "Everywhere I go, he's tailing me. The other day I was at a reception trying to talk to a very beautiful woman, and he kept following me around and talking to me and always sitting next to me."

"Who's that, Sameen?" asked Malak.

"This asshole doesn't have anything to do with me, we're not friends, but everywhere I go he sticks to me like glue. He's always by my side. I swear, all I have to do is sit in an empty seat and the next second, I find him next to me. And he's about twice as fat as I am."

"But is that even *possible*, Sameen?" asked Malak sweetly.

"Bitch," he replied in English. Malak just smiled at him.

People were getting more and more drunk, and on Haroun's signal, Sayed started to pour champagne into crystal glasses. High customs duties vastly inflated the market price of champagne, so it was a real luxury—or sign of decadence—to be able to drink it in Egypt.

All of a sudden a booming voice from the door proclaimed, "Hello, hello, hello! I missed you all soooooooooooo much!" It was Nour, the actress, making her typically grand entrance. She had taken a few steps into the room and then stopped, instinctively finding the best light just as if she were on stage.

Now that she had commanded everyone's attention, she repeated in formal Arabic, "My beloved friends, I have missed you all so very much!" She then swept into the room and went to kiss everybody hello, working counterclockwise from her right. She appeared to have come straight from the theater because she was still in her professional makeup, painted on Kabuki-thick. She was wearing a long skirt that was slit all the way up the thigh and a tight sweater that buttoned up the front and was covered with sparkly rhinestones. She was spilling out of her clothes, and between each button the sweater gaped open boldly, revealing the folds of flesh of her breasts and belly underneath and a lacy bra.

Farouq was ogling her, as usual; he had a taste for large women. He loved fleshy thighs, breasts, buttocks, stomach. He leaned over and muttered to Haroun, "I'd love to take those tits of hers and stick them in my ass." Haroun laughed.

When Nour had sat down, Haroun said to her, "You know, Madame Nour, Farouq was just telling me . . ." Farouq tried to shush him, clutching his arm, but Haroun shook Farouq's hand off. "Farouq was just telling me that he would like to put your breasts in his ass. Technically speaking," he continued, with an appreciative glance at her bosom, "I don't know exactly how that would work, but that's what he said to me."

The actress smiled sweetly over at them both. "Really, Farouq darling? You'd like me to fuck you in the ass with my tits?" Alia's eyebrows shot up half a centimeter. But Farouq was neither shocked nor embarrassed.

"I swear by the prophet, I'd love that," he replied. The judge was looking on disapprovingly. Farouq leaned over and said to him in a drunken stutter, "What . . . what . . . what about you, sir, wouldn't Your Honor love to take those tits of hers and stick them right in your ass?"

The judge, poker-faced as always, just stared at him for a moment, silent, and then said, "No." Others tittered with laughter.

Malak turned to Nour. "Doesn't it offend you when people talk to you like that?"

"Oh, honey, I'm used to it by now. When you are an actress, you are a sex symbol, and when you are a sex symbol, you have to be prepared to hear such things."

I was listening quietly in my seat next to Malak. Aside from the young girl who had come with Zizi, I was the youngest person there, and the only American. I put a leaf of arugula in my mouth and started to chew.

Snorter had been watching me. All of a sudden he spoke very loudly, in English. "And you, why don't you talk?" My eyes jumped to him and

I blushed, trying quickly to swallow. Staring directly at me, he spoke to the others. "You know, someone that pale, you can see even the blood under the skin in her thighs."

"It's true, in my shoulders and arms you can see the veins under my skin." I pointed to a faint blue line that branched underneath the strap of my camisole.

"No, in the thighs! The *thighs*!" he cackled. "Where are you from?"

"America."

He frowned. "I know you're from America. Where are you from in America?"

"Virginia."

"Ah! A virgin!" He cackled again. "You know," he continued to the others, "Americans don't know how to lie. She can't lie. She can have an affair with her husband's best friend, and then she'll go to her husband and tell him, 'I'm sorry, honey, I slept with your best friend.' It's true, isn't it? You can't lie, can you?"

Regaining my composure, I nodded at him gravely. "You are quite right. I never lie. It is completely impossible." Alia looked at me sharply, and Malak smirked. I put my arm around Malak and kissed her cheek, thinking about the lies I had told to my own husband, and I thought of all the people sitting around me, some friends and some not, and about all the stories I had told them. I wondered if once, long ago, I had ever been that mythical American who didn't know how to lie.

The lies were for my husband and his obsession with female respectability before our marriage had ended. The stories were for the other men around me. The men who came to Haroun's gatherings would always flirt with me, since I was considered fair game if I was at Haroun's. I had to find novel ways of politely rebuffing them. I soon learned that certain lines of conversation were never innocent. Chief among them were questions about my living situation. "Are you living alone or with roommates?" That translated to, "Would we be able to have sex in your apartment, or do I have to pay for a hotel?"

At first I considered just telling people that I had a roommate. But that was too directly dishonest, and I also had to consider that there might be a second translation for the roommate question, namely, "If it doesn't work out with us, maybe you could introduce me to a friend." So I decided to create an altogether different set of home companions, fantastic, unbelievable, to whom nobody would ask to be introduced. To some people, I said that I had a two-meter-long snake. "I wrap it around my neck to keep it warm in winter, and it sleeps in my bed at night." Most Egyptians had no concept of the idea of keeping a snake as a pet.

The idea of one sleeping in my bed frightened and repulsed them. (I did have a pet snake for a while, but I didn't sleep with it—I might have squished it.)

I told other people that I was living with Nubians. I tried this out one night at a dinner party with a man I was talking to. He did a double take and asked me what in the world I was talking about. "I invited a Nubian family to come live with me," I told him. "I'm an anthropologist and I wanted to know more about Egyptian culture. To live it, firsthand. Everyday life."

He had a look of amazement and incredulity on his face. "Where did you find these Nubians?" he asked.

"Well this lady was a maid for one of my friends, so I asked if she wanted to come with her family and live with me."

"Ah," he said, with a look of dawning understanding. "___ her to clean for you." That made it okay, if she was a se___

"No, she doesn't work for me. She's my guest." He ___ again. "She and her husband and their little baby; t___ year-old son. He's really cute!" I enthused. "I love to pl___ hardly ever cries!"

"A woman and her husband? What does her husband___

"He's a mechanic."

His mouth was literally hanging open. He reached over the arm of a friend of his who was sitting nearby, a medical doctor named Qasem. "Listen to this story. Lisa has Nubians living with her!"

But the doctor was not surprised at all. "Yes, I traveled a lot in the south of Egypt and I saw lots of foreigners living with the Nubians. They love Nubians." He went on to tell some anecdotes about Nubian traditional medicine and how they handled scorpion stings. The doctor's credulity clinched it for the others. He thought it completely normal, so even if they couldn't affect his blasé attitude, at least that moved the story into the realm of possibility. But because I could never talk about the Nubians without laughing, they also didn't know whether I was serious or pulling their leg.

From then on, that became my trademark story. From a small family, they gradually grew. "There are thirteen Nubians living with me." When people would balk and say, "Thirteen?!" I would say, "Well, really it's ten, but three of them are pregnant so I'm trying to get used to the idea that soon it will be thirteen." The Nubian roommates story disturbed Egyptians' established ideas about privacy, class relations, and race relations. It verged on the unbelievable because they could never imagine such a situation, but at the same time they couldn't quite discount it as a possibility because everybody knew that foreigners did crazy things.

Another story I liked to tell was that I was about to move to the City of the Dead. My inspiration for this story came from hearing about some Italian anthropologist who was living in the graveyards and doing her research there. So when people asked what part of town I lived in, a question partly designed to assess my social class, I would say, "Well, right now I'm living in Zamalek"—a posh and expensive island in the middle of the Nile where many foreign diplomats live—"but next month I'm moving to the graveyards. There's an Italian anthropologist living there and she's moving out, so I'm going to take her flat. It's only one hundred pounds a month." People found this story more alarming than the Nubian story, but less so than the snake story.

Sometimes I combined the stories. "I have to move out of my flat in Zamalek because it's just getting too crowded with Nubians. Thirteen of them! Well, really only ten, but three are pregnant. So I found a very large place to live in the cemetery. It's actually several places, several adjacent graves, you know. But there's plenty of living space around the tomb. The tomb really only takes up very little space in the center of the room. The Nubians are going to live next door."

Alia would play along, to convince people of the story. "What's wrong with living with Nubians?" she would ask. "Doesn't Haroun have Nubian servants? Well, then! Not such a big difference!" Or, "What's wrong with living in the City of the Dead? It's very sensible, actually. She'll save a lot of money on rent."

Now people were getting up from the table and going over to sit on the couches. I wondered if they would make Malak dance. Usually after dinner Farouq or Haroun would try to persuade her to dance, and she complained to me that she was their performing monkey. Now Malak came over to sit next to me and complain more about her current boyfriend. She and Farouq had split long before, when Farouq started a relationship with the actress Lulu. Malak had started to date Galal, but their relationship was officially a secret because, he said, he didn't like people talking about him. I thought that it was more probably because he wanted to be able to keep his options open rather than be identified with one woman, and Malak suspected that it was because he didn't like to be publicly associated with a dancer.

"I tell you," said Malak, "I'm not very pleased with the group in general these days. Haroun's friends. You know, most of the men in this group, with the exception of Haroun, they are all snobs and they do not like me. Why? Because I am a dancer. These men, they cannot move outside their own social class. They see me as inferior. And most of these men, they are fundamentally unable to deal with women; they can't even talk to women. Even Haroun, for example, he only knows how to joke around; he can never speak seriously with a woman. He likes women only when they're saying something funny, but he can't listen to them talk seriously about anything."

I nodded. "Yeah, he's the same with me, I've noticed. He's always laughing and patting me on the back, but no real conversations about anything. But maybe that's because we're foreigners, not because we're women. I mean, he and Alia seem to talk normally, about everything. But you know, they're both in business, they have a lot more in common. Maybe also he doesn't know how to talk to us because we have such different professions than him, you know? That, and the fact that we're foreigners."

"Maybe, maybe," she considered. "But no, I think he can only talk to Alia because she is his lover. I never saw him talking with any other Egyptian women seriously, never. I think it's partly the whole masculinity issue. Also, usually Egyptian women don't have anything interesting to say."

I laughed at Malak's outrageously sweeping prejudice. "Or maybe it's because Haroun is trying to put barriers between himself and other women who he's attracted to, you know? He doesn't want to create threatening personal connections and attachments, so he tries to just keep everything on a light, humorous level."

"Hmm. That may be true, also. He is attracted to every woman he meets, so he has to have some mechanism to put distance between him and them, especially if he wants to stay with Alia. And in the end, he may be attracted to other women, but I think he really loves Alia so much. He knows that he will never find someone else like her, someone who is so loyal and devoted to him."

Haroun had a strange power over people. Alia, for example, had a very strong personality, but she appeared completely bound to Haroun's will. He was the only person in the world who could control her; she would do anything he asked, willingly. Jump through the most ridiculous hoops. Even other men in Haroun's circle became almost fawning in his presence.

Malak said, "In the end, maybe it's not a question of me being a woman. I think that most men of their type and social class will never feel comfortable around me because I was a dancer. A *ra"āsa*."

I said, "Even though you're a foreigner? Doesn't that put you in a different social category than an Egyptian *ra"āsa*?"

But Malak said, "You know, deep inside it is basically the same. I'm still a *ra''āsa* for them."

Haroun came over to us now, handing me a glass of white guava juice. I thanked him for being so considerate. He bowed and then asked Malak to dance with him. They put on some slow music and stood up to dance. When they finished, Haroun led Malak over to the sofa, and then he asked me to dance as well, as if it were an afterthought. I was amused. He made it seem like he had just noticed a wallflower and charitably decided to show her a good time. I stood up to join him.

As we danced, he kept a polite distance, but after a minute, he slipped his right hand under my jacket, and then under my camisole, so that his hand was resting on my bare skin. "That's nice, isn't it?" he said to me, with a wink, and I glanced at him uncertainly. Haroun had a silencing effect on me. He had such a strong personality, and I didn't really know how to talk with him. Especially how to respond to such a statement. Alia was watching us dance with a small smile on her face and a wineglass in her hand. She could see that his hand had snaked under my jacket.

"You know, I'm really quite fond of you," he said to me now, speaking in a low voice next to my ear, without looking at me. "You did realize that, didn't you? Didn't you?" He seemed determined to get an answer out of me, so I decided to not give it to him. I just leaned my head back far enough so that I could catch his eye, and raised my eyebrows as if surprised to hear it. He laughed abruptly. "Oh, come, now. You must know that I want you. I think it is quite obvious. I think I have made it clear enough." I wondered what he was talking about. True, he flirted with me, but I had always thought that he was an equal-opportunity flirt, flirting with everyone he invited to his gatherings. What had he done to make clear his interest in me? Was he referring to the pretty gold ring that he and Alia had together given me for my birthday? Still I didn't speak. I just raised my eyebrows further in an even more exaggerated show of surprise.

"Oh ho! Now I see. We are playing games? But I do not like games. I am a straightforward man. I like directness."

"That is good," I said. "I like directness as well."

"Then tell me, What is your reaction to my proposal?"

I furrowed my brow. "What proposal?"

He frowned at me. "Oh, come, now." Then he spoke as if to himself. "Does she know what I'm talking about? Or is she playing dumb?"

There is a verb in Arabic for "to play dumb." I hadn't heard it until just that moment, but I knew the root of the word—*'abeeta*, which was part of Sara's favorite name for me, Lady Idiot,—and there was a verb form that meant "to pretend to [do that action]," so I could figure out the meaning from the structure of the other letters arranged around that root. I smiled to myself. I was smiling at my own linguistic accomplishment, but Haroun thought I was smiling at what he had said.

"I think that she knows very well what I'm talking about," Haroun said, continuing to talk about me in the third person. "The question is, Why doesn't she reply? I'm hoping for a clear answer. I'm a man who likes clarity."

I leaned back and looked at him. "You want a clear answer, but you have not given me a clear question!"

"Let me be clear, then," he smiled. "I want you to join me tonight."

"And what about Alia?" I asked. He had led us over so that we were dancing right in front of Alia.

"Join us both!" he said, loud enough for Alia to hear. "Right, Alia?"

"Yes, join us both!" she said with a warm smile. Haroun kissed me on the cheek.

Now I was really confused. I thought quickly about how to respond. None of the stories I used to deflect men's advances were of any use here. The snake and the Nubians and the apartment in the cemetery— none of them would work with Haroun because Alia knew that none of them were real. I had never expected an advance from Haroun, who was always friendly but distant with me. Certainly I never expected to be invited to join a threesome. All I could think of to say was, "I am a married woman, Haroun."

"Are you?" he said. "But where is your husband?"

"He is in America."

"Why didn't he come here with you?"

"He has his work in America. I go to visit him there."

"He's an Arab, isn't he?" I was surprised that he acted like he didn't know these things, since I had told them to Alia during our long phone conversations, and once Alia had told me that she called me on fact-finding missions for Haroun, who had urged her to establish a friendship with me. My mind was racing, trying to figure out how to interpret all of this, and I was distracted by his hand stroking the bare skin of my back.

"And you love him?" he asked.

"Yes, I love him." I hadn't told anyone except Malak about the end of my marriage.

"Good. I am a married man. And I love my wife. What will be between us, it is, shall we say, 'between brackets.' Separate. Something different. It doesn't mean that you don't love your husband, or that I don't love my wife."

The music ended, and I stepped back from him. I smiled. "Certainly, I will join you and Alia for a drink on the sofa tonight." I picked up my guava juice and sat down next to Alia. "Thank you very much for the dance, Haroun Bey, and thank you for the kind hospitality, as always." I raised my glass of juice to him. He groaned at my determination to politely play dumb and sat down next to me, putting an arm around me. Alia leaned toward me and put her hand on my thigh. Malak raised her eyebrows at me from across the room.

Everyone's attention was caught by the loud voice of Snorter. He was complaining about people who act like they can succeed on faith alone, to the exclusion of actually working. So he appealed to the judge, who was known to have a bent toward sports; he had played soccer in his youth, and still played it weekly with his friends at the club. Snorter said to him, "So, Abdallah Bey, tell me. Suppose you have a soccer player who is very pious. He prays five times a day, he does extra fasts, he has a prayer mark on his forehead, and he is *mustangee kwayyis*. Does that mean that he's going to win the match and score goals even if he's missing practice?" Abdallah started laughing. It was a rhetorical question, of course, no need for a reply, but what he was laughing about was the word *mustangee*. It appeared to have special comic value.

Abdallah said to Snorter, "For the sake of the foreigners here," nodding to me and Malak, "why don't you tell them what *mustangee kwayyis* means."

Alia laughed and whispered in my ear, "It means that he's cleaned his ass well."

Snorter started to explain but was cut off by Qasem, the medical doctor who had once discoursed on foreigners' fetishization of Nubians. Now Qasem took it upon himself to offer an academic explanation of what it meant to *yastangee*, or clean one's ass (as Alia put it), with the aim of attaining a state of ritual purity before praying. I sensed that he wanted to give a full description of the process, but suddenly he became aware of the presence of a lovely and polite woman sitting next to him and he turned shy. So Qasem cut short his explanation and merely said, "After one uses the toilet, one must wash properly before one can pray."

I put on my most naïve look and, pretending that I hadn't been enlightened by Alia, said, "But I don't understand. You have to wash your hands after you go to the bathroom?"

Haroun and Alia grinned, Qasem looked embarrassed, and Snorter seized the moment, saying very loudly in his flat, American-accented

English, "It means that after you shit, you wash your ass." Ms. Lovely and Polite turned up her nose at his frank explanation and vulgar discussion of bodily functions, making it clear that she did not expect to hear the words "shit" or "ass" spoken in her presence. Everyone else who didn't have to pretend to be respectable laughed and laughed.

The next morning when I woke up back in my apartment—which was not in the City of the Dead and was empty of Nubians and snakes—I sprinkled sugar over the butter on my toast and went to sit on the balcony to eat, peering over the railing to the street below. I watched the guard sitting on a wooden chair in front of the ministry building at the end of the road. His gun was propped against the wall next to him, and he was dully scraping in the sand with the toe of his boot, ignoring all the people walking past. My upstairs neighbors lowered an empty basket on a cord and hauled it up again full of leafy green vegetables. Saeed, the old doorman who was back from a trip to his natal village in the south, watched the basket ascend safely and then slowly plodded off on other errands. To the right a woman with very shiny black hair was yelling at a thin man who held a bike by the handlebars. He kept quiet, head down, resigned to her scolding. I leaned forward, trying to figure out what he was in trouble for, but I couldn't hear what the woman was saying. If ever I needed to campaign against the stereotype of Egyptian men dominating women, this woman could be the face of the campaign.

I finished my toast and decided to visit Sara in the hospital. She had finally gone to the hospital for her operation three weeks ago, although they hadn't operated until a week after that because they were having trouble finding enough blood of her type, which was relatively rare. It was Sara's family that was having trouble finding the blood, not the hospital, because although she was being treated in a public hospital for free, patients were still required to supply their own blood and medicine, and if a donor was not available from the family, the blood had to be bought by the pint from various blood banks in town. Then the patients or their families had to carry the frozen blood to the hospital in bags, and it slowly defrosted as they made their way across Cairo on the subway or the crowded buses.

When I had first visited, shortly after the operation, I was shocked at how much pain Sara was in and how much liquid of various colors was oozing through the bandage over her knee. Sara could barely talk through the pain and the haze of drugs, and all I could do was sit next to her and pat her hand.

Now it was two and a half weeks later. I walked into the hospital in

Abasiyya and paid my two-pound entrance fee. I walked through several courtyards to reach the wing where Sara was being kept and up several flights of stairs. Then I walked down a litter-strewn hallway toward Sara's room. There were wadded-up pieces of paper, cigarette butts, and an empty potato chip bag on the floor. In one corner someone had dripped blood all over the floor and it had dried to dark brown circles.

I found Sara at the far end of her room watching TV on a small portable set that her mother had brought in from her home. The mattress she was lying on was stained yellow, and some of the stuffing poked out the ends. An orderly had just delivered the afternoon meal: two pieces of whole-wheat pita bread, one container of plain yogurt, and one boiled egg. Sara greeted me with four kisses on alternating cheeks and tried to prop herself up in bed, tugging the thin floral pillowcase back over the yellow, crumbling foam pillow and placing it behind her back. "Mama, raise the bed so I can sit up and talk to Lisa." Her mother, who had been sitting cross-legged on the floor reading the Qur'an, readjusted her head scarf, then got to her feet.

Sara was better than before, but still in a lot of pain. The wound hadn't quite healed. It was still swollen and continued to ooze blood and pus, sometimes more and sometimes less, and now she told me that the doctors were saying that she would probably need another operation to "clean up" the wound. They were trying one last round of intensive antibiotics first in an attempt to avoid surgery. She groaned as her mother cranked the bed up higher. Sara suddenly shouted out in pain as her leg was jostled. She let loose a torrent of abuse at her mother, who threw up her hands and stalked out of the room in protest. The woman in the neighboring bed was silent a moment, then said, "Sara, you need to speak more respectfully to your mother; she's only trying to help you."

Sara shouted back at her, "You don't know how ill I am! I'm in so much pain and nobody feels for me at all, nobody!" She started to cry.

The woman spoke soothingly. "Never mind, I know, but try to bear it. Everyone here is in pain, but you can't yell at your mother like that." Sara just stared up at the ceiling, blinking back tears. The woman tactfully changed the subject. "One of your favorite movies is on TV, Sara."

Sara sniffed and turned toward the television. She kissed her hand and pressed it to the television screen over the male actor's head. "I adore him."

One of the sets for the movie was the apartment or villa of someone very wealthy; it had checkered marble floors, a grandly curved staircase with an elaborate balustrade, and sweeping green satin curtains in the background. Sara sighed. "I wish I lived in something like that." She turned back to me and, wincing, sat up and eased one leg over the edge of the bed. "I'm glad you came," she said with a tired smile. "I need to talk to you."

"Here I am."

"But we can't talk here. Too many listening ears." The hospital room had twelve beds and seven of them were taken. It was visiting hours, so the room was full of people sharing food, making coffee on little gas burners on the ground, and talking in a loud cacophony of voices.

"I doubt that anybody could hear us over the general noise level."

But Sara was already gingerly lifting her other leg, the bandaged one, over the side of the bed. "Let's go outside and sit in the hallway. Get me the walker." There was one walker shared by all the residents in the room. I brought it over to the bed, and Sara slowly stood up. We made our way out to the hallway, where Sara eased herself into one of the plastic chairs in the hall, panting from the effort of moving so much. I sat next to her and patted her arm awkwardly. Together we watched two young boys who were playing together in the hallway. One boy was small and hunchbacked, with a head too large for his body. He walked awkwardly but nevertheless moved very fast.

"He's always running around," said Sara. "He's about to have an operation for his legs, then he won't be able to run anymore. Poor thing. His mother is that tall, thin woman in the room in the bed across from mine. Did you notice her?" The woman stood out, tall and thin as she was. She had the classic, gaunt, pharaonic features that can be seen in some Egyptian villages but rarely in Cairo; she looked like a painting from an ancient tomb, but she was dressed in a galabiyya, the traditional long robe that rural men and women wear, with a scarf on her head. "She's pregnant again. Did you know, she has six children, and all of them except for one girl have something wrong. Two are blind, three are crippled in various ways. But she just keeps getting pregnant. She and her husband keep trying, hoping for one normal boy."

The small boy, the tall woman's son, was very silent, for all his activity. He was playing with another boy who, Sara said, had had six operations so far after having been injured in a car accident. One operation was on his head, and the hair was still growing back; the other operations were all on his leg. He was in a wheelchair, and the little hunchbacked boy was pushing him up and down the halls. The little hunchbacked boy could barely reach the handles of the wheelchair and couldn't see where he was going, so the other boy would steer with his hands on the wheels and tell him to stop when they were about to run into a wall. They were racing around at top speed and laughing with exhilaration. It was terrifying to watch, since they always seemed to be about to run into a wall, and the boy in the wheelchair was too short to fit in it properly, so his fragile, skinny little feet stuck straight out in front of him; it looked like his delicate ankles would take the brunt of any crash, but for the whole time we watched, the boys somehow, perhaps miraculously, managed to avoid injury.

They made their way over to where Sara and I were sitting, and the boy in the wheelchair spoke to me. He was very skinny and had a big head; there was a wide grin on his face. He said, "You speak foreign?"

I laughed. "Yes, I speak English."

"But now you're speaking Arabic."

"I learned Arabic later but English is my mother tongue."

"You are a foreigner?" I nodded. He said, politely, "It doesn't show at all!" It was said in the same tone of voice that one would reassure someone that a pimple was barely noticeable.

"Thank you," I said, laughing again at the odd compliment, and then they sped off again.

Sara was reaching into a pocket of some inner layer of clothing. She looked me in the eye. "I'm going to show you something; I want to know what you think it is."

"Okay."

She pulled out a piece of gauze and started to unwrap it. She finally reached an inner layer, a thick rectangle of gauze that was folded in thirds. She opened it up and showed it to me. Inside were two thick pieces of something bloody and mucous-like.

"That's disgusting. What is it?"

"That's what I want you to tell me. What do you think it is?"

I leaned over and looked more closely. It just looked like a clot of blood, but there was something fleshy about it too. But still it didn't look like anything identifiable. "I have no idea."

"It came out of me."

"What? Is that from the operation? It's really disgusting. Why are you keeping it in your pocket?"

"No, not from the operation. I didn't have my period for three months, since before I entered the hospital. And then all of a sudden my period started and I had really bad cramps—they were terrible—and I went into the bathroom and this came out. It's not just blood; it's a big piece of something. Do you think that it's a baby?"

Now I looked at it even more closely. It still didn't look like anything, but I supposed it could be a fetus. It was too squashed into the mesh of the gauze to look like anything now. "You were pregnant? My God, Sara. With Ali?"

Sara was starting to cry. "I think so. I think so. I hoped I was pregnant."

"Are you crazy? You wanted to be pregnant? You aren't married! Your brothers would kill you!"

"We were married *'urfi*. Secretly. Unofficially."

I paused to take that in. "You still would have been in big trouble. If you really were pregnant, then you're lucky you miscarried."

"But I wanted the baby. I wanted to have a baby with Ali. I wanted to be the mother of his children. He'd have to stay with me then. I could have left home, run away to a different town, maybe Alexandria. My brothers wouldn't have to know."

"Sara, maybe, maybe you could have run away. If you weren't in the hospital. But Ali can't run away. He's already married and he has children. He's not going to run away with you."

"I wanted to have a baby with Ali," she repeated stubbornly. She wiped away her tears with her hand. I fished around for some tissues in my purse.

"Does anybody know?"

"I didn't show it to anybody but you."

"But I mean does anybody else know that you were secretly married?"

"No, nobody except for you."

"Why did you tell me?"

"I had to talk to somebody. You're a foreigner. And I know you won't tell. You like gossip but you don't spread it."

"No, I won't tell." I smoothed the hair back from Sara's forehead and patted her cheek. Sara looked away, embarrassed by her tears, and blew her nose, then stared at the wall in front of her. "Ali doesn't even visit me in the hospital. He came only once since I came here. He says he's too busy with work and with his family. I can't even talk to him on the phone. And now there's nothing. Now I have nothing from him."

I didn't know what to say to that. I just kept patting Sara's shoulder, her arm, her hand, and murmuring, "Never mind. Everything will be okay."

For weeks I couldn't get the image of that piece of blood and flesh, mashed into the gauze, out of my head. How long would Sara carry it around with her in her innermost pocket, secretly taking it out to examine when she was alone, to look for a small hand, a head, anything identifiable as flesh? Her last tie with Ali, reduced to two bloody chunks of something, maybe and maybe not an aborted fetus, folded up into a piece of gauze. She was married to him, secretly, as his second wife—his irrelevant wife, his unimportant wife, his disposable wife. Once she had gone into the hospital, he disappeared. Now that she was an invalid, he was too busy with work and with his family. He hadn't been too busy when she could meet him secretly, when he could have sex with her.

A few months later I was sitting on my bed under the mosquito netting typing up field notes. It was nighttime, and the blue glow from my laptop was the only light in the room. I stopped writing and leaned back against the headboard. I reached a hand out from under the netting and pulled the phone onto the bed and dialed Sara's home number. She had been discharged from the hospital a few days before, after an extraordinarily long hospital stay that had involved multiple operations, several serious infections, and a blood transfusion in which they mistakenly used the wrong type of blood; she had had a violent reaction that nearly killed her. A man's voice answered.

"Is Sara there?"

"Just a moment," he replied, and I heard retreating footsteps and a tinny voice shouting, "Sara!"

I could hear music in the background, then the footsteps becoming louder and louder again, and then Sara's voice, "Hello?"

"How does it feel to be back home from the hospital?" I asked.

"Oh, it's you. It's hard to walk up and down the stairs. We live on the fifth floor. I don't get out much. But soon, God willing. I can walk pretty well with my cane."

"You didn't sound very happy to hear my voice," I said dryly.

Sara laughed a little. "Sorry, never mind me. I was just hoping that it was Ali on the phone."

"What, he is calling you now?"

"He couldn't call me in the hospital, you know. No public phone there, and you know I don't have a mobile. I'll get one next week with the cooperative money. But now that I'm home, he can call. My love!" she exclaimed happily.

"And what about when your mother or your brother answers the phone?"

"Ali's sister calls, and then he takes the phone from her to talk to me."

"His sister knows about your relationship?"

"No. I don't know. Maybe she has an idea."

The sound of music in the background got louder.

"What is that music?"

"I came to sit in front of the TV. There's a Fifi Abdou movie on. She's the best belly dancer in Egypt, you know. She's one of the people, you know. She used to be poor. And she was married about eight times, all ʿurfi marriages, secret marriages!"

"Like yours?"

"Be quiet!"

I sighed loudly. "Nobody can hear me, you know." I changed topic. "So, you like this belly dancer. What about dancing, do you like to dance?"

"I can't dance in front of anybody."

"Why not?"

"Just because. No good."

I persisted. "You mean it's no good because you don't like to dance, or you like it but it's ʿayb, shameful?"

"ʿAyb. Of course everyone likes to dance, who doesn't? But it's shameful."

I pulled my computer toward me and started taking notes, cradling the phone between my shoulder and ear. "Who can you dance in front of, your family?"

"No, not even my family. Only in front of Ali."

"Who is around you right now while you are saying that?" I could hear voices in the background.

Sara just said, "There are people here, family members."

"You can talk about Ali like that in front of them?"

She said, "Yeah, I'm not afraid."

I was typing furiously. "Not even of your brothers?"

"I'm bold; I'm not afraid of them," Sara said defiantly. "Well, only a little afraid."

"Can they hear what you're saying right now?"

"Of course not!" Sara said, and laughed.

I stopped typing and thought. "Do they know about your relationship with Ali?"

"Of course not!"

"So what would happen if they knew?"

"They would kill me if they knew."

"Truly?" I asked with interest, thrilling at the idea of an honor killing. I started typing again. But Sarah just laughed.

"No, you idiot foreigner, not truly. But they would forbid me from leaving the house and they would forbid me from talking on the phone. And that would kill me."

CHAPTER 8

Kinship, Honor, and Shame

Note just how masterful was Sara's reaction to my slightly horrified, slightly titillated, and absolutely sensationalist assumption that she actually feared for her life should her brothers find out about her affair with a married man. In one breath, Sara casually flicked aside the assumptions of an "idiot foreigner," at once exposing the absurdity of the anthropologist's expectations about honor crimes in Egyptian families and revealing the importance of love and desire in her life. What would kill her if her affair were exposed would not be her brothers. What would metaphorically kill her would be getting cut off from her lover, the destruction of her romance, the thwarting of her desire.

This anecdote suggests not only the importance of taking love and desire into account when developing an anthropological model of kinship in Egypt, but also the fact that it is impossible to consider Egyptian kinship and the "honor-and-shame" complex (I won't continue to use problematizing quotes, but readers should keep in mind their ghostly presence) without taking into account the way the theories of Western anthropologists shape what anthropologists look for when studying Arab societies.

In this chapter, then, I want to consider these anthropological theories—about kinship and gender, honor and shame—in light of the ethnographic material presented. And in turn, I hope to show that applying unconventional ethnographic data to classic anthropological theories can illuminate what is valuable, and what is obscured, by those theories.

I start with a classic anthropological theory of kinship, that of the great French structural anthropologist, Claude Lévi-Strauss. Kinship, Lévi-Strauss argued, was, at its heart, the gift exchange of women, with fathers, uncles, and brothers marrying off their female kin to build up the social networks of men. It is a provocative theory, and one that feminists have used to describe the cross-cultural oppression of women, even as they have critiqued it as "phallocratic." But what if we tried to apply this theory to Haroun's gatherings of powerful men and women of the demimonde who are having extramarital affairs? Can this theory about kinship explain what is happening in a social system where there are no blood relations and where women's sexuality circulates outside marriage? And what does the existence of such a demimonde say about anthropological theories of honor and shame in Arab cultures? Finally, what is at stake politically when social scientists build theories about the cultural complex of honor and shame and the patriarchal control of women's sexuality by Arab men?

Kinship as the Exchange of Women

Lévi-Strauss's theory of kinship is at once elaborately argued and elegantly reductive. He examines kinship as part of the more fundamental problem that he spent his many-decades-long career trying to theorize: the relationship between culture and nature, between society and psychology, and the link between the infinite variability of social structures and the universal workings of the human mind. In a nearly-five-hundred-page anthropological masterpiece called *The Elementary Structures of Kinship*, Lévi-Strauss (1969) makes a simple argument, backing it up with ethnographic case studies from just about every exotic kinship system that anthropologists have ever documented. The argument, in essence, is that human society is built around men's gift exchange of women.

To set up this argument, Lévi-Strauss poses "the problem of incest," as he calls it. The rules governing whom one can and cannot marry vary enormously from culture to culture, with one society's marriage ideal constituting another's incest violation. Yet for all that variation, the incest taboo itself is a cross-cultural universal, as fundamental to human society as language is. Why, he asks, is this so? Lévi-Strauss (1969, 13) wittily dismisses modern theorists who explain the incest taboo as a cultural means of preventing the genetic abnormalities that can result from consanguineous sexual relations:

> This theory is remarkable in that it is required by its very statement
> to extend to all human societies, even to the most primitive, which in

other matters give no indication of any such eugenic second-sight, the sensational privilege of knowing the alleged consequences of endogamous unions.

The answer to the problem of incest is not, Lévi-Strauss says, to be found in nature (that is, in biological selection) but in culture. Or rather, to be more precise, the incest problem is culture's answer to a very different problem of nature: not the evolutionary need for genetic diversity but the human psychological need for social interaction. The incest taboo requires people to marry outside their families or small social group (that is, exogamy), thus binding groups together and preventing society from fracturing and solidifying into narrow family alliances.

> Exogamy provides the only means of maintaining the group as a group, of avoiding the indefinite fission and segmentation which the practice of consanguineous marriages would bring about. . . . The biological group can no longer stand apart, and the bond of alliance with another family ensures the dominance of the social over the biological, and of the cultural over the natural. (Ibid., 479)

There are hundreds of different kinship systems and cultural ways of organizing marriage and sexual reproduction, but what they all boil down to, Lévi-Strauss tells us, is men exchanging women:

> The rule of exogamy . . . tends to ensure the total and continuous circulation of the group's most important assets, its wives and its daughters. . . . Exchange [of women] provides the means of binding men together. (Ibid., 479–480)

Lévi-Strauss is riffing on sociologist Marcel Mauss's (1966) *Essay on the Gift*, which argued that the exchange of gifts (or "*prestations*," depending on translation) structures society. Unlike commodities, gifts engender feelings of obligation to reciprocate, and these ties of reciprocity are the essence of the social bond. Anthropologists and philosophers have critiqued and applied and tweaked Mauss's theory to explore the way economies work (finding that there is a lot more gifting mixed up with the ostensibly free market exchange of commodities than most people acknowledge) and the relationship between things and people, in everything from the art market (Hyde 1983) to the pharmaceutical industry (Oldani 2004) to sperm donation (Tober 2001) to the logic of philanthropy (Douglas and Isherwood 1979). But Lévi-Strauss's (1969, 481) contribution to Mauss's "supreme rule of the gift" was so simple that it is either elegant or vulgar, depending on one's perspective. Lévi-Strauss argued that the greatest gift that men can give is women. Women, he repeatedly tells us, are society's "valuables *par excellence*." As such, women are principally a means to an end—namely, the strengthening of bonds among men. He illustrates this with extensive examples of the various kinds of kin bonds among men and their "brothers-in-law," a figure that is portrayed as a kind of synecdochical prototype for the kin bonds created among men through marriage.

He makes an analogy with that other great human universal, language. Women are like signs (that is, words): socially, they are worthless unless they are circulated. "Women themselves are treated as signs," he tells us, drawing on the ideas of linguist Ferdinand de Saussure, "which are misused when not put to the use reserved to signs" (Lévi-Strauss 1969, 496). It is in considering his analogy with language that Lévi-Strauss very briefly recognizes—though not until the second-to-last page of the large tome—that women have agency as more than just objects being exchanged:

> [Women] . . . on the one hand, [are] the object of personal desire, thus exciting sexual and proprietorial instincts; and, on the other, [are] the subject of the desire of others, and seen as such, i.e., as the means of binding others through alliance with them. But woman could never become just a sign and nothing more, since even in a man's world she is still a person, and since in so far as she is defined as a sign she must be recognized as a generator of signs. In the matrimonial dialogue of men, woman is never purely what is spoken about; for if women in general represent a certain category of signs, destined to a certain kind of communication, each woman preserves a particular value arising from her talent, before and after marriage, for taking her part in a duet. In contrast to words, which have wholly become signs, woman has remained at once a sign and a value. This explains why the relations between the sexes have preserved that affective richness, ardour and mystery which doubtless originally permeated the entire universe of human communications. (Ibid., 496)[1]

This brief acknowledgment of women as subjects is anomalous, but not necessarily because Lévi-Strauss sees women as agentless objects. That is to say, though he describes women as a *category* as valuable, his theory is no more concerned with women as *individuals* than it is with men as individuals. His point is that the value of an individual (or a group of individuals) is subsumed under the broader psychosocial dynamic creating the structures that bind people together in a society.

Yet it is, of course, this reduction of women to the category of traded objects that has drawn the attention of feminist critics.

Feminist Assessments of Lévi-Strauss's Theory of Kinship as the Exchange of Women

Many theorists have applied and critiqued and commented on Lévi-Strauss's theories, and the study of kinship is a large and traditional subfield in anthropology that has recently been revitalized by new work that examines kinship not in terms of marriage (which is the word Lévi-Strauss uses metonymically to refer to kinship as a whole) but in terms of gay, lesbian, transsexual, and other nonheterosexual kin partnerships, and in terms of the impact of new reproductive health technologies on kinship systems.[2] Here, though, I want to focus on a couple of key feminist theorists and what they have had to say about Lévi-Strauss's theory of kinship as the exchange of women.

Perhaps the most famous interpreter of Lévi-Strauss's theory is Gayle Rubin. Nearly twenty years before she actually received her PhD in anthropology, Rubin become known in academic circles for her 1975 essay "The Traffic in Women: Notes on the 'Political Economy' of Sex," which describes Lévi-Strauss's theory as an "implicit theory of sex oppression." The essay, published a year after she received her master's degree in anthropology (and still her best-known essay), puts Lévi-Strauss in critical dialogue with Sigmund Freud's theories about gender roles through a Marxist-inspired, feminist analysis. Lévi-Strauss's analysis is, she notes approvingly, a "radical questioning of all human sexual arrangements, in which no aspect of sexuality is taken for granted as 'natural'" (Rubin 1975, 179), and, unlike Karl Marx, Lévi-Strauss is very much concerned with the importance of sex and gender in understanding how societies are stratified and how one group oppresses another. However, Rubin argues, the theory needs a bit more critical thinking to extend it to its logical end.

This end is an understanding of kinship as the oppression of women (although Lévi-Strauss and Rubin use different terminology; what Lévi-Strauss calls kinship, Rubin calls the "sex/gender system"). If the incest taboo is a cultural universal and if that taboo arises out of a social imperative to exchange women in order to foster social bonds among men, then the oppression of women is also a cultural universal. Taking Lévi-Strauss's analysis to its logical conclusion means understanding that "the social organization of sex rests upon gender, obligatory heterosexuality, and the constraint of female sexuality" (Rubin 1975, 179).

Rubin sees Lévi-Strauss's theory as "a seductive and powerful concept" that is "attractive in that it places the oppression of women within social systems, rather than in biology" (ibid., 175). On the other hand, she argues wryly that Lévi-Strauss doesn't go far enough. Referring to the second-to-last page of his book, where he briefly acknowledges women as agents in their own right as well as exchange objects, and his intriguing suggestion that it is in this duet between women's social role as objects and their agented personhood that romance arises, Rubin asks, "Why is he not, at this point, denouncing what kinship systems do to women, instead of presenting one of the greatest rip-offs of all time as the root of romance?" (ibid., 201).

The other feminist interpretation of Lévi-Strauss I want to consider here is that of philosopher Nancy Hartsock (1998) in her book *The Feminist Standpoint Revisited, and Other Essays*. In two essays, the first addressing Lévi-Strauss's theory and the second Rubin's interpretation of it, she accuses both of "phallocratic theory." She critiques Lévi-Strauss's theory as "an expression of abstract masculinity" (1998, 173) that turns concrete and sensual experiences into symbolic abstractions devoid of agency and subjectivity. The resulting model of human society, which arises out of a "masculinist" denial of the productive power of women, is riddled with logical errors:

> The strangeness of all this is only a little compounded by the counterfactual on which the whole theory of the exchange of women rests: Women are not fully human. Why would reasoning, sign-producing beings, possessed of their own needs and desires, consent to becoming rather than possessing valuable objects? To becoming rather than producing signs? If we begin from the realities of women's lives, it is hard to imagine that women are not humans, but are the means by which humans (men) communicate and establish a social synthesis. On the basis of a division of labor analysis, one can see that the reality is the reverse. Women are not, as Lévi-Strauss would have it, the creation of an intentional act of the male mind, the invention of a symbol by means of which to construct society and to distinguish it from nature. Women

are the literal and material producers of men, who in turn like to imagine that the situation is the reverse. (Ibid., 183)

Hartsock is also critical of feminists who have used Lévi-Strauss's theory as a starting point for their own theories. Building upon his theory "leads toward a phallocratic mystification of women's material lives and a location of women's oppression in the sphere of ideology rather than material social relations" (ibid., 172). Lévi-Strauss does not accord women humanity, Hartsock argues, and she rejects feminists who have tried to defend him on this point.

All feminists who have written about Lévi-Strauss, and Lévi-Strauss himself, have tried to argue that he was not maintaining that women were not human. Yet given his stress on the transaction of the exchange of women as a relation between men, and given the fact that only once in *The Elementary Structures of Kinship*, and in a single sentence, does he make the statement that women might be human, these arguments are unpersuasive. (Ibid., 190n63)

Ultimately, interpretations of Lévi-Strauss depend on whether we think he was describing the reality of female oppression (this is Rubin's interpretation) or whether we think he came up with his theory of kinship as the exchange of women because he simply couldn't imagine men being exchanged rather than the exchangers (this is Hartsock's argument: "It is curious that women but not children are circulating commodities. . . . One can only conclude that this is a result of Lévi-Strauss's unwillingness to see any males as commodities" [ibid., 179]). But setting aside this unanswerable question, let us turn from abstract theory to ethnographic realities. It is somewhat ironic, considering that Hartsock is a philosopher and not an anthropologist, that one of the main critiques she levels against Lévi-Strauss is the type of critique that anthropologists frequently level at philosophers: his kinship theory is too abstract and disregards the experiences and subjectivities of actual people. (She repeatedly declares that Lévi-Strauss's theory is premised on the "death of subjectivity.") Both Lévi-Strauss's theory and Rubin's reading of it, Hartsock argues, are abstractions and ideal models that fail to take into account the concrete realities of women's lives, instead treating "women as unreal beings who are at bottom simply symbols created by the male mind" (ibid., 171). Yet Hartsock's critique is also an abstraction.

What can Lévi-Strauss's, Rubin's, and Hartsock's theories tell us about the ethnographic material I have described for turn-of-the-millennium Egypt? And what can ethnography tell us about the usefulness of these theories? In particular, can Lévi-Strauss's theory of kinship as men's exchange of women apply to nonkinship or quasi-kinship situations, such as Haroun's demimonde gatherings, or Sara's *'urfi* marriage to an already-married man?

Applying Kinship Theory to Extramarital Affairs

Lévi-Strauss's definition of kinship offers a useful perspective on what was taking place at Haroun's gatherings—to a degree. Lévi-Strauss (1969, 480) argues that the exchange of women "provides the means of binding men together." As outrageous as that sounds, it is a surprisingly apt description for Haroun's gatherings. Women were indeed circulated in this group to lubricate and extend men's social networks.

Consider: the hours that Haroun, Farouq, Galal, Sameen, Abdallah, and Qasem spent together flirting with women and watching belly dancers perform were opportunities for them to spend time with other men and build their friendships in shared, risqué intimacy. The male friendships and intimacies established at these gatherings lasted far longer than those they built with the women in the group. The women (with the exception of Alia) came and went, while the roster of men who attended Haroun's parties was much more stable. These gatherings generated male solidarity not only because they were opportunities for socializing but also because they were semi-illicit, binding the men together in shared secrets kept from wives and family.

Of course, the liaisons being created at Haroun's parties were extramarital, and Lévi-Strauss spoke almost exclusively of marriage. The women in Haroun's group were not related to anyone in that group and never would be, since none of them were respectable enough to marry. (Even Farouq's multiple marriages to belly dancers were clearly regarded as a different kind of marriage than that to his first wife, the "mother of his children.") Yet even outside formal kinship structures, we can see how men use women to bind other men to them socially. Indeed, such evenings with not-respectable women homosocially bound men together precisely *because* they went beyond kinship systems, giving men a shared secret. Haroun took great delight in introducing new women to the men in the group. His central role as the social linchpin of the group gave him power and authority vis-à-vis the other men.

Haroun, Farouq, Galal, and Sameen all had business dealings with each other. The judge, Abdallah, and the doctor, Qasem, were wealthy and powerful men whose friendships might offer benefits at some point in time, even if there was no immediate business relationship binding them together. In any event, we need not resort to vulgar materialism to explain the value of these men's social network (and Lévi-Strauss would be the first to tell us so). Building friendships and creating a social network can be an end in itself, independent of any immediate financial benefit.

The fact that women are exchanged by men for extramarital sexual affairs isn't at odds with Lévi-Strauss's theory. The anthropologist undoubtedly only used "marriage" as synecdochical shorthand, and he described an astonishing range of variations on marriage in different cultures. (In fact, virtually every theorist who has commented on Lévi-Strauss takes pleasure in recounting some of the peculiar sex and marriage customs that Lévi-Strauss used to support his theory; even Rubin, otherwise remarkably on track in her writing, can't resist digressing to recount the exotic sexual arrangements of various tribes in Papua New Guinea, ranging from oral sex between men and boys to the process of collecting semen from a woman's multiple sexual partners in a coconut shell. It would be an unprecedented break from anthropological tradition in writing about kinship if I failed to mention at least a few of these cultural practices here.) Kinship, after all, is not a neatly bounded category of human relations, as anthropologists such as Kath Weston (1997) have pointed out, redefining the field of kinship studies. 'Urfi marriage is what we might call a paramarital relationship, meeting some of but not all the qualities of a more conventional marriage (Wynn 2016), and it finds echoes in other paramarital relationships in the region, such as "temporary" (sigha, or muta'a) marriage in Iran (Haeri 1989). As classic treatises on the topic (such as Lévi-Strauss's) have taught us, kinship fundamentally refers to the multiplicity of ways that societies formalize relationships with both genetically and nongenetically connected people (and even, in some cultures, with animals and supernatural beings).

Nor does this extramarital exchange of women that I have described upset Rubin's theory. In fact, it supports it rather well. Even though the exchange occurred outside formal kinship structures, the way that women were circulated at Haroun's parties can be read as an expression of male power and privilege that are solidly entrenched as part of the cultural organization of the sex/gender system in turn-of-the-millennium Cairo. Men are allowed extramarital affairs, but women are not. Of course, such a simplistic claim must be hedged about with all sorts of caveats, since neither Islam nor Coptic Christianity condone extramarital affairs for men, and since Egyptian women of course have extramarital affairs too. But for a woman to have an affair is considered shocking, whereas a man's having an affair is unexceptional, so even if it is condemned by religious orthodoxy, it is popularly accepted in many Cairo subcultures. Women are, Kerim and Zeid said over and over again, divisible into two categories: respectable and unrespectable; the respectable ones are married and protected; the unrespectable ones are not married and not protected.

In short, Haroun's group was not a kinship system, and it did not guarantee the kinds of permanent relationships among men that Lévi-Strauss describes as being generated by marriage, but it is clearly a case of women being used to build male solidarity through an arrangement of sexual mores that was unequal in its expectations of men and women.

But, following Hartsock, let us trouble Lévi-Strauss's and Rubin's theories a bit more with this ethnographic case study. Was it only men who exchanged women? To answer this question, let us review the logistics of how women circulated through this group, since that might not have been explicit in the ethnographic narrative of preceding chapters.

Haroun's mistress Alia and Farouq's girlfriend Malak were primarily responsible for recruiting new women to the group. Retired belly dancer Malak introduced to the group an American anthropologist (me) and belly dancers from England, Australia, Germany, Sweden, France, and Morocco. Alia introduced a divorced Armenian tour guide, a married (but not very faithfully) Egyptian tour guide, an attractive housewife going through a divorce, an American-Egyptian banker who vacationed in Egypt several times a year, and two Egyptian bankers, one a divorcée and the other an unmarried, veiled spinster (she was in her late thirties, locally considered a late age to have never been married). Other women, such as Zizi, Nour, and several other dancers and actresses, were introduced to the group by Farouq after his relationship with Malak ended.

Once the women had been introduced to the group, Haroun and Alia assessed their social suitability to decide whether they should get repeat invitations to Haroun's parties, which he held two or three times a week. Then, if the women weren't already Alia's friends, Haroun instructed Alia to befriend them and gather more information about them. As she did with me, Alia would call these women regularly to chat, and during these conversations she would extract information while she cheerfully shared her own life story. Maintaining these relationships was an ongoing, time-consuming endeavor, and whenever I saw Alia, she seemed to spend half her time on the telephone. Haroun felt it was inappropriate, and possibly offensive to Alia, to interact with these women himself, so he used Alia as a proxy. They were, incidentally, explicit and open about this: Alia told me that she conveyed the content of our conversation to Haroun and told me that he asked her to call me and other women he was interested in gathering information about. Her calls served the purpose of building Haroun's social network.

Yet these phone conversations did not only serve Haroun's purposes. Alia and I developed a friendship that lasted long after I stopped attending parties and went back to America, even after Alia and Haroun's relationship ended. I continued to call and meet with Malak and Alia long after I had stopped seeing Haroun and the men in his social circle.

This brief sketch immediately suggests two caveats to Lévi-Strauss's theory about men exchanging women to build social relationships with other men, and about women being society's prime valuables. First, it may appear that women are the ones who are exchanged, rather than men, since the male members of this group were stable but women came and went with little stability except for one or two core members. Yet it hardly seems accurate to say that *men* were the ones who exchanged women, since it was two *women*—Alia and Malak—who introduced to the group at least two-thirds of the women who circulated through it.

Second, while the introduction of women to this group built male social networks, the women benefited at least as much as the men did from these social exchanges, and perhaps more. Malak introduced her friends, mainly foreign belly dancers, to the group; in exchange for the opportunity it gave Haroun and his friends to flirt and to enjoy their exotic feminine charms, the women ate for free and drank alcohol that was expensive and hard to get in Cairo and gained opportunities to socialize and network, and Farouq frequently took them out to nightclubs to see other belly dancers, which they couldn't afford to do often on their own. Malak enjoyed the prestige among her friends of knowing wealthy and powerful men; her friends reciprocated by inviting her out with their own wealthy patrons. Alia's friends enjoyed similar benefits. Alia worked on Haroun's behalf in getting to know the women Malak brought to the group, and clearly Haroun benefited from this, but so did Alia, as she developed her own lasting friendships and social networks (not to mention receiving extravagant gifts of diamond-and-gold jewelry and a car, gifts that Haroun gave her to signal that she was his valued partner). In short, both men and women gained socially, but only women gained immediate economic benefits from these social situations, somewhat balancing the fact that they had less economic power than the men (but also binding the women to the men in affective ties that were created and strengthened via gift relationships).

The ethnographic account also raises the question of whether it is only women, and not men, who are exchanged. In her interpretation of Lévi-Strauss, the Belgian psychoanalytic philosopher and feminist Luce Irigaray (1985, 171) asks, "Do women have no tendency toward polygamy? The good anthropologist does not raise such questions. . . . Why are men not objects of exchange among women?" Irigaray asks the question only to dismiss it, but it is an important one. In my account of Haroun's social network, it might appear as if it is only women who circulate and are exchanged because the group was a stable group of men who regularly met in one location, but we could just as easily argue that women circulate men for their own purposes.

For example, I have described that Alia introduced her friends to Haroun's group and briefly mentioned one Egyptian housewife in the midst of a divorce. Alia brought this housewife, Nadia, into the group at a time when she was battling her husband in court over distribution of resources and custody of their children. (Rania Salem's 2011 dissertation gives an account of how difficult it is for Egyptian women to gain both a divorce and the property rights that their marriage contracts supposedly guarantee.) When Nadia joined the group, she immediately attached herself to the judge, Abdallah. She was a strikingly attractive blonde, and while there were several moderately handsome men in the group, the taciturn judge had all the physical attractiveness and personality of a toad. Everyone assumed that she hooked up with the judge so that he would help her with her with her court case, which he did. Shortly after her divorce was settled, Nadia stopped attending Haroun's gatherings. Clearly Alia had introduced her to the judge to benefit her friend, and Nadia discarded the man once he had outlived his usefulness. We could argue that the Alia and Nadia had exchanged this man to benefit one of them, in the process strengthening the relationship between the two women.

Or to take another (somewhat more personal and embarrassing) example, I remember a conversation I had with Malak after a dinner I had had with Samir, a man whom I was interviewing for my PhD research on tourism. Samir owned a couple of tourist resorts, and we had arranged to meet at a hotel restaurant for the interview (my standard protocol for interviewing people I didn't know). I thought it was all business and planned to pay for the meal as thanks for his time and for sharing his expertise with me. But the man clearly had other ideas; he insisted that dinner was on him and proceeded to order a vast quantity of dishes to impress me in a potlatch-like display of extravagant waste. Then, sidestepping my questions about tourism, he spent the evening telling me that he had just split up with his mistress because she didn't appreciate how well he treated her (he described in detail the party he had thrown for her birthday and its cost and listed the gifts of jewelry he had given her over the course of their relationship), declared that he was looking for a replacement mistress, and made vulgar comments in the guise of (utterly unfunny) "jokes" that alluded to the financial benefits that would accrue to any woman who had a sexual relationship with him. ("How can you tell if a woman really wants a new piece of jewelry? She swallows.") Nauseated, I escaped as soon as I politely could, but as we parted he gave me his card and insisted that we go out another time, suggesting that I could invite all my friends too.

When I got home, I called Malak and told her about the evening. We laughed; she commiserated. Then she commented that it was a pity the man was such a buffoon, since he clearly was willing and able to spend on his mistress, and she knew I wasn't looking for a man, so if he had been halfway appealing, I could have introduced Samir to her and she could have enjoyed his generosity (she had recently split with Farouq and was looking for a replacement). "Well," I told her, "he *is* a jackass, but I can introduce you and maybe you can go out a few times and you might meet some other people through him, and at least he'll pay for a few nice dinners if you can stand his company." She considered briefly before deciding that it wasn't worth suffering a fool in exchange for free dinners and the unpromising social networking possibilities that Samir represented.

In this case, two women contemplated exchanging a man, and though they ultimately decided that he had too little value to be worth it, it is clear that not only do men exchange women, women may also exchange men (and other women) to build their own social networks, and these exchanges happen both within and outside marriage and other normative relationships leading to marriage, such as courtship. (See Peletz 1987 for a discussion of marriage in nineteenth-century Malaysia as the "exchange of men.")

Agency and Affect

The ethnographic material reveals what is missing from both Lévi-Strauss's and Rubin's accounts: agency. That much is patently obvious, and it is at the core of Hartsock's (1998), Marylin Strathern's (1981), and many other feminist critiques of Lévi-Strauss's theory of kinship. But it also shows *why* agency matters in developing a theory of kinship. The importance of agency in kinship theory is not just a difference in perspective—an Archimedean, structuralist view versus a phenomenological, subjective account of kin relations. When we neglect agency, we fail to understand how and why people, both men and women, circulate through social networks and bind themselves to other people, not to mention how men and women are bound together in affective relationships of love and desire in which they coconstruct each other as men and women (Joseph 1999; Ghannam 2013).

Women and men are not only exchanged; they are their own agents, who circulate *themselves* strategically for gain. The pretty blonde housewife decided to attend Haroun's parties to find a powerful ally to help in her divorce, and she stopped attending once she had achieved her goals. I went to dinner with a man who I hoped would give me information about the tourism industry in exchange for a free meal and pleasant company, and he went to dinner with me hoping that I would prove to be sexually available if he demonstrated he could spend enough money on me. For every character in the preceding narratives, I could identify a range of material incentives driving men and women to seek out association with each other.

Yet there is still something missing when we dwell on the material benefits that women gained as they circulated through this group. As Holly Wardlow (2006, 15–19) points out, material and social self-interest cannot form the sole basis for a theory of agency in a kinship system. Describing kinship primarily in terms of agency and exchange is a reduction that evacuates the powerful emotional content of kinship relations. Cases of mercenary opportunism—such as the ones I have described, the divorcing housewife exchanging her personal charms for legal assistance or Malak considering whether free evenings on the town would be worth dating a vulgar jackass—certainly exist, but liaisons that were motivated purely for gain were rare in the broader terrain of interactions between men and women. Indeed, the instances I have described were cases of failed intimacy: the relationship severed when its utility had ended; the date never made with a jackass. But the relationships that lasted, whether they were normative (such as that of Ayah and Zeid, who eventually married) or nonnormative (such as Alia and Haroun's long-term extramarital affair) blended sexuality and material exchanges in socially binding gift economies (Mauss 1966) that were mediated by affect that was far from mercenary in the pursuit of material (or other) gain.

Consider, for example, Alia's feelings for Haroun. I have described her deep attachment to him and her willingness to experiment sexually and make her social life revolve around him and his own social goals. But one incident really illustrates the extent to which she was willing to sacrifice for this relationship and the extent to which her attachment to Haroun was *not* materially driven.

A small group of us had a conversation about sexually transmitted infections (another of the topics, like applying chili paste to the genitals and other alleged aphrodisiacs, that was taboo in polite Egyptian company and that I only ever heard discussed by Haroun's entourage). Alia commented that any woman who knows her partner has HIV should insist on condoms when they have sex. At that, Haroun became visibly angry. He declared that a woman who thinks of protecting herself when her partner is dying instead of wishing to die with him clearly wasn't showing enough loyalty and love because if she truly loved, she would not think of protecting herself. He reduced her to tears in the argument that followed, as he threatened to leave her for not being sufficiently loyal, and she argued that she wasn't just thinking of herself; she had children and needed to keep herself alive so that she could raise them to adulthood. Alia eventually submitted, tearfully groveling for Haroun's forgiveness in an ugly scene that was embarrassing to everyone else there—including, incidentally, other men in the group who took Alia's side and disagreed with Haroun's insistence that a woman must share the burden of disease with her partner. And Alia submitted (or at least gave a convincing appearance of submission) even though she was an independent and defiant woman in other aspects of her life (as in her attitude toward her family, who demanded that she end her extramarital relationship with Haroun, which was well-known and embarrassed the family).

If we think of this as a story about material gain or pseudo-kinship structures, then it becomes incomprehensible why Alia—an independent woman who was a banker, had a high-paying job, owned her own apartment in an upper-middle-class part of town, and was raising her sons as a single mother—would remain with Haroun after an argument like that. Clearly it is not a story about a woman engaging in a risqué sexual relationship in order to further her own self-interest through social advancement or material benefits. Haroun expected Alia to be willing to die to prove her love to him, and she declared herself willing to do so (though we can doubt whether she really would have).

What bound Alia and Haroun together was not only self-interest but also a deep emotional attachment that rendered one of them, at least, willing to act against self-interest and to submit to humiliation at the hands of the partner she loved. Alia was a beautiful, sensuous woman who independently supported herself and her children. She did not need the gift of a car and gold and diamonds from Haroun. Setting aside need, even if she simply wanted to consume luxuries beyond what her own salary could provide, she could have dated any number of men other than Haroun. She was a banker who invested money for wealthy clients, and men regularly made advances toward her at work. She could have been another man's mistress, or she could have found someone who would marry her and thus made herself (more) respectable in the eyes of society. But it was Haroun she wanted, Haroun she loved, and this was enough to make her agree that she would have unprotected sex with a sexually promiscuous partner (and it takes no great leap of imagination to see how Haroun imagined himself in this hypothetical scenario) to prove she was willing to share his suffering in whatever sexually transmitted disease he might have.

Or consider Sara's passionate love for Ali, her willingness to stand by the sidelines loving him as his secret second wife, when there was no material or social benefit whatsoever to be gained by pining away for a lover who had neglected her, who abused her, and with whom she had no socially respectable future. She was a beautiful woman who could have rejected the illicit relationship in hope of a respectable marriage. Even Malak, who was quick to see men in terms of what they could materially provide for her, was constantly in search of a companion, someone to talk about the day with, and perhaps even love.

In short, what mediates, transcends, and occasionally completely overturns the logic of material or social benefit and "rational" self-interest is some combination of love and desire, two of the most powerful emotions binding humans together. How can we dismiss these emotions as extraneous to the more fundamental process of exchanging women, when it is the emotions of love and desire that explain the romantic entanglements of men and women, the sacrifices they make for each other, and women's willingness to sacrifice social respectability in order to be with the men they loved, or men's willingness to sacrifice material wealth in order to gift and support their mistresses and wives?

Submission and discipline may give pleasure, as demonstrated by Sara's happiness at a slap from her jealous partner. This is a simple argument that has been elaborated in many ways by thinkers ranging from the Marquis de Sade to Michel Foucault. Yet Alia's submission to

Haroun was not the sadism of sexual pleasure. It was the sadism and pleasure of love. Love was, for Alia, sacrificing and at times painful but also elevating, euphoric, and fulfilling in ways that we only catch the barest glimpses of (for reasons I discussed in chapter 2). Love can compel people to act in ways that may appear to be against their own best interests and those of other loved ones, as when Alia professed her willingness to suffer an incurable disease with her lover, even if it put her children at risk. Or, on the other hand, love can drive people to protect their loved ones at their own expense, as we see when parents sacrifice careers to care for a disabled child.

In short, love is a lot of things—indeed, it can probably be whatever one makes of it, depending on individual and ethnographic context—but it is at the heart of many of the intimate relationships that are (mostly but not entirely) subsumed under the category "kinship," and clearly love is something far more complex and deeply embodied than simple rational self-interest or the psychosocial need to create social ties outside one's own kin group. This is the Deleuzian "primacy of desire over power" (Biehl and Locke 2010) that we see in Sara's accounts of her relationship with Ali, a relationship where she sacrificed and submitted to his controlling jealousy, even as in other contexts Sara could generically insist that she didn't let men become too controlling and urged me to do the same.

But it would also be too simplistic to say that love overrides self-interest. Affect in general, and love in particular, are complexly *intertwined* with self-interest and economic exchange, as we can see in Malak's search to find a boyfriend who could be a friend and confidant and at the same time show his affection by providing some financial support, in the expensive gifts Haroun gave his mistress Alia, or in the show of financial capacity that Zeid had to demonstrate to Ayah during their courtship period.

Just because love is embodied does not mean it is only an individual, psychological phenomenon. Love is deeply, personally, individually felt, but love is also culturally constructed and socially constrained, as Berlant (2012) argues. And it is that combination of embodied, subjective emotion and sociocultural norms that together make up what anthropologists call kinship. Or, to return to Lévi-Strauss and Rubin's critique of him, it is in the tension between structure and agency that desire is generated, leading to the creation of formal kinship structures, or leading people to act outside those formal structures.

Of course, to say that women have agency is no great ethnographic insight. Not only has it been demonstrated by multiple feminist critiques of Lévi-Strauss and numerous ethnographic studies of women in the Middle East, a handful of which I have discussed here, but also, as I have pointed out, Lévi-Strauss acknowledged it himself in that intriguing single page of a five-hundred-page tome. But because everyone "knows" that women have agency, some contemporary anthropologists are too quick to dismiss the enduring value of Lévi-Strauss's work. Yet people *do* get exchanged. People are both agents and objects. People are circulated for gain, just as they circulate themselves and others for gain. Despite the fact that Lévi-Strauss's argument has been appropriated by feminists like Rubin and Irigaray to describe the structures of patriarchy, my ethnographic material shows that women also exchange men. Moreover, these networks of exchange are mediated by affect that powerfully binds women to brothers and fathers and lovers and husbands. Love and desire in turn-of-the-millennium Cairo show both the ways that this classic structuralist argument about marriage can be productively applied to other nonkinship relationships and the limits of the structuralist perspective. Women's (and men's) respectability—their exchange value, in structuralist terms—is a simulacrum (Baudrillard 1988). It is unreal, in the sense that it is constructed at a distance from people's actual behavior or characteristics, even when it claims to be built on that behavior or those characteristics, whether it is a man's perceived ability to support a family based on how often he goes out to nightclubs, or a woman's virginity simulated through hymenoplasty after sexual activity (Wynn and Hassanein 2017). But it is also more real than real, because it has enough social power to determine their exchange value.

From a Universalizing to a Regional Theory of Kinship

Lévi-Strauss's theory of kinship offers us a springboard for exploring some of the ways that individuals and groups exchange other individuals and groups in order to accrue social benefits ranging from gender solidarity to social influence to emotional fulfillment. (I am indebted to Michael Jackson, personal communication, for this insight.) His theory of kinship as the exchange of women actually hasn't gained much traction in Middle East studies. Perhaps this is because both Lévi-Strauss's enthusiasts and his critics focus too narrowly on his claim that men exchange women, rather than seeing its broader implications—and after all, anyone who has spent time in the Middle East knows how influential mothers, aunts, and grandmothers are in the family and particularly in arranging marriages. How could anyone imagine that marriage only furthers men's alliances when they have seen that it is *women* who negotiate with female friends to select brides and grooms for their sons and daughters? Who could see marriage in terms of male social networks after seeing the way a mother mediates between a daughter who is passionate over a boy she's fallen in love with and a strict father who is less than pleased to hear that his daughter has been dating someone without his knowledge?

What *has* been influential in thinking about kinship in the Middle East is the theory of honor and shame (Abu-Lughod 1993). Yet the classic formulation of this regional theory owes much to and suffers from precisely the same flaws as Lévi-Strauss's theory of kinship as the exchange of women: both have a distinct tendency to ignore the way both agency and affect—specifically, love and desire—mediate this cultural complex.

Both anthropologists and the general public have a kind of fascination with the so-called honor-and-shame complex, particularly when it culminates in a much-publicized "honor killing." Yet Sara's story shows that while women may fear having their brothers and fathers find out about their sexual lives and may fear being shamed or embarrassed or scandalized, they rarely fear for their lives. Even when Sara was actually pregnant and miscarried in the hospital, her principle concern was with what it meant for her relationship with Ali and her desire to bear children, not with what her brother would do if he found out (her father was dead and a brother acted as family patriarch). This raises some interesting questions about the everyday ways that both men and women negotiate cultural concepts of honor and shame.

But what is this cultural complex of honor and shame that I have suddenly introduced into this ethnographic text? The words "honor" (*sharaf*) and "shame" (*'ar*) have not appeared in the ethnographic narrative; they only appear in this text when I overlay the ethnographic data with anthropology's theoretical lens. That should sound a few warning bells for the reader. Let us therefore approach the concept carefully.

Honor and Shame

The classic formulation of the honor-and-shame complex is usually attributed to Jean Peristiany (1965) and Julian Pitt-Rivers (1965). Peristiany edited a book called *Honour and Shame: The Values of a Mediterranean Society*, to which Pitt-Rivers contributed a key chapter. As these two anthropologists describe it, this cultural complex, found throughout the Mediterranean region, consisted of an overriding concern with public "face" and reputation, which was enhanced by men's performance of key cultural ideals (such as generosity and hospitality) and lost through women's sexual transgressions.

In other words, if a man generously fetes the village at his virgin sister's wedding, he gains honor. If his sister gets knocked up before she is married, he is shamed.

In this formulation, honor was an inherently male attribute and shame a female one. Protecting women's sexual chastity was a paramount goal for men seeking to maintain their honor. Furthermore, because women were a potential threat to men's honor, men in these cultures were particularly concerned with controlling women's behavior in order to preserve the men's honor.

In other words, a brother had better keep a close eye on his sister to make sure she doesn't get knocked up before he can marry her off.

The honor-and-shame literature often depicts a culture that sees women as sexually insatiable, and thus a threat to society, and/or fundamentally lacking in honor (Delaney 1987). For example, Carol Delaney wrote of the honor and shame complex in Turkey:

> Women . . . are, by their created nature, already ashamed; the recognition of their constitutional inferiority constitutes the feeling of shame. Shame is an inevitable part of being female; a woman is honorable if she remains cognizant of this fact and its implications for behavior, and she is shameless if she forgets it. A man's birthright is honor; he can lose it if he cannot protect the boundaries of "his" women. At the most reduced level, the boundary of a woman is her hymen. (Ibid., 40)

Several feminist and Marxist anthropologists have thus described the honor-and-shame complex as an ideological tool of mystification that enables men to control and subjugate women (in addition to Delaney 1987, see, for example, Sherry Ortner's 1978 article "The Virgin and the State," and David Gilmore's 1987 summary of the honor-and-shame literature).

Seeing Arab cultures in terms of honor and shame isn't just part of the history of Western anthropology. Moroccan theorist Fatima Mernissi's (1975) landmark (and controversial) book *Beyond the Veil* is part of this literature. Mernissi weaves together a historical account of the coming of Islam to the Arabian Peninsula, and the effect this had on women's freedom and sexuality, with a sociological perspective on the way Arab cultures interpreted and transformed Muhammad's teachings to increasingly oppress and control women. But Mernissi's complex and at times even subtle analysis usually gets reduced to this simple polemic: women's sexuality was seen by male Muslim theorists as a threat to the order and stability of society and had to be contained through practices of segregation, veiling, polygamy, and repudiation. Although Mernissi was writing about Morocco in the 1970s, the enduring influence of her work in understanding Middle Eastern societies is apparent at the beginning of this book, where we see Ayah reading Mernissi as part of her sociology studies at the American University in Cairo and using it to critique the sexist norms of respectability for men and women.

A number of revisionists have challenged the classic anthropological (and sociological) formulation of the honor-and-shame complex. Michael Herzfeld (1980), for example, critiqued attempts to use the concepts of honor and shame to describe the Mediterranean as a culturally unified system, arguing that such generalizations obscure more than they illuminate. Norwegian anthropologist Unni Wikan (1984) compared ideals of feminine honor and sexual behavior in Egypt and Oman to show not only how different these are in different Arab societies (Wikan shows that in Egypt, women gossiped mercilessly about the supposed sexual transgressions of others, whereas in Oman, women considered it honorable to keep one's mouth closed and not be judgmental about other women's sexual lives) but also the extent to which women saw honor in themselves, not only in men. Lila Abu-Lughod's (1993) influential ethnography *Writing Women's Worlds* also showed how Egyptian Bedouin women themselves value and maintain their own honor, at once contesting the assumption that honor is a male domain and showing that women are not passive sexual objects being controlled by men but active agents in the assertion of their own sexual modesty.

All these theorists have warned anthropologists that certain theoretical concepts become so hegemonic in academic approaches to particular areas of the world (in the Mediterranean and Arab world, it is honor and shame; in India, caste; and so on) that they then influence what we look for and what we find. That was certainly the case when I went to do fieldwork in Egypt. I fully expected to find honor and shame as central cultural concepts. It threw me when I didn't. In fact, for a while it made me wonder if I was somehow a defective anthropologist because I wasn't seeing things that other anthropologists had seen. It took three years of living in Cairo, fluency in Egyptian Arabic, and continual immersion in discussions about the morals of men's and women's sexual behavior before I was willing to consider that maybe, just maybe, the defect wasn't in my ethnographic research skills. Maybe the defect was in the prejudices I had absorbed from reading the anthropological classics.

I still remember the day during my second year of living in Cairo when I figured out the Egyptian Arabic translations for honor (*sharaf*) and shame (*'ār*) and realized that in spite of the *constant* discussion of female respectability and sexuality that I heard, I had never once heard any of my Egyptian informants use either of these terms around those topics. The closest I came to ever hearing the word "shame" was the term *'ariānā*, which means "naked," and derives from the root *'ār*. But *'ār* itself? I never heard it, whether associated with female sexuality or in any other context.

What I *did* hear frequently was the Arabic term *'ayb*, which is generally glossed in English as "shame" or "shameful." This term generally signals a minor infraction against cultural norms of propriety and can be used to admonish a teenage girl who dresses immodestly, a boy caught mooning the neighbors, or a toddler who throws her food around (to mention just a few of the instances when I heard it used). Etymologically the term connotes a defect, as in a defect of culturally appropriate behavior, but it can equally be used to describe a defective toaster. It was applied to men just as often as to women—though of course the types of behavior that were considered inappropriate and thus shameful differed according to gender and age.

And instead of "honor" (*sharaf*), what I heard people constantly talking about was *respectability* and its lack. Men and women were both frequently described as *muhtarim* or *muhtarima* (or *ghayr / mish muhtarim*; that is, "not respectable") and both women and men strove toward respectability.

Incidentally, it is not just people who are respectable. A store or even a beach resort can be considered respectable or not respectable. (Sharm el-Sheikh, crowded with five-star resorts where wealthy Egyptians vacation with their families and Arab leaders hold summits: reasonably respectable. Dahab, known as a backpacker's haven and the place to go for hashish and *bango*—that is, cannabis: not respectable.)

As with the term *'ayb*, though the label can be applied to men and women (and beach resorts) equally, the types of behavior that are considered respectable or shameful are contingent upon gender, and a woman's respectability is more fundamentally connected to her sexuality than a man's. Men are admired, not shamed, for being Lotharios, and sexually speaking, the only thing that seems to bring them public shame is the vulgar public display of an extramarital affair. (So a man like Haroun, who discreetly maintained a mistress and attempted to recruit her American friend for group sex while nevertheless supporting his family and honoring his wife, was respectable. But the heir to the Aboul Fotouh BMW franchise, who secretly filmed himself having sex with belly dancer Dina, a tape that was then leaked to the internet, was definitely *not* respectable.) Men can also be described as "not respectable" if they fail to perform certain expectations of masculine responsibility, such as caring for their dependents.

In contrast, a woman's respectability is fundamentally determined by the way she manages not only her sexuality but also the male sexual predators around her. A man's respectability revolves around how he cares for and manages his female kin and prospective kin. Recall that Zeid thought that Ayah's friend was not respectable for driving around alone at midnight, and that Ayah protested the injustice that labeled a woman who had never been kissed "not respectable" while a man could stay out late and have sex with prostitutes every night of the week and still escape censure. (Women's respectability, like men's, also hinges on the care and affection they show for their children.)

Maybe, I thought as I considered the disjuncture between the anthropological literature and what I was seeing in Cairo, I was being deceived by language; after all, people call the same things by different words in different parts of the Arab world. Maybe the fundamental cultural complex of honor and shame was still there, even if urban Cairene culture did not use the Arabic terms *sharaf* and *'ar* very widely. Are *ihtiram* (respect) and *'ayb* (shame) merely local substitutes for *sharaf* and *'ar*? Or to put it another way, can we consider Cairenes' interest in female respectability, its link to female sexuality, and the way it reflects on and must be protected by male kin to be part of this broad cultural complex of honor and shame, albeit a distinctive variation on it?

Well, yes and no. Overall, there seems to be some overlap between Cairene ideas about "respectability" and the classic honor-and-shame model: women are indeed judged according to their sexual behavior, women's extramarital sexual activity is judged far more harshly than men's extramarital sexual activity, and women hide their sexuality from the men of their family for fear of reprisal and shame.

Yet there are also significant differences between the classic model of honor and shame and the ethnographic evidence in Cairo. Emic accounts (that is to say, the "native" perspective) do not speak of *male* honor and *female* shame, as much of the classic honor-and-shame literature does. Emic accounts speak of respectability, and respectability is something that both men and women work toward and that *all* women claim as their own (even women whom others labeled "prostitutes"). Women do not see themselves as fundamentally lacking in respectability or honor. Nor did I ever see any evidence that men saw women as categorically lacking in respectability. And just as Wikan, Abu-Lughod, and other anthropologists have shown elsewhere in the Arab world, women in Cairo seek respectability for their own sakes, not just for the sake of their brothers' and fathers' reputations.

Another way that the ethnographic account I have drawn in Cairo differs from classic depictions of the Mediterranean honor-and-shame complex is in its link with family economies. Peristiany (1965), John Davis (1977), and Jane Schneider (1971) have all described female honor as an economic commodity exchanged by men (for a summary and critique of this literature, see Gilmore 1987, 4). In these theories, control over women's sexuality is closely tied up with family economies. The more women are financially dependent on men—and, even more critically, the more men are financially dependent on being able to marry off their daughters and sisters—the more men will seek to control women's sexuality.

Yet the economic value of chaste sisters and daughters is doubtful in turn-of-the-millennium Cairo. A woman in the family who is respectable may potentially net her father and her brothers a valuable alliance when she marries, but this is by no means guaranteed, as arranged marriages are less and less common. Meanwhile, families expend considerable sums to marry both their sons and their daughters (though it is more expensive to fund a son's marriage than a daughter's), and the older generation gains little, economically speaking, in return. What the older generation *does* gain through their financial sacrifices for their children is a measure of control over the younger generation, who usually cannot marry without considerable financial assistance from their parents.

In my Egyptian ethnographic material, it was apparent that the more financially independent a woman was, the less beholden she was to kin and to men's ideas about respectable behavior. As a banker, Alia's financial independence freed her from having to depend on a husband (though extracting herself from the abusive marriage was a long, painful process that took her years), and her financial independence also ensured that she did not have to bow to her brothers' demands that she end her extramarital relationship with Haroun. The retired belly dancer and entrepreneur Zizi and the actress Nour both behaved in completely outrageous ways without any fear of social reprisal or rejection by kin because they were powerful and economically independent women. Sara was poor, but she had her own job, which ensured some independence from her brothers, though she was also careful not to create conflict by flaunting her romantic and sexual liaisons in front of them. Indeed, Kerim considered any woman who lived on her own to be categorically a whore, suggesting an equation (in his mind, at least) between financial independence and sexual freedom.

But that is another generalizing statement that half the time turns out to be wrong. The link between respectable behavior and women's wealth was never so simplistic. I knew many middle-class working women who earned considerable salaries of their own yet who played a conservative role of dutiful and respectable wife and mother, and I knew others, completely dependent on their fathers or husbands for financial support, who engaged in a series of premarital or extramarital affairs. It is not just economic independence but also some level of personal, individual inclination that determines how much women bow to or rebel against dominant norms. However, it is economic independence that allows women to publicly flaunt the norms; women who are dependent on male relatives for support work harder to hide their transgressions, as they are more vulnerable to retribution.

In sum, the ethnographic material from turn-of-the-millennium Cairo indicates that despite a cultural fascination with women's sexuality and the concept of respectability, there is only a very partial fit with the classic anthropological formulation of the cultural complex of honor and shame. Yet that classic formulation is powerful enough to shape what the anthropologist expected to find, to the extent that when I heard Sara saying her brother would kill her, a common phrase of hyperbole in both Arabic and English, I immediately thought of media coverage of honor killings and anthropological theories of honor and shame. It is, itself, like women's respectability, a simulacrum: an anthropologist sees an honor-and-shame complex even when talking to an informant who was having an extramarital affair. What the theory purports to describe has only minimal relevance to the ethnographic data, and yet this classic theory has the power to shape not only academic but also popular media representations of the Arab world, as I shall argue below.

What Is Respectability?

Even if we accept the cultural dominance of this concept of the "respectable woman," what is respectability, anyway? I spent three and a half years trying to define it. I eventually realized that even though women are continually being conditioned by relatives to seek and live up to an absolute definition of the term, "respectability" was a continually moving target. It has no absolute meaning. It is defined differently by different people and even by the same people at different times and in different contexts. What is more, no woman gave up on the concept of "respectable," no matter how far she found herself from some bourgeois consensus of what constituted respectable behavior. Malak was striving toward a respectable identity when she was embarrassed by her doorman's pimplike behavior toward a new boyfriend. I strove to be a respectable wife of an Arab man, even when I was hanging out with belly dancers and their male patrons, whom my husband regarded as beyond the pale of respectability. And Alia never accepted her family's criticism of her as not respectable because even if she was having an affair with a married man, she loved him and was faithful to him and she was a good mother who was raising her sons with love and the material comforts of life.

Ultimately, we can't consider separately the cultural *ideal* that there is an absolute definition of respectable woman from the cultural *reality* that respectability is a receding event horizon toward which women must perpetually strive and which they must perpetually define themselves against. What is important is the way this cultural ideal and reality intersect. It is in their intersection—the negotiation of real behavior against the pressure of hegemonic ideals—that we see the real workings of the sex/gender system that Rubin (1975) describes, enforced by both men and women. The concept of respectability disciplines women. It reminds them that they are constantly being morally judged by how they contain or share their sexuality. Yet it is also in the gap between ideals and reality that we see patriarchy creatively defied, subverted, and renegotiated.

Respectability is not just something that men impose on women as a disciplining cultural force. Women also judge each other, as we saw when Malak, a European who generally seemed to have radically liberal attitudes toward sex and money, criticized other dancers for being whores, or when Alia criticized some of the other women who came to Haroun's *wakr* for gatherings, or when Ayah pointed out to me other women who were "prostitutes."

Another thing that shapes definitions of respectability is kin relations. Or, to put it another way, a man's perspective on respectability depends a great deal on how he defines himself in kin terms vis-à-vis a woman. A man who has premarital sex with his fiancée might see her as completely respectable, as long as he believes that she has only ever had sex with him. (Or he might take it as a sign that she is fundamentally untrustworthy and break the engagement.) Her brother or father might consider this completely unrespectable behavior, if they ever found out. A man is more tolerant of the behavior of other unrelated female friends, though he may act protective and employ fictitious kinship terms to define a close but nonsexual relationship (as Kerim and Zeid did with me, frequently describing themselves as "like brothers" and warning me about my behavior—though never as stringently as my husband did). The closer a man is to a woman in kin terms, the more rigid are his expectations of her and the more demanding is his definition of respectability—but also, the greater is his sense of obligation to protect her.

Yet as the example I have given of male-female friendships suggests, with recommendations given to me by platonic male friends couched in the form of brotherly advice, there is also a range of ways that men and women are mutually obligated to each other by cultural notions of respectability outside formal kinship structures, which illustrates the plasticity of "respectability." For example, Haroun never would have talked in front of other people about putting chili paste in his wife's vagina, as he did with Alia. He also would never have tolerated his wife staying out until late with belly dancers, actresses, and such women. Yet did that mean that Haroun did not respect Alia? He was both protective and demanding of Alia in ways that he was not with other women, he made it clear that he would not tolerate insults to Alia, and he never would have described Alia as "not respectable" in front of his friends.

Haroun also got angry if he ever thought Alia was flirting with other men or if she went out late at night in a group of men and women without him (as she occasionally did with her banker colleagues, which always caused conflict between them), so even though he allowed (and indeed, expected) her to act in ways that were very different from the behavior he expected from his respectable wife, he also exerted a measure of jealousy and control over her behavior that most Cairenes regarded as a mark of a man's affection, regard, and respect. Alia said that she and Haroun treated each other "like husband and wife," though she clearly had less claim on him than a wife did: he bought her gifts, sometimes wildly extravagant ones, but he did not pay for her apartment or consider himself responsible for giving her a living allowance (as he did with his wife), and she clearly behaved in ways that were not compatible with his ideas about wifely comportment. For her part, Alia considered herself respectable, even as she rejected in both word and action prevailing bourgeois norms of female respectability.

In short, what all these examples show is that respectability and its lack are not magnetic poles. They are not even points on a continuum, unless we accept that each person has a different continuum and different definitions of respectability that change at different times in his or her life and according to whose behavior is being judged. Perhaps the only sense in which we can see a continuum is in the ways that different women hold themselves to different behavioral standards, shifting strategically according to circumstances and opportunity.

Or, to put it another way, the concept of respectability exists not as an organizing principle of culture but, rather, as a language for talking about self and society, about moral behavior and the appropriate gendered expression of sexuality. Everyone uses this language. (Even European belly dancers in Cairo quickly learned to speak this language.) But everyone is constantly trying to redefine the meaning of the terms. And ultimately, these definitions of respectability are simulacra, loosely tied to behavior around sexuality, love, and desire, which are interpreted through a relentless scanning for signs but are distinctly separate from women's actual sexual behavior yet are so powerful that these signs' realness eclipses the signifiers themselves.

On Representations of Islamic Societies and Arab Men

I keep thinking back to Lévi-Strauss's comment about romance emerging out of the duet between a woman's agency and her value as a social object of exchange. Isn't that, after all, the underlying premise of most historical romance novels? They are all about women or men who are obligated by societal rules to perform in a particular way according to narrow societal strictures and who either rebel against those rules and find true love or follow those rules but somehow find love in spite of them (as in the popular stories where the hero and heroine fall in love after an arranged marriage).

Every time I read a historical romance novel,[3] I always wonder why there is such a market for romances set in Regency and Victorian En-

gland and yet very little Western market for romances set in the contemporary Arab world. In many, perhaps most, historical romances
set in England, the heroine is a young lady whose chastity is fiercely
guarded by her father and brothers. She falls in love with some virile
rake who guards his own sisters just as fiercely but spends the rest of his
time happily debauching any other woman he can get his hands on. In
the process of debauching the lovely heroine, he realizes that he loves
her, and he guarantees her respectable position in society by marrying
her. Or, alternatively, he desists from his impulse to debauch the heroine
because he realizes that he loves her, so instead he marries her so he can
have sex with her without destroying her position in society.

There are a few similarities between the characters in such the romances and the people I have described in this ethnography. Rakes
abound, from Ali to Haroun to Zeid. (Although Zeid remained a virgin
until his marriage to Ayah, he dated widely and frequently until he met
her and even after he met her, during their frequent breakups.) These
rakes indulge their sexual appetites mostly with less-than-respectable
women, but they occasionally fall for a plucky young woman (like Ayah)
who sneaks around behind her father's and brothers' backs to engage in
romance while nevertheless maintaining enough of an aura of respectability that the hero never loses his respect for her and protects her by
marrying her.

Of course, there are rather few unambiguously happy endings in all
the romantic entanglements I have described here, and the role of hero
is a fleeting one. Love and desire often result in portraits of humili-
ated, subservient women, like Sara, abandoned in a hospital and miscar-
rying a child that she hoped with desperate futility would bind Ali to
her. They play out on a cultural terrain characterized by a deep sexism
that penalizes women but not men for extramarital affairs, and requires
young men like Zeid to labor to the point of exhaustion to prove their
worth to demanding fiancées and their families.

Nevertheless, the reality of women's lives has never stopped a fiction
writer from crafting a happy love story. And all the cultural elements
that drive the tension in most historical romances—a cult of virginity;
the judgmental gaze of society, ever scrutinizing the moral behavior of
young women and prepared to cast out any girl who falls from grace; ra-
pacious men who spend their nights pursuing sexual adventure but who
might be persuaded to settle down by a spirited young woman who earns
their respect; domineering fathers and brothers who both oppress and
jealously protect their female relatives—all these abound in the portrait

I have drawn of turn-of-the-millennium Cairo. Yet in the mainstream romance market, virtually the only novels set in the Arab world are either historical romances featuring harems and love slaves (as in the oeuvre of Bertrice Small, who is otherwise known in romance circles for her innovative use of the term "manroot") or more contemporary romances where the white woman is kidnapped by some Bedouin sheikh in the desert. And even these types of stories are a very small and not terribly popular subgenre. (See Teo 2012 for an extended discussion of romance novels with an Arab setting.)

On the contrary, with few exceptions (such as the movie *Aladdin*), most Western representations of Arab society portray the men as patriarchal oppressors (not romantic heroes) and the women as oppressed (not plucky, independent heroines navigating their way through the constraints of culture).

The Syrian writer Rana Kabbani (1986) has used the lens of Edward Said's theory of Orientalism to show how the West has represented Arab sexuality as being the opposite of whatever the prevailing Western sexual norms are. During the Victorian era, when Western bourgeois society was sexually repressed, Western society depicted the Arab world as sexually licentious, with harems full of lusty sheikhs, dancing girls, and concubines (e.g., Flaubert 1996). Then, with the sexual revolution of the 1960s and 1970s, Western representations of the Arab world reversed themselves, rendering a geography of sexual repression as a foil to Western sexual freedom.

But what unites this shifting history of representations of Middle Eastern sexuality is a portrayal of dominating, oppressive, and occasionally violent Arab men.

This is a dominant representation of Arab sexuality today, and nowhere is this more visible than in media coverage of so-called honor killings in the Muslim world and diaspora. The literature on honor killings portrays these and other "crimes of honor" as violence motivated by cultures of honor and shame (Welchman and Hossain 2005, 4), and media coverage of such crimes have undermined multicultural policies in Europe and triggered waves of Islamophobia (Fekete 2006). Here again we see that representations of the Middle East are driven by the assumption that these societies are driven by a paradigm of honor and shame. As Lama Abu-Odeh (1997) wryly notes, what is called a "crime of passion" when committed by a Westerner is called a "crime of honor" when committed by an Arab or Muslim. The implications are far-reaching. As Purna Sen (2005, 61) notes, "The contemporary discovery of, and subsequent opposition to, crimes of honour in the West have meshed together the perception of a foreign concept (honour), an alien and terrorist religion (Islam) and the bogey of violence against women into a politically potent mix." Such depictions ramped up in the wake of 9/11 and the US invasion of Afghanistan and later Iraq.

I thus titled chapter 7 "Honor Killing" ironically, to show that the Western anthropologist had certain expectations about the outcome of Sara's sexual liaisons rooted in a literature on honor and shame, one that is simultaneously academic and political, and that sees the ultimate expression of this cultural complex as violent murder (Inhorn 2012). Sara's blasé and derisive response to my "idiotic" credulity when she said that one of her brothers would kill her points to the absurdity of this perspective.

What the ethnographic material I have presented here suggests is that so-called honor crimes are actually astonishingly rare, considering how often illicit sex takes place. Sara feared her brothers' finding out about her relationship with Ali, but she didn't fear for her physical life; she feared for her social life. Alia's family knew about her affair with Haroun, and the worst damage it caused was a degree of tension at family gatherings. I knew of many other cases (which I have not described here) of women who had premarital sex or extramarital affairs, including unmarried women who got pregnant (usually their mothers helped them arrange an abortion). My sample, obviously, was not representative, but this fact should nevertheless give us pause.

Western Representations of Arab Women

Reports of honor crimes in Western media perpetuate an image of Arab women as oppressed and subjected to violence by Arab men (Inhorn 2012; Naguib 2015). As anthropologist Laura Nader has argued, representations of the oppression of women in Arab societies do little to improve the status of women in those societies. Instead, Nader reminds us, comparing two societies to see which treats its women better is an ultimately futile exercise that draws our attention away from the ways that women are disadvantaged in both societies.

Most anthropologists probably know Nader from her famous article "Up the Anthropologist: Perspectives Gained from Studying Up," in which she urged anthropologists to study elites, the affluent, bureaucracies, the powerful, and the colonizers rather than the poor, the downtrodden, and the colonized (Nader 1972). But she has another article that is a cult classic among scholars of gender in the Middle East. In "Orientalism, Occidentalism, and the Control of Women" (Nader 1989), she points out that the same sort of criticism of the status of women in the Muslim world that is so popular in both "liberal" and conservative Western circles is mirrored by similar rhetoric in Middle Eastern countries.

For example, when I lived in Saudi Arabia in the 1990s, the Saudi English-language press was replete with denunciations of the vile treatment of women in the West. Consider this excerpt from an article in the *Saudi Gazette* circa 1992:

> It is one thing to clamour for the rhetoric "women are equal to men," but when that very equality means in pure and simple language exploitation of the privacy and unique beauty of women, such as is witnessed in advertising anything from a screw to a tractor with a semi-clad beauty, the attitude of Islam begins to take on a new dimension—even for non-Muslims. ("Islam Treats Ladies with Real Respect," *Saudi Gazette*, April 24, 1992, 5)

Other articles published in the *Saudi Gazette* iterated statistics on domestic violence and sexual assault in North American and European countries.

Nader (1989, 324) expands Said's "observations that the Moslem world exists for the West, to include the notion that the West also exists for the Islamic world and serves as important contrastive comparison." She then goes on to argue that claims of "our women are better off than your women" is an essentially male discourse that serves to distract women from the real issues and from the processes that serve to control women in both worlds. "By taking a position of superiority vis-à-vis the other, both East and West can rationalize the position of their women" (ibid., 328).

But gloating or pious assessments of the oppression of women in Arab and Muslim countries do more than distract attention from the epidemic of violence against women in both parts of the world. The representation of male Muslims oppressing Muslim women has been used to justify Western military intervention, in an extension of the colonial logic of "white men saving brown women from brown men" (Spivak 1994). For example, images of oppressed Afghani women were mobilized on the eve of the invasion of Afghanistan to justify the American invasion as an intervention to free poor Afghani women from their bur-kas. Laura Bush declared that "the fight against terrorism is also a fight for the rights and dignity of women" in a November 2001 radio speech describing the plight of women under the Taliban (Gerstenzang and Getter 2001).

The same rhetoric continued to appear throughout the US occu-pation of both Afghanistan and, rather more perplexingly, Iraq. Con-sider, for example, this contemporary white-male fantasy of saving brown women from brown men, which appears in an article by Fred Thompson (2007) entitled "America, Saving Muslim Women's Lives." Thompson criticizes the deaths of schoolgirls in Mecca, the oppression of women under the Taliban in Afghanistan, and "the horrors of life for millions of women in pre-liberation Iraq." He vaunts the reduction of infant mortality in postoccupation Afghanistan as a result of American intervention and concludes:

> The next time I'm reminded of the suffering women endure in too
> many radicalized Muslim cultures, or apathy toward their plight back
> here at home, I'm going to conjure up the image of 40 or 50 thousand
> Muslim mothers smiling into the faces of healthy babies. You might try
> the same—and remember, while you're doing it, that these babies would
> not be alive today if it were not for the U.S. and Coalition soldiers.

Thompson's article also claims that "in Iraq, the health-care and ed-ucational statistics are even better," and breezily mentions that "there are, of course, still many areas of life that need to improve in both coun-tries, but," he concludes, "we're moving in the right direction."

Thompson is not specific about those areas that need improvement, but one area of life that might need to improve in Iraq, for example, is the mortality rate: the deaths of hundreds of thousands of Iraqi chil-dren, women, and men are directly attributable to Coalition forces, and more than half a million deaths are attributed to other causes related to the occupation, such as increased sectarian violence and lawlessness and the degradation of health care and infrastructure (Burnham et al. 2006, 1).

The relationship between politics and Western portrayals of Arab masculinity and femininity is illustrated definitively by Smeeta Mishra, who analyzed representations of Muslim men and women in the *New York Times* between September 11, 2001, and September 11, 2003, and found a dominant discourse portraying Muslim women as "victims in need of Western liberation, which was sometimes defined narrowly as the exercise of individual choice in the purchase and use of consumer goods such as nail polish, lipsticks and high-heeled shoes." She concludes that these portrayals "established the need to intervene to rescue the women and control the men" (Mishra 2007, 1). (However, Shakira Hussein [2013] documents a shift from "rescue missions" to "discipline" in Western discourses on Muslim women, though the "rescue" narrative hasn't completely disappeared.)

This is all to say that we have to be wary of the political implications behind Western representations of Arab and Muslim men and the sexuality of Arab women—a literature of which this very book is a part.

And, not so incidentally, this also explains why there isn't a popular genre of romances set in the contemporary Middle East. It is too much of an uphill battle to portray Arab cultures romantically when our society has so much at stake in maintaining a very unromantic image of male-female relations in the Arab world.

Conclusions: Romance, Love, and Desire

As Abu-Lughod has convincingly argued (1991, 1993), the problem with many ethnographic accounts of so-called honor-and-shame cultures is the way they describe culture in terms of general characteristics. They claim, for example, that a man's honor is created and maintained by the actions of his agnatic kin and that a woman's behavior determines the honor of both her male relatives' and her husband's families (Abu-Zeid 1965). In my ethnographic account of pre- and extramarital liaisons in turn-of-the-millennium Cairo, we see a much more complex range of behavior and relationships between men and women than we could imagine if we were working from prescriptive models. (That said, comparing a Bedouin village like the one Abu-Lughod describes in the early 1960s with a megacity like Cairo at the turn of the millennium is like comparing apples and gigantic watermelons.)

These are stories about romance, love, and desire, but they are not particularly romantic. They are stories of female initiative and cunning, but the women don't always come out the winners, and they don't always resist male control. They exercise, as Michel de Certeau might say, the tactics of the weak, not the strategies of the powerful. Yet even that concept presupposes relatively stable hierarchies to be subverted. That does not do justice to the complex ways that women and men weave their way through romantic and kin relations, sometimes submissive, sometimes openly defiant, other times sneakily subversive. As Laura Miller (1997, 32) points out in her critique of James Scott's concept of "weapons of the weak," "structural analyses that divide the population into the powerful and the powerless are . . . limited because they do not account for coexisting multiple hierarchies of power."

Remember that Sara urged me to not let my husband become too controlling, to carve out my own space of independence in defiance of his desire to ensure my moral status and his, even as she submitted to her own lover's control over her behavior and thrilled when he slapped her face. George called Sara a man with a combination of admiration and discomfort for the way she fiercely defied cultural propriety by openly pursuing a relationship with a married man. Alia, too, openly defied her family and continued to date a married man after they found out about her affair. Malak epitomized a different way that some Egyptian women—particularly belly dancers like Fifi Abdou, whom both Nesma and Sara admired, but also actresses like Nour who attended Haroun's gatherings—defined sexual and moral integrity. This was the skill of a belly dancer or artist or woman from what Egyptians call the "popular" (*shaʿabi*) class who is so accomplished that she is called a *muʿallima* (which connotes learnedness), someone who has such great social mastery that she needs no male protector, someone who can handle every situation with deftness. Nour's sexuality was so open and so powerful that she was invited to fuck a man's ass with her tits, a symbolic inversion of sexual gender hierarchies that simultaneously offended bourgeois codes of female respectability (to be openly sexually propositioned would provoke most respectable women to storm haughtily from the room) and elevated Nour's sexuality to that of a man's, the penetrator rather than the penetrated. Her potent sexuality, rather than being something dangerous and in need of protection (or suppression), here became empowering; her breasts were metaphorically converted to a phallus. Nour the *muʿallima* responded not by acting offended, as Malak and I rather expected, but by at once joining the judge in gently mocking Farouq's symbolic emasculation and graciously accepting Farouq's compliment to the power of her sexuality and her status as an accomplished actress. (Farha Ghannam discusses the Egyptian valorization of what are seen as masculine attributes in women and the contexts in which masculinity is seen as a negative attribute. When a woman is strong, firm, supportive, fair, and honorable in keeping her word, she is described as *sitt bi meet ragul* [a woman worth a hundred men], but when she dresses in ways that are masculine, she earns the negative label of *"mistargula"* [manly] [2013, 54–55].)

But even these daring women, whom I admired, were not always models of independent defiance. Remember that Sara submitted happily to discipline by Ali, who hit her and ripped her clothes to teach her to be more modest (but also to express jealousy and thus his passionate attachment to her). Or consider the curious mixture of dependence and independence of Alia, who divorced her cheating, abusive husband and started an affair with another man, in open defiance of her relatives, who threatened to disown her over her relationship with Haroun. Alia was game for any sexual novelty that Haroun wanted to try, whether it was chili paste in the vagina or a threesome with one of their mutual friends. Yet Alia also submissively bowed to Haroun's rules about whom she could socialize with, and in any disagreement, while they might have a spirited debate, he always had the final word and threatened to leave her if she did not ultimately defer to him.

What these stories illustrate is a huge variety of female role models and expressions of appropriate female sexuality. While Egyptians may gossip about dancers and many say they would never let them marry into their families, they also invite them into their most important and most joyous family events. Flamboyantly transgressive actresses like Nour and Fifi Abdou are widely admired, even by women who claim to hold themselves to rather different standards of female behavior, as we saw when the shop employees expressed their veneration for Fifi Abdou's life of serial marriages and affairs. And women both rich and poor—from Alia, who wore diamonds and gold and lived in the wealthy neighborhood of Heliopolis, to Sara, who lived in a slum on the outskirts of Cairo where uncollected rubbish piled up in house-sized mounds on the streets and there was only running water for two hours every day—navigated public opinion and their own internal moral codes as they engaged in extramarital affairs.

Feminist theories of honor and shame, whether by Mernissi or Schneider, share both the advantages and problems I have described for Rubin's interpretation of Lévi-Strauss's theory of kinship as the exchange of women. From a certain angle, these theories offer a useful perspective on cultural dynamics. As feminist critiques, they are powerful.

On the other hand, like Lévi-Strauss's theory, classic formulations of the so-called honor-and-shame cultural complex fail to take into account the significance of both agency and affect in mediating powerful cultural norms. As Abu-Lughod (1993) and Wikan (1984) point out, these theories fail to see women as actors, as personally invested in creating and maintaining their own reputations, as active in managing the sexual advances of men. They fail to account for powerful women like Zizi and Nour and Malak and Alia who defined respectability in their own terms, who defied bourgeois ideals of female behavior and yet carved out social niches where they were respected and loved. They rarely acknowledge that women strive for respectability and value it as their own, not just as the property of the men in their lives. They also ignore the ways that women navigate their social world using emotion and ties to other people; loving men yet also criticizing them; and, although aware of cultural rules of behavior, tacitly understanding that these could be manipulated, tweaked, twisted, and sometimes even turned upside down in actual intimate relationships. And in failing to recognize the power of love and desire—and the way these emotions influence the complex ways that women submit to and resist the social norms that constrain them—they struggle to predict the possibilities for, the forms of, and the limitations of feminine resistance to patriarchy.

CHAPTER 9

Love, Revolution, and Intimate Violence

It took more than a decade for Sara to tell me that two of her boyfriends had helped their friends rape her.

I suppose this shouldn't surprise me. One estimate holds that about 15 percent—nearly one in six—American women have been raped in their lifetime (RAINN, n.d.), and though I have known hundreds of American women, none have ever told me about being raped. I use American data because there are no reliable estimates of the rate of sexual assault in Egypt. According to the European Institute for Crime Prevention and Control, the rate of sexual assaults recorded by police in Egypt was 0.2 rapes per 100,000 people (Harrendorf, Heiskanen, and Malby 2010, 38). Sara's account will illustrate how little these figures reflect the reality of unreported rapes in Egypt.

Perhaps the surprising thing is that my Egyptian friend eventually *did* decide to speak about that kind of trauma that so few women and men share with others.

What triggered her revelation?

It was 2012 and we were sitting in my Cairo hotel room talking about a completely different research project, one on hymenoplasty, for which I had hired Sara as a research assistant. She had little formal schooling (some high school), but she was smart and socially savvy, someone I trusted better than most to help me figure out how to talk to people about this sensitive topic. Also, Sara, who lived in a poor part of Cairo in a two-room apartment that she shared with five other relatives, would give me far better access to poor Egyptians than my university-educated research assistants could. We were planning to travel to Alexandria to visit Sara's relatives and in preparation we had drafted a set of interview questions, which we decided to test with a mock interview. I held my voice recorder between us and asked Sara the questions, and she answered them briefly, commenting sometimes on my wording or on the types of answers she thought I was likely to get.

"Some people," she warned me after I asked the last question, "will be shy to speak about the topic. People might say they don't know anything about this. And, you know, it's impossible that someone will tell you that she erred with someone." ("To err" was Sara's euphemism for having sexual intercourse outside marriage.)

I murmured agreement. We had talked about this at length. We had decided to ask people not about any personal experiences but, rather, about their general opinions about the surgical procedure: who they thought sought it out, how, and under what circumstances.

There was another pause, and then Sara said, matter of fact, "Do you know how many men I slept with? So many."

In the audio recording, you can hear my voice rise half an octave. "You?"

"Yes. I wrote about it in the life history I've been writing for you."

Sara knew that I was writing this book about love and desire (separate from the hymenoplasty research project), and I had asked her for permission to write about her. For the past year we had been talking about what to write and what details to change to protect her identity. She was enthusiastic about appearing in the book and had insisted that she should write down her life history for me to serve as background and context to the things that I had personally observed. She had given me the first part of this life history, which included a dramatic account of being circumcised when she was eight years old (she hid behind the couch in terror when the midwife came), but she kept alluding to far more dramatic revelations that I would read about in the second part of her life history, which she had not yet completed.

"Seriously?" I repeated myself like an idiot. I knew about two of her lovers, but not about "so many." But I wasn't so much surprised to hear about her active sex life as I was confused about the sudden change in topic. I wondered if she was thinking of telling me her life story on tape rather than writing it down.

"Yes," she said, almost cheerfully. "There were so many I loved. But they did bad things to me." Here her voice became more somber. "Because they were not good people. I don't even want to remember who they are."

"Really?" I gathered that she didn't want to speak about individuals, so I decided to tease her a little in an attempt to lighten her mood. "How many is 'a lot'? Like, say, fifty?"

She laughed. "No, no, no. Not that many! You know the situation here isn't what it's like where you live. Abroad you can do what you like, but here, someone would be afraid, aware that everyone is watching him. For example, I might love someone and he, for example, he doesn't love me but he wants me. He wants to sit with me somewhere," she added euphemistically. "But because he doesn't love me, he lies to me. He takes me to, for example, his friend's house. So I have to sleep with his friend, and then sleep with him."

"*Yaaa!?*" I made a sound of surprise and question that drew the short word out over about three syllables.

"That's how it is here. Do you understand?"

I understood the words, but I was still struggling to grasp the implications of what she was telling me. I suspected that Sara wasn't speaking in the hypothetical. "This happened before?"

"It happened to me twice. But against my will [*ghasban 'anni*]. A boy from Harat El-Yehud [a quarter of old Cairo where many goldsmiths' shops are located], Sameh, I used to love him. We went to the beach, and he took pictures of me, we went here and there, and then he said, 'Come over to my friend's house; we'll spend some time together.' And I went."

"Did you know you were going to sleep with him?"

"Me and him only. And then I found him there with two of his friends . . ."

"Hang on a sec. You slept with him before that? Before that trip?"

"Yes, before the trip. So I went there. I didn't know he was going to bring his friends. And then I was shocked when they pulled their knives on me. I hemorrhaged; I was bleeding a lot. And then I went home. And I decided that I don't know him anymore. That was around ten years ago, or more."

Sara's voice was matter of fact, though you can hear my expressions of surprise in the background of the recording. There was a long pause as I tried to assimilate the fact that my friend had just described being gang-raped at knifepoint. I blame my shock for the inanity of the next questions I asked her.

"Did you know him [Sameh] from the *souq*?"

"Yes, but not from the area where I work."

"Do you worry about him talking about you, what it would do to your reputation?" Sara's current boyfriend worked in the *souq* and I wondered if he knew about any of this. Though it had been rape, I knew knowledge of it would damage her reputation, and I also knew that Sara was working very hard these days to present an image of conservative respectability in the hopes that Hassan, her (married) boyfriend, would eventually marry her as his second wife.

"No, I doubt it. I avoid that whole area where he [Sameh] is."

"Didn't you want to go to the police?"

"No." She said it definitively, with an emphatic glottal stop that made the word into two syllables.

"Why not?"

"I'm the one who was in the wrong. What will I tell them? I'm the one who went there [to that apartment]."

"*You* were in the wrong?! But . . . they're the ones who did it! Didn't you say they had knives?"

"Yeah. They were bad men. Anyway, I decided I didn't know them after that."

In this audio recording, Sara never actually described these events as "rape" (*ightisab*), but the phrase she used, "against my will" (*ghasban 'anni*) has the same root in Arabic. Yet it is strikingly unclear whether her inability to report the first rape was because she believed herself complicit in the suffering she endured (to paraphrase Cynthia Mahmood, describing a common reaction of rape survivors; see Mahmood 2008) or because, pragmatically, she was aware that the police would not help her and would blame her. As Veena Das reminds us, defining acts of violence—in this case, pinning down the event as "rape" or sex "against [Sara's] will"—is not as important as understanding that the instability of the definition is "crucial for understanding how the reality of violence includes its virtuality" (Das 2008, 284), for seeing violence as "both actuality and potentiality" (ibid., 285). Also crucial to the relationship between violence and gender, Das tells us, is the "deep connection between the spectacular and the everyday" (ibid., 284).

That uncanny connection between spectacular and everyday is evident in the audio recording of this interview, where the matter-of-fact dismissiveness in Sara's voice and the mildness of the terms she used to describe the situation ("they were bad men . . . I didn't know them after that") contrasts with the shock and rage and astonishment in mine.

"Didn't you want to kill them? If it were me, frankly, I'd want to kill them."

Sara clicked in dismissal of my absurd suggestion. "That's abroad, not here in Egypt."

I tried to convert this revenge fantasy into kinship terms, thinking that that would make it more locally relevant. "I would tell my brothers, and they would kill them. And they wouldn't kill them quickly, no! They would first torture them!"

Sara laughed but didn't think much of my attempt at cultural translation. "I've never talked to anyone about this before. Not a single person. Only you."

"Not even Nisreen?" Nisreen was Sara's cousin, a close friend, and she slept with many men in exchange for money or gifts. If Sara could tell anyone in Egypt about this, I figured it would be her.

"Not even Nisreen. I can't. No one."

"You said this happened to you twice."

"Yes. The second time was with Ali."

"Ali? The one that you used to love when I was living here in Cairo before? Before you had your operation?" The book I was writing focused extensively on Sara's relationship with Ali.

"Yes, right, you remember him. It was when you were first living here."

"It happened with *him*? How is that possible?"

"Yes, I went with him to his cousin's house, and his cousin was there . . ."

"Wait, this was before the operation or after it?"

"Before it." My inability to listen to her narrative without interrupting hints at the cognitive dissonance I was experiencing at hearing that the man she had loved for so long had been one of the two boyfriends who had helped their friends rape her—and at hearing not just that she had loved him but that she had *continued* to love him *after* he made her body available to his friend, "against [her] will."

"I went with him and I had to sleep with his cousin first before I could sleep with Ali, because we were in his cousin's house. I was crying so hard. That he would do that to me . . ."

There was a long pause as I tried to assimilate what she was telling me with what I thought I knew about Sara and Ali's love story. When I eventually spoke, it was something between a whisper and a stutter. "But . . . but . . . but how . . . how could he . . ."

"I don't know. Because he didn't love me."

"Wait, this was *before* the operation? But . . . you still loved him then, when you were in the hospital."

"Yeah."

"Remember in the hospital? Remember how you wanted to marry him? Remember?" If I kept repeating myself, it was because that particular scene in that hospital (which I recounted in chapter 7) was, to me, utterly unforgettable in its tragedy and sadness.

"Yeah. Yeah." She shrugged. "So that's it. I left Ali, too." But not, it seemed, immediately after this violation, because that had happened before Sara went into the hospital for surgery and for the several months she was hospitalized and even after she got out of the hospital and returned to work, Sara had talked continually and repeatedly about how much she loved Ali.

"He still visits me sometimes in the shop where I work. Says hi to me. I say hi, that's it."

There was another long pause. "Now I want to kill him too," I commented darkly.

"Nisreen, you know, she sleeps with men because she wants money. Wants to dress well, buy things for her children, go out, have a good time."

"And you?"

"No. I do it only for love. Otherwise I won't. Not for money. Never in my life have I taken money [for sex]. Only if I want him. Not all girls are alike. Not everyone thinks alike. I could even pay *him* if I wanted to sleep with him! Know what I mean?" We laughed and clapped hands together, enjoying a moment of levity.

Listening again to this recording I am struck by how quickly she moved between talking about love and desire to talking about rape and then back again, contrasting her own sexual desire with that of her cousin Nisreen. Nisreen used her body for material gain; Sara freely gave hers to those she loved and also actively sought and took pleasure from those whom she desired.

"How many do you think are like Nisreen, and how many are like you?"

"Eighty percent do it for money. Because everything is about money these days. Twenty percent, they sleep together for love. But otherwise, no. It's all about money."

"And how many girls do you think sleep around before marriage?"

"Not many. There are good girls, you know, who don't have sex before marriage."

"But how would you know, realistically? Probably people say the same about you, say that you're a good girl. Hassan thinks you're a good girl."

"He doesn't know anything about me, nothing at all! But he loves me."

I remembered, even if Sara didn't, that she used to say the same thing about Ali, a decade earlier.

Ethnographic Contingency

To paraphrase Appadurai (1997, 115), ethnographic interpretation is "always a work-in-progress, wrested from the corrosion of contingency."

This moment in a Cairo hotel room illustrates the extent to which ethnography is a process, sequence, and accretion of intimacy, and it reveals the unevenness and contingency of the tempo through which stories unfold. Both fieldwork and its interpretation are contingent on the intersection of temporality and connection between anthropologist and informants and on the contexts structuring that connection.

The context in this case was partly Sara's ongoing work on her life history, which would contribute to the book she knew I was writing about her (among others); partly our discussion about hymenoplasty, a procedure that women sometimes seek in order to hide the fact that they are not virgins when they marry; and partly a Turkish soap opera, *Fatima*, which Sara and I had been watching before we started recording the hymenoplasty interview that turned into a narrative about love, desire, and sexual violence.

Over the past half decade, Turkish television serials dubbed in Arabic have become incredibly popular in Egypt, and Sara watches them avidly. In 2012 (when I recorded Sara's narrative), *Fatima* was a huge hit in Cairo. It is a story about a woman who is gang-raped by friends of her fiancé, who then leaves her because he cannot bear the idea of marrying a woman who has been violated by his friends. Another friend of both the fiancé and the rapists marries her to preserve her honor, but their marriage is not sexually intimate, though the man slowly falls in love with her. The television series tracks her trauma, the slow process of her recovery, the justice that is (eventually) meted out to her attackers, and multiple competing social ideas about female purity and marriageability. Egyptians consumed it avidly and talked about it frankly. Sara's decision to talk about the rapes she had survived more than a decade earlier was partly triggered by this soap opera and our discussions of it. As Lila Abu-Lughod (2005) describes in her book *Dramas of Nationhood*, Egyptians often narrate their lives through the language of television, a process that shapes the ways they experience their own subjectivities as a result of television serials' emphasis on interior emotion. Sara often narrated her life dramatically with reference to Egyptian television serials, and perhaps this particular show gave her the vocabulary for talking about a secret trauma that she had suppressed for a decade.

But it is not just ethnographic knowledge that proceeds in this uneven and contingent tempo. Also temporally contingent is the elaboration of anthropological theory based on ethnographic data. Rena Lederman (2006, 485) characterizes the methodology of anthropology as "systematic openness to contingency," and Allaine Cerwonka and Liisa Malkki (2007, 15) note that "the tacking that ethnographers undertake is not so much between the part of culture and . . . the whole of a culture. The tacking . . . is . . . moving in our interpretive analysis between theory and empirical social facts in a dialectic that often reshapes our theoretical ideas as well as our view of the empirical data." Yet this openness to contingency, this dialectical tacking between empirical facts and theory, can be just as uneven and fraught as the tempo of ethnographic knowledge in the field. Sara's revelation came just as I was finishing a draft of this book, and it temporarily derailed that project. For months I stopped writing as I struggled to rethink what I thought I understood about love and desire, and I realized that despite my efforts to avoid a romanticizing notion of love relationships, I had nevertheless failed to appreciate the extent to which violence and pain could be intimately wedded to love and desire.

Sara's revelation and my reaction to it illustrate the messy terrain of affect, the difficulty that an anthropologist faces in finding an encompassing theoretical framework for understanding love and desire and sexuality that takes into account both power and social hierarchies (including local ideologies of masculine power and female purity that partially account for the logic of a man facilitating the rape of a girlfriend with whom he has sexual relations) and affect (for example, Sara's account of continuing to love Ali even after he forced her to have sex with his cousin, which is wholly unexplained by seeing their relationship in terms of power and hierarchy). As Ghassan Hage (2013) points out, if a social scientist only looks for ways that one person or group dominates another, "she will be missing an important resource that people, and especially subjugated people, have, to constitute themselves as viable human beings outside the relations of dominations in which they are grounded," and being in love is one of those ways that women and men constitute themselves outside a relation of domination, even as they are fully grounded in gendered social hierarchies. This is one of the problems with theoretical positions, such as those discussed in chapter 8, that attempt to flatten social relations into "domination" or "subordination." (I am indebted to Abu-Lughod, personal communication, November 2014, for this insight.) My dilemma speaks more broadly to difficulties that anthropologists have in taking the complex events of life—with all their violence and illogic and painfulness and idiosyncrasies—and neatly packaging them into a coherent account that we can place in dialogue with critical and anthropological theory.

Sara knew I was writing this book, and she insisted that I should incorporate her account of rape into my ethnography, but I wondered if it was possible to do so and still do justice to Sara's feelings for Ali and her other boyfriends. Can an observer understand the love that one person feels for another if that observer focuses on the violence and pain that was part of that relationship? The conventions of ethnographic writing ensure that it is far easier to empathize with the pain and suffering of an anthropological informant than with her feelings of love and desire (a disciplinary bias that I discussed in more detail in chapter 2). Wouldn't writing about how Sara's boyfriend enabled his friend to rape her overshadow everything else I could say about that relationship and make it impossible for us to understand the love that Sara felt for him?

Then again, can we really understand love and desire without seeing how violence and pain can be a central feature of both? Das (2008, 284) argues that we can find "every conceivable kind of emotion . . . as part of the experience of violence," including courage, heroism, despair, grief, anger, laughter, parody, longing, love, hate, horror, fear, pain, and suffering. But my material suggests the possibility of inverting Das's formula. In Sara's experiences of love and desire are entangled multiple affects. Her love affairs encompassed violence, pain, parody, longing, hate, despair, suffering, grief, anger, laughter, joy, exuberance, and hope. Her love story with Ali was not an idealized, fantasy love that lives happily ever after. But it is not always a tragic love story, either. It is a much more complex interweaving of love with both spectacular and everyday violence.

My dilemma was not only how to understand love and desire in the context of sexual violence; it was also a dilemma about the politics of representation. Knowledge production is a confrontation between the ethnographer's political agenda and the unpredictably idiosyncratic specificity of a field site and set of informants. My theoretical-political agenda had been to examine how Egyptian women in pursuit of love and desire deftly navigate, manipulate, and defy moralizing cultural norms that penalize women who have sex outside marriage as unrespectable social pariahs, even as they applaud for their virility men who do so. I conceptualized this as a project in the spirit of Michel de Certeau (1984, 96), who sought to document the "multiform, resistant, tricky and stubborn procedures that elude discipline without being outside the field in which it is exercised," but also in the spirit of Abu-Lughod (1991, 1993) and her insistence that ethnographers attend to individuals' unique experiences instead of creating generalizing, prescriptive models of culture. Yet Sara's account of being raped threw into doubt just how free and deft women were in their efforts to evade social controls on their sexuality. It revealed the moments when they are violently penalized for not adhering to such cultural ideals. I feared that readers would focus on a sensational act of violence and ignore all the other evidence of women who *do* successfully navigate this terrain in pursuit of nonnormative sexual relationships.

Beyond that theoretical agenda, there are broader politics of representation at stake when a white American-Australian woman writes about gender violence in the Muslim world.

First, while there are clearly political and legal structures that enable rape (and the nonreporting of it) in Egypt, examining cultures of violence against women in Muslim and South Asian countries has been historically used to justify military interventions and occupations—white men saving brown women from brown men, to paraphrase Gayatri Spivak (1994, 101)—and I didn't want my portrayal of Egypt to fuel that phenomenon. As Das (2008, 289) points out, Western justification for war in Muslim countries in terms of these regimes' violence against women is "so often used to make the complicity of Western regimes in supporting those very regimes less visible to the public." (Ironies abound: since female soldiers in the US Army experience sexual assault at rates much higher than women in the US population at large, and given the army's long and thoroughly entrenched tradition of gender discrimination, how, we might ask, could an institution that has a history of failing to protect its own female soldiers be suited for the task of protecting Afghani and Iraqi women from sexual violence and gender discrimination?)

As Abu-Lughod compellingly argues (2013), Western media accounts of gender violence in the Muslim world are inevitably harnessed to imperialist projects of conquest and colonialism, leading just as inevitably to more violence.

Second, there is violence against women all over the world, in all kinds of cultural contexts and legal-political systems, and a portrayal that focuses on violence against women in a far-away country or region is often a representational legerdemain that draws our attention away from structures of violence at home, as Laura Nader (1989) has argued with particular reference to Western representations of the Middle East and Middle Eastern representations of the West.

And third, though there are structures and cultural norms that enable violence against women in Egypt, there is also a culture of respecting and protecting women in Egypt. Writing about male violence when most of the Egyptian men I know love and respect women would, I worried, do an injustice to my male informants.

The Western media is hungry for critiques like that of Mona Elta-hawy's (2012) famous article "Why Do They Hate Us?" which, Arab feminist critics have argued (e.g., Errazzouki 2012), flattens the region into a monolithic caricature of every Western bogeyman, from face veils to female circumcision to the Saudi ban on women driving. I did not want to feed that hungry beast, which is always eager for more stories of misogyny and male oppressors in the Arab world.

On the other hand, downplaying or ignoring violence because it is relatively rare and focusing on the culturally commonplace is no useful way of doing anthropology. How, I wondered, could I undermine a flat understanding of social life that reduces gender relations to domination and hierarchy, and instead look at complex ties, while nevertheless giving due attention to the violence that Sara (and others like her) experience as women?

A False Dualism and a False Equation

As I struggled with how to understand and represent the relationship between violence and love, I realized that my difficulties arose out of the creation of one false dualism and one false equation. The false dualism is the assumption that love is antithetical to violence and pain. But as we can easily see from a vast corpus of romance novels, songs, and movies about love (in popular culture in both English and Arabic), love and pain can and do coexist and may even mutually constitute each other. Sara's Facebook page is full of sayings about love: "Love is my heaven and my hell" (*el-hubb ganniti wa nari*). "Love: if you have not suffered you will not learn" (*el-hubb: in lam tata'allam lan tata'allam*). "Love is the ailment and the remedy" (*el-hubb da' wa dawa'*). "My situation is worse than that of this country right now, and all because of love; I die a million deaths every day; my soul cries out, and I cry inside," she recently wrote.

Sara opened a Facebook account in January 2011, and it is no coincidence that she did so at the start of the Egyptian revolution, when political activism thrived on the use of social media. Even very poor Egyptians who had limited access to computers (like Sara, who uses a computer and accesses the internet at work) opened Facebook and Twitter accounts. Yet Sara's Facebook page is strikingly apolitical and consists mainly of aphorisms and poems about love, photos of celebrities, and pictures of adorable children (usually male, often wearing miniature tuxedoes and holding roses). In the Arabic aphorisms that she posts, the antonyms (heaven and hell) and phonetic similarities (ailment and remedy, suffer and learn, have done and will do) invite us to consider the ways pleasure and pain are closely intertwined. If love and pain coexist, if pain and conflict can, in fact, drive the intensity of the emotional experience of one's intimate attachment to another person, then it is only a small step from love-and-pain to love-and-violence, a step that is enabled by cultural norms and legal structures that encourage women to accept male violence and that convince them that they either *are* to blame for it or they *will* be blamed for it. (This is reflected in the legal structures I described in chapter 6 that shape the way prostitution is identified and prosecuted.)

In short, to collapse this false dualism we must direct our analysis to asking what kind of *ecology*—to adopt Tim Ingold's (2000) use of the term—creates a situation in which love and violence coexist. I use Ingold's term to signal that I am attempting to emulate his theoretical approach of collapsing apparent dualisms not only in an attempt to understand what links them but also to ask *why* we think of them as dualisms and why we misrecognize the links between them.

To put it in the terms of this book's theoretical agenda, we have to examine how the conditions that make possible women's manipulation of cultural norms, their ability to love and desire outside the structures that attempt to constrain nonnormative sexual relationships, are at the same time the conditions that enable violence against them, the shame and secrecy surrounding both love affairs and rape. Simply put, Egyptian women and men secretly engage in sexual relationships to avoid the social stigma of sex outside marriage, but the very secrecy that enables these nonnormative sexual relationships is what makes the women (and gay men) vulnerable to violence, as it removes them from the social networks that constrain them but that also protect them.

As Sarah Pinto (2014) argues, the paradox of kinship is that it intimately binds care to confinement, and sometimes to violence as well. It is this relationship between care and confinement that this book seeks to understand, as it describes how women deal with controlling and domineering—and occasionally violent—brothers and fathers and boyfriends and husbands while simultaneously enjoying the protection and love and attention and support that men offer to their female kin and lovers and wives. This book also examines the extraordinary pressures on men to care for their female kin, both morally and financially, by a society that evaluates men's masculinity and moral worth in terms of their ability to both support and protect their sisters, wives, and daughters (Ghannam 2013).

The false equation I was making was the assumption that reporting an act of violence by an Egyptian man is a betrayal of nonviolent Egyptian men. That equation is an insult to the majority of Egyptian men who condemn rape. It also accepts as inevitably dominant the widespread portrayal of Arab men as patriarchal, violent oppressors. It assumes that there is no way for an American-Australian anthropologist to report Sara's narrative of rape without contributing to that stereotype, rather than seeing anthropology as an activist discipline that works to combat stereotypes that paint Arab and Muslim men as patriarchal, violent oppressors. Not only does ignoring violence dismiss Sara's horrific experience (and that of other women), but it also means ignoring the work of the many Egyptian activists, women and men, who are working to challenge the political structures and cultural norms that perpetuate gender violence in Egypt.

These male and female Egyptian activists have been responsible for publicizing and condemning acts of gender violence during political demonstrations. For example, Yasmine al-Barmawi appeared on al-Nahar Television to describe an attack by a gang of men on her and one male and one female friend when they were participating in a strike in Cairo's Tahrir Square; she described her male friend being attacked and injured as he used his body to try to shield the women, and she drew hundreds of thousands of viewers to a greater awareness of the violence threatening women protesters.[1]

These female and male Egyptian activists have been responsible for critiquing the actions of the state, which has punished political protesters through acts of violence on women's bodies. For example, Samira Ibrahim sued the military for subjecting her to forced "virginity testing" after she was detained while protesting in Tahrir Square. This act of sexual violence and humiliation against female protesters by the military recall Razack's (2005, in Das 2008) analysis of the acts of torture committed by American soldiers against Muslim prisoners in Abu Ghraib, where "sexualized violence accomplishes the eviction of the tortured from humanity" (Das 2008, 290)—in Abu Ghraib, through "an eviction from masculinity" (ibid.) and in Egypt, through an attack on the female protesters' respectable femininity. After a military court exonerated the accused military officer, hundreds of protesters demonstrated in Cairo.[2] These protests and Ibrahim's brave legal battle against the Egyptian army led to an Egyptian court ruling banning "virginity testing." The case was brought to court in part through the efforts of several Egyptian human rights and legal aid organizations (Lindsey 2011). And since the revolution, several organizations of male and female volunteers formed to protect women protesters and journalists in Tahrir Square in the wake of dozens of sexual assaults.[3]

These male and female Egyptian activists have been responsible for speaking out against the daily sexual harassment faced by Egyptian women in the streets. For example, twenty-four-year-old male actor Waleed Hammad dressed up as a woman and walked in the street while a collaborator secretly filmed what men said to him to document and raise male awareness about sexual harassment.[4] A group of Egyptian men contributed to a powerful video published on YouTube in which they condemn sexual harassment and tell their peers, "*Kifaya!*" (Enough!, the slogan of the Egyptian Movement for Change, which was a powerful actor leading up to the 2011 revolution; the repeated use of the term *kifaya* thus equates their condemnation of sexual harassment with the goals of the democracy movement and likens men who harass to the corrupt military autocracy).[5]

In drawing public attention to these women's experiences of gender violence, these activists, female and male, prevent the victims from experiencing gender violence in isolation, they identify the cultural and political roots of the violence, and they bring it to national and international attention in their efforts to effect systemic reform. The irony is that international attention often translates these activists' efforts into fuel for the stereotypes that demonize Arab men (Amar 2011; Abu-Lughod 2013). A comment below an article in *al-Akhbar English*, for example, states, "Many Egyptian men simply think they have authority and are right. They are the bosses and can do no wrong. Its [*sic*] the women who keep the place running and do all the work. Gross generalisation, I know. But the tendency is there and can lead to other things" (comment to Kareem 2013).

What is striking is that this commentator (who identifies himself as "John X") can simultaneously recognize the gross generalization and yet embrace it ("the tendency is there"). Instead of saying, Look what a vibrant civil society of activists and reformers Egypt has! or Look at all these Egyptian women *and* men campaigning against gender violence!, he takes what activists make visible and reduces it to that tired old Orientalist trope of harem master. The work of the Egyptian male activists and feminists (as in the case of the male television broadcasters on al-Nahar or the male lawyers who argued Samira Ibrahim's court case pro bono or the many men who have contributed to anti-sexual-harassment campaigns) is magically erased and replaced with the generic image of the lazy Oriental despot.

The perverse result of Egyptian activism against sexual violence is to raise Western awareness of violence without, apparently, raising awareness of the work of activists.

In such an international economy of representations, how, then, might we proceed to examine structures that enable the oppression of women without creating a category of passive Egyptian women who are oppressed (thus missing the ways that women successfully defy male dominance and the ways that men refuse or fail to dominate)?

How do we examine sexual harassment and violence against women without letting them become "the 'essence' of an invented idea called 'Egyptian men'" (Kareem 2013)?

How can we understand a multiplicity of violences, ranging from the verbal harassment of women on the street to sexual assault at knifepoint, without rendering them as one monolithic concept of "male violence," yet still stay attuned to the power that the whole *assemblage* (Deleuze and Guattari 1987) of violences have to both discipline female behavior in Egypt *and* organize Western thinking about the Middle East?

And finally, how do we create a theoretical space where a woman who is forced to engage in sex against her will and still loves her boyfriend afterward makes sense without rendering her a dupe—that is, recognizing the intensity and complexity of those affective ties while also recognizing that she is fully in possession of the critical faculty to perceive and reject gender violence and hierarchies?

The solution is to document the complex ways that women and men relate to each other intimately, in both love and conflict, recognizing a range of strategies and tactics, in the de Certeauian sense (de Certeau 1984), that structure and resist gendered hierarchies of domination.

This entails recognizing the long history of feminism in Egypt (Abu-Lughod 1998; Al-Ali 2000; Badran 2009; Baron 1997; Bier 2011; Booth 1998), the contemporary activism of a vast range of indigenous Egyptian organizations that campaign for women's rights (Abu-Lughod 2010), and the individual women who vocally resist domination—that is, *strategies* that overtly confront gender violence, from the dispersed and low-level violence of verbal harassment on the streets to the state-sanctioned and brutal violence against women activists and political prisoners.

This also entails recognizing *tactics*: the ways that women navigate social expectations, cultural norms, and legal structures that penalize them for pre- and extramarital relationships of love and sex, the ways they manage to skirt the rules, often hiding their sexual activity and occasionally publicly embracing it, while nevertheless managing to claim the label of "respectable woman"—even if their definition of what constitutes a respectable woman differs vastly from the dominant social definition. These are subtle maneuvers and manipulations that do not confront dominant norms; rather, they subvert them (c.f. Rosaldo and Lamphere 1974; Ortner 1978; Strathern 1981).

It further means attending to other structures of social hierarchy, such as class and education and age and ethnicity, that crosscut gender hierarchies and enable women to dominate men, for a portrayal of Egypt in which men are always dominating women is laughably absurd.

In so doing, we must not waste our time looking to divide up Egypt into "good" and "bad" men or women; rather, we must discern how legal, political, economic, and social structures enable or discourage particular opportunities for domination. Through close ethnographic examination of the ways that men and women are bound in love and desire, we can bypass the temptation of constructing monodimensional heroes or villains and instead see complex men and women who both care for and constrain those they love. Also, instead of reducing an entire country or society to a single and simplistic label like "patriarchy," we can view social systems as complex *assemblages*, where at one moment the military can forcibly impose "virginity tests" as a punitive tool against women protesters and at another moment male and female activists can protest against this, leading to a state judge ruling virginity tests illegal.

And finally, we must look at the ways that men and women relate outside and beyond relationships of power, even as they are deeply embedded in them (Hage 2013). This means trying to appreciate how women love family members and boyfriends and husbands even if they chafe against the constraints of kinship and male authority, and how men love family members and girlfriends and wives even if they chafe against the heavy financial responsibilities (among other responsibilities) of caring for them. It means recognizing the depth and power of those affective ties and not reducing them to false consciousness.

Ultimately, we must proceed via a delicate balancing act. On the one hand (to return to the example of Sara), we can understand Sara's continuing love and desire for a man who subjects her to violence, humiliation, and, eventually, abandonment as a kind of "cruel optimism" that organizes her "relation of attachment to compromised conditions of possibility" (Berlant 2006, 21). In this view, desire appears to be a kind of pathology that nevertheless has its own internal logic. How else can we explain a love that persists in the face of violence and humiliation other than by recourse to a language of pathology? Even Sara, in retrospect, narrates the history of her love for Ali as a dystopia.

Yet a perspective on love and desire that reduces it to pathology, to relations of domination, to conflict, and to pain is grossly inadequate. It is inadequate for explaining not only the why of love and desire but also the emotional intensity, the giddiness, and the joy they offer. So we must also stay attuned to the way, for Sara (and the other women we've met in this ethnography), love and desire promise hope, offering a horizon of possibilities, "lines of flight" (Deleuze and Guattari 1987, 277), "a source of creativity that produces new optimism, new narratives of possibility, even erotic experimentality" (Berlant 2012, 43), and the promise to be able to reorganize worlds (ibid., 14).

In short, both of these perspectives—desire as pathology and cruel optimism; desire as joy and possibility—can teach us different, and useful, things about the ways that women and men are bound together in love and desire and in shared yet also contested cultural norms that render individuals "respectable" or not.

Fifteen Years Later

Much has been written about the value and limitations of ethnography, anthropology's methodology of long-term participant observation. Though the intensity and scale of the method mean that a single ethnographer can never gain access to enough people to be able to draw representative conclusions about an entire population, the depth and intimacy resulting from knowing a small group of people for many years give a more fine-grained portrait of lived culture at an individual level than could ever be gained by representative, quantitative surveys or even by other qualitative methods such as in-depth interviews and oral histories.

The portraits I have drawn here of people whom I have known for more than a decade do not represent all aspects of Egyptian culture. What they do illustrate is a range of the ways that men and women navigate love and sexuality in Egypt, constructing meaningful moral identities for themselves along the way. Yet when I first published an early formulation of chapter 6 in *American Sexuality* and *Alternet* in 2008, some readers reacted with hostility. A few online commentators indignantly asserted that what I wrote about was not "real Egypt," that I had gathered around me an exceptionally deviant, disreputable set of informants, that I had, in classic Orientalist fashion, focused only on deviance and on Arab sexuality, thus painting a distorted portrait of Egypt.

This argument assumes one of two possible methodological flaws in my approach. The first is that I coincidentally fell in with a group of Egyptian deviants and, because I knew too few Egyptians to be able to tell the difference between what is "normal" and what is not, I ended up accidentally portraying the "wrong" kind of Egyptians. Setting aside the moral argument implied in this critique, the methodologi-

cal assumption is false. I knew many dozens of Egyptians from all social classes, from poor slum dwellers to middle-class white-collar workers to some of the wealthiest businessmen in the country. I met them
through multiple points of contact: in the village next to the pyramids
or through the archaeologists I met through my dissertation fieldwork,
through contacts at the American University in Cairo and the University of Cairo, through old friends from Saudi Arabia who had families
in Egypt, or at hotels and markets where I was doing my research. Others I met without intermediaries (for example, while shopping or in my
neighborhood). Each point of contact branched out as I got to know
people's families and friends. To put it in more methodologically precise terms, I used snowball sampling from multiple starting points. It is
statistically unlikely that every starting point led only to a rare, anomalous subculture. Moreover, what I describe here is consistent with what
is written about the lives and loves of Egyptians by the great Egyptian
novelists, from Naguib Mahfouz to Alaa Al Aswany.

The second methodological critique is the possibility of selection
bias: that I allied myself with deviants and avoided mainstream Egyptian lives, or that I cherry-picked those stories to represent exceptions,
while avoiding describing more conventional lives. This is a more complex argument to consider. I have deliberately reproduced my arguments
about this with my ex-husband, and his own accusations of Orientalism,
to explore such a possibility. I was certainly intrigued by women whose
lives did not conform to the normative ideal of female sexuality. I also
selected a small number of people to write about from the many I knew.
Within the constraints of a single ethnography, I couldn't describe the
romantic lives of all my informants and portray them with the depth
and history that I aimed for.

All these facts are why critical anthropology of the past half century has explored bias in anthropological writing. The body of the anthropologist—the way she looks and acts, her gender and perceived social class, her religion, her nationality—all shape whom she knows, how
they perceive her, what she asks, and what people tell her. Postmodern-
ist and feminist anthropology understand this as a political fact. Phenomenological anthropology understands it as a perceptual and psychological fact: intersubjectivity, or the way that meaning is created by
individuals in their interaction with their environment (Csordas 1994;
Katz and Csordas 2003). This point is one of the core messages in chapter 4. It is why I have spent so much time presenting the anthropologist—myself—in this text, describing how what my informants told me

was shaped by their perceptions of me, my research interests, and my own relationship to love and desire. Portraying that is simultaneously a methodological and a political decision I have made in writing this ethnography.

Nevertheless, the fact that I was fascinated by women and men who deviated from normative ideals of sexuality does not mean that I only portrayed the most deviant of all my informants. Some of the people I portray had very normative monogamous relationships (Ayah and Zeid, for example). Meanwhile, some of the people I chose *not* to write about were far more "deviant" than those I focused on here. These included a housewife who had an affair with her daughter's fiancée; a television personality who fell in love with her dentist and his gentle hands over the course of several dental appointments, married him as his second wife, and then maneuvered to get him to divorce his first wife so she would have all his attention; a woman who worked in tourism who had an affair with her married boss who got her pregnant but refused to marry her; and Sara's cousin who is a sex worker.

If my portrayal of Egyptian lives looks so different from the respectable lives that these critics take to be "the norm," I would argue that there is far more sexual diversity in urban Egypt than this "norm" presupposes, and I have been able to describe intimate and sometimes deviant lives that are usually hidden behind the more respectable facades that most Egyptians present to the world. In other words, the assumption that there is a "respectable" norm is itself a selection bias.

There are two key explanations for why I was able to collect such intimate accounts of people's sexual lives and gather stories that most people hide so that they can present a respectable persona. First, people tell the foreign anthropologist things that they do not share with other Egyptians because they perceive non-Muslim foreigners to be less sexually inhibited and less judgmental about sexual deviance. They saw me as an outsider, less embedded in their social networks and thus less likely to reveal their secrets to those who would judge them. They also, hopefully, believed me when I assured them of confidentiality as a basic principle of ethical research practice. They knew that I would write about them, but that I would change names and disguise identities to protect them, and as I have noted, many participated collaboratively in that project.

Second, the length of time that I knew people and the degree of intimacy we shared allowed me to gather information about people's romantic and sexual lives that usually remains hidden behind the facade of respectability that most Egyptians work hard to maintain. This is apparent in my account of Sara, who took years to reveal her most painful, intimate secrets. It is one of the great benefits of long-term participant observation as a research method.

Setting aside the critiques of my own research practice, however, there are three key problems with this "exceptionalism" argument that dismisses nonnormative sexualities as not relevant to understanding contemporary urban Egyptian lives. First, it assumes that any practice that is not condoned by mainstream social mores—that is, any deviant behavior—is by definition not appropriate for anthropological analysis. But anthropologists have always been interested in subcultures and in minorities of various kinds, including sexual minorities. Just because a person is not statistically representative of the majority does not make his or her life irrelevant.

Second, this kind of exceptionalism, which dismisses people or social phenomena by portraying them as abnormal and deviant, seems to be particularly applied to women who do not subscribe to normative cultural ideals of female respectability. In this respect, the critique is part of the same phenomenon that I describe—namely, the silencing of women's loves and desires in favor of an account of a contained, socially unthreatening female sexuality.

And third, even if all the people I wrote about were quite exceptional, it would nevertheless still be the case that they lived their lives successfully in a particular sociocultural milieu and that they navigated the same norms as everyone else (including all those respectable, supposedly nonexceptional people that we might look for). The core insight of deviance studies is that deviance tells us as much about normative society as it does about the deviants themselves. Studying minority subcultures tell us a great deal about how they are contained by, and push back against, more dominant cultures. Defining deviation from the norm is inherently also a process of defining the norm; by describing people who carve out a life for themselves at the margins of marriage, we better understand the boundaries of marriage itself. And it is for that reason that, regardless of how typical or exceptional my informants may be, there is still much of anthropological value in examining their lives.

The value of an in-depth, ethnographic, longitudinal study that follows the same set of informants over time is that we see how events in their lives and relationships unfold (here represented in a simulacrum of real time and real, transcribed conversations, even though most of the conversations I described were reconstructed from memory several hours later, when I typed up my field notes), rather than capturing just one moment in time. The value of a longitudinal study—or, as one anonymous reviewer of this manuscript calls it, a "slow ethnography"—is that we also see how their interpretations of events and relationships change over time. In particular, we see how their emotions, the affective level of these interpretations, transform over time. One of the most striking things about Malak, for example, was the way her general cynicism about men repeatedly gave way to infatuated optimism as she fell in love again and again, and then turned back to cynicism as she was disappointed. If I had merely interviewed her at one point in time, I would have captured only one aspect of her attitude toward men, love, sex, and money. I would have seen her in only one relationship. But by talking to her over and over again for more than a decade, seeing her in the thrall of infatuation and falling in love and then out again, I can capture a much more nuanced view of how a woman navigates love and desire in turn-of-the-millennium Cairo.

While Malak's approach to love and desire changed cyclically, others' views seemed to fundamentally transform over time. They reinterpreted the past against the foil of the present, and the present against the past. Sometimes they changed their opinions; other times their views became more entrenched; in some cases, they stopped worrying and talking about things that previously had preoccupied them. (This was particularly true when several of my younger male informants got married and stopped worrying about the major cultural dilemma of finding a suitable spouse for life and thus stopped obsessively theorizing about female respectability.) Yet even as their opinions about the relationship between men and women transformed, what often remained the same was a shared set of concerns about what needed to be observed and interpreted: the nature of love, what constituted a respectable woman or decent man, how to negotiate desire within gendered cultural norms, the social constraints that people did or did not subscribe to, and external scrutiny from neighbors, friends, and family members.

The events described in the passages of ethnographic narrative mainly took place over a decade ago, but through the technological wonders of email and Facebook and Skype, I have kept in touch with most of the individuals described. I have visited them on yearly or twice-yearly return trips to Cairo from 2008 to 2014, congratulated them on marriages and births and divorces, given them copies of my first book in English and Arabic, and I have consulted with them over how to represent them in this book. Thanks to such technological wonders, it seems to me that there is no excuse to not make this consultation an ethical imperative in my writing,

The person whose story I was most reluctant to write about is Sara. In 2014, during a visit to Egypt, I discussed it with her in my typically fumbling fashion:

"You know I am writing a book," I told her (holding an audio recorder between us), "and I have been writing down notes about you for ten years. But this is the first time you've told me about these bad things that happened with these men. So I just want to make sure that you are comfortable that I write about them."

"Yes," she replied, "because there are many like me. And there are those who suffered more than me. For example, I didn't run away from home; there are others who could have made the mistake of running away from home. She could've worked here or there, worked in wrong places, worked as a belly dancer, did wrong things, stayed in furnished apartments [that is, worked as a prostitute]. So many people suffer more than me."

"That's why I feel that it is important that people hear your story. But I want to make sure that you are comfortable with the idea that I write about you and . . ."

Sara interrupted me. "Write about me, it's okay."

". . . And that no one knows who you are. So I will change some information, I will say that you work in . . ."

"Any field," she interrupted again. "Even if you say my real field, no one will know."

"But I will write about the time you spent in the hospital; what should I say you were in the hospital for?"

"You can tell the truth, that I was in for my leg."

"But if I say where you work and say that you were in the hospital for your leg, people will know who you are."

"No, they won't. No, no, no. No one will know."

"You think?" I said doubtfully. Then I brought up the bigger issue of the politics of representation.

"Imagine if there is an American or an Australian person who reads about the rape and the bad things that happened to you, what are they supposed to get out of this story? What kind of idea will they have about the life of an Egyptian woman?"

"By God, women here suffer a lot. A woman suffers from her childhood until she gets married."

"But honestly," I said to her, "I am a little scared to write about the rape because there will be people in the West who will say, 'See, the men in the Middle East are bad people, and they control women,' and so on. And I don't want to help fuel this kind of talk. Because for example, the American government when they invaded Afghanistan and Iraq, they said it's because we want to save the women."

"In Iraq they used to rape men," Sara interjected. "In prisons they used to rape men," she added.

"But what I mean," I attempted to clarify after a confused pause, "is the American government tells the American people that 'we are protecting the women in the Middle East. That's why we have to invade . . .'"

"No, no, no," she said, dismissing my concerns.

"But people do say that," I insisted, "so I am worried if I write about the rape in my book, people will say that men in the Arab world are bad and control women. . . ." When she continued to make faces, indicating that she didn't think much of my worries, I asked, "Aren't you worried about what people in the West will say?"

"You mean talk about us? Why? What will they say? The whole world is talking about us anyway. That we are savages. Savage people. Uncivilized. And truly we are savages."

Sara was adamant that I should share her story. She had experienced brutality and hidden it for years. Once she decided to talk about it, she didn't want to suppress it anymore.

I had similar conversations with most of the other people I have written about here. I made a draft of this book available to them in English, and I used grant funding from the Australian Research Council to have the manuscript translated into Arabic by Metalingual (a superb academic translation company) to ensure that everyone could fully understand what I had written. I told them that if there was anything I had written about them that they wanted me to cut from the book, or if they wanted me to change anything in order to better protect their identities, I would happily comply. Astonishingly, no one requested any changes.

Consultation, however, does not imply that any one character in this book agrees with all that I have written. For all I know, they might have decided my academic prose was too boring and stopped reading it before finishing. All the usual caveats apply about the author taking ultimate responsibility for interpretation and any mistakes. I am incredibly grateful to all those friends who agreed to let me portray their private lives.

As a final postscript, I want to conclude by revisiting all the characters in this book and catching up with their lives.

Sara

Sara remained in that grim public hospital for months and months, through several operations, iatrogenic infections, and a transfusion of the wrong blood type, which nearly killed her.

Sara and Ali broke up long ago. After that, she dated a few men that she met in Ammoula, briefly married and divorced a cousin, and then spent five years in a relationship with Hassan, a married man. Hassan kept promising to marry her as his second wife. Each time I visited Cairo over the five years they were together, Sara would catch me up on the state of their relationship. She would tell me that Hassan was going to marry her on the next feast day (*'eid*). I would come back six months later and she would tell me that they still hadn't married. "Next feast," she would say.

Hassan was unwilling to tell his wife and his father about his engagement to Sara because his father, who controlled his son through the salary he paid him for working in the family business, would cut him off financially if he knew. (His wife is a cousin on the paternal side, so his father's loyalty was to Hassan's wife.) And he kept claiming he didn't have enough money to marry Sara. During this period, Sara went heavily into debt to help Hassan financially, giving him money to pay his rent and to buy gifts and medical care for his daughter. Every year, I warned her that he was using her, that as long as she kept giving him money, he would keep stringing her along but never marry her. She disagreed. "He loves me," she said stubbornly. When I asked her how she knew that, she said, "I can just tell. It's not about money, *ya* Lisa. Nobody is truly supportive [*gada'a*] these days. Every woman wants a man's money, but if a woman stands by her man during the hard times, he'll remember that."

Sara convinced Hassan that she was a virgin. He knew she had been married to a cousin, but she told him the marriage was never consummated, and she never told him a thing about any of her other past relationships. For the first four years, the only physical intimacy they shared was holding hands and one kiss. She was determined not to sleep with him because she wanted to marry him. "Believe me, Lisa," she said, "if you have sex with an Egyptian man before marriage, he will never ever marry you." She planned to have hymenoplasty surgery before they got married to appear to be a virgin.

I kept visiting Cairo twice a year. She was never married, and every month or so I had to send money to help pull her out of debt. She didn't make enough to support herself and Hassan's family too.

Then a few events happened that changed everything. Hassan's wife got pregnant and had another baby. Sara was furious and depressed because, with another child to support, Hassan would never have enough money to marry her. She stopped giving him money. Hassan was angry with his wife (who had secretly gone off contraception to get pregnant) and for months refused to register the baby's birth under his name.

Then one night Sara and Hassan had sex in the shop where he worked, after his father had gone home for the night.

"Will he still marry you?" I asked her when she told me. She said he would, but she didn't sound very certain. If he didn't, she said, she would douse herself in gasoline and set herself on fire outside his shop. It would shame him, and he would have to live for the rest of his life with the guilt.

I don't think such a thing would have occurred to her before she encountered the media coverage of the Tunisian man who had set himself on fire to protest his treatment at the hands of police, triggering a wave of revolutions across the Arab world (the so-called Arab Spring). In Egypt too, several individuals set themselves on fire in protest (Amar 2011, 300). Previously Sara's fantasies of suicide-revenge had revolved around dosing both herself and Hassan with rat poison.

Not long before the political demonstrations that led to the July 2013 army coup against the Muslim Brotherhood presidency, Hassan and Sara broke up, leaving her deeply depressed. Now in her late thirties, she doesn't think there is time to find someone else to marry her and still be young enough to have children. Having children is her desperate, and now seemingly impossible, goal. In 2013 Sara started participating regularly in the mass demonstrations in Tahrir Square. Previously she had been afraid to participate in political demonstrations (which have resulted in a number of deaths, injuries, and rapes), but in 2013 she did so with a kind of suicidal nonchalance that emerged from the hopelessness generated by the intersection of her failed love life and her desperate financial situation (because the antiques business was hit hard by the economic downturn in the wake of the 2011 revolution). "If I die, remember me always because I really love you, Lisa" she said in one email, and then in another, in response to my expressions of alarm and concern, she said, "I've decided to live alone [that is, without Hassan], and I'm going to go to Tahrir tomorrow [to join the demonstration]. I'll be fine, and if I die, no biggie" (". . . *wa lau hamut, 'adi giddan*").

Again and again we see how Sara's love life intertwines with political events in the region, from her adoption of Facebook at the start of the Egyptian revolution to her suicide fantasy to her participation in the Tahrir demonstrations with the vague idea that, one way or another—whether it resulted in political change or death—it would be a distraction from her failed love life.

She didn't die. In November 2013, she asked me to send her money to help pay for an abortion. In January 2014, she wrote to me, "I met someone new. He knows about my previous relationship with Hassan and I'm with him now and I started the relationship with him for the sake of money. I've become just like my cousin; I sell myself for the sake of money, and nothing matters to me now after the story of my failure with Hassan. I'm exactly like my cousin now; there's nothing to differentiate us. I exist. I don't want my heart to be broken again." For Sara, the decision marked a major turning point in her corporeal and affective experience of love and desire, a search for intimacy and financial security amid the failure of love and the unreliability of men, the embracing of her status as a not-respectable woman who can no longer hope for marriage and children but who can at least enjoy intimacy, companionship, and gifts from a man.

On February 14, 2014, she posted this status update to her Facebook page: "Happy Valentine's Day . . . if there's such a thing as love, anyway" (*"Kulli hubb wa intum tayyibeen . . . da lau kan fi hubb aslan"*).

Ayah and Zeid

Ayah and Zeid are now married and have three children. Ayah fully inhabits the role of respectable wife, cooking Zeid dinner every night (when they met, she scarcely knew how to cook at all) and taking primary responsibility for the children. Zeid now plays the role of provider-husband and proud father with the same air of ironic detachment that he applies to everything and everyone he loves. He still complains about how "hectic" it is at work and that he is too tired and too broke to go out at night, but now Ayah is just as tired as he is. He tells her exactly how much money is in their bank account and gives her a debit card so she can take money out herself, rather than giving her a fixed household allowance, and he tells me that he is unique among his friends in this regard. It is a canny solution to their previous arguing about money, because now that they are part of a shared household economy, she feels just as broke as he does.

More than anything, it is the kids that stop them from going out now, so they no longer argue about Zeid wearing sandals. Zeid doesn't provide Ayah with much relief from the toils of child rearing. When I visited Cairo after their first child was born, I took Ayah out for dinner alone and Zeid stayed home to babysit. She wouldn't leave until after she had put the baby to sleep herself because Zeid, she laughed, was a complete disaster when it comes to taking care of children. She then recounted a very funny story about going out once for lunch with some relatives, leaving Zeid in charge. When she got back, she found their baby asleep on a cushion, half naked and soaked in urine. The rest of the house was a complete disaster and there was shit smeared all over the bathroom.

Actually, it doesn't sound that funny when I write it, but Ayah is a master storyteller and when she told me, she had me in stitches.

Despite his short temper, their bickering, and his uselessness at domestic chores, they are still in love, and Ayah remains convinced that Zeid isn't a cheater, unlike so many of the other men she has known through relatives and friends, partly because of his love for her but also because he fears God's punishment. He has become deeply religious. He talks to me sometimes about his religious passion, but he is never preachy or proselytizing. He does, however, like to cheerfully speculate about who is going to go to hell (in a word: politicians).

Kerim

After one failed engagement and after dating several glamorous women whom he affectionately cared for but jokingly called "prostitutes" and after insisting he would never marry, Kerim finally got engaged. Before I met his fiancée, he warned me over the phone that she wasn't the gorgeous blond type that he had always aspired to marrying, but she was a nice, respectable woman. I couldn't tell whether he was expressing his own disappointment over settling or trying to brace me for a really homely fiancée. Thus I was surprised to be introduced to a quite attractive and glamorous (if not blonde) woman, who is indeed very nice and respectable.

These days, Kerim seems much less interested in evaluating every woman he sees and determining whether she is a "case study" or not. That was the obsession of a particular time in his life, when he was on the marriage market and much was at stake as he tried to hone his individual tastes and cultural sense for what constituted a good marriage partner. Now he and his wife have children, and he is more worried about the state of the economy in Egypt and how to support a family on his meager salary. He drives home in Cairo's miserable traffic congestion after a long day of work and tries to give his tired wife some relief from the children in the evening (he is much more conscientious about helping his wife around the house than Zeid is), and when they go out together, it is to an outdoor café in Mohandiseen, taking the children along. The nightclub scene, he declares, is dead in Cairo. (Of course it thrives, but it is dead to him and his cohort as they have married and had children and no longer have the energy or the inclination to stay out until two in the morning.)

George and Nesma

George left the antiques shop and works in a telecommunications company. The last time I saw him I almost did not recognize him because I was looking for a skinny man with hair on his head. He attributes his new girth to the comforts of marriage.

Nesma also left the shop and has started her own business in silver jewelry. She was successful for a time but then lost her money to a lover who had a cocaine addiction and sold off her stock to fund his habit. She is still recovering financially from the theft and emotionally from the betrayal.

Malak

Malak taught belly dance in Egypt for another decade before returning to Europe amid the economic uncertainties that followed the January 25 Revolution. Some of the dancers she introduced me to are still in Cairo; others have moved back to Europe, Australia, or the Americas. Many of the foreign dancers can no longer perform on stage in Cairo because the law was changed to make it more difficult for foreign dancers to obtain work visas. The change in law is said to be the result of one politician's determined effort to clear the field for a new generation of Egyptian belly dancers, who were being pushed out of the field by the hoards of aspiring foreign dancers trying to make it big in Egypt. Now foreign dancers can only get permission to work in Cairo if they have exceptionally good *wasta* (political influence) or if they are dancing in coastal resort towns such as Hurghada or Sharm El-Sheikh, where Egyptian dancers rarely perform. But there is a steady stream of foreigners coming to Cairo who want to learn to dance, and several foreign expatriates make a living teaching belly dance to these tourists.

Malak is more financially independent than she was fifteen years ago, but for as long as she was in Cairo, she still relied on men to take her out at night, which helped her stay on top of the belly-dance scene in Cairo. She has cycled in and out of relationships, still looking for love and companionship, but she is serially disappointed by the men she dates. She has finished her master's degree and still reads voraciously. I remain completely in awe of her wit, her gentle beauty, and her analytical mind.

Alia and Haroun

After more than ten years together and many gifts of jewelry and a new car, which Haroun gave Alia when her old car started giving her trouble ("I don't want to have to worry about her breaking down on the road alone while she's driving home from work," he told me; "I can't rest thinking about what might happen to her"), Alia and Haroun broke up several years ago. She caught him in the act of cheating on her one evening. He had told her he would be at a business meeting, but she found his car parked on the street in front of his *wakr*. Alia recounts the discovery grimly, as though every minute of that evening will be etched on her memory forever. For a brief moment of fury, she seriously considered calling Haroun's wife and telling her exactly where to find him and the "low-class prostitute" he was sleeping with, because there would be no graver punishment for Haroun than to be caught cheating again by his wife. But somehow at the last minute Alia restrained herself, sensing that to do so would be seen by Haroun as the ultimate betrayal and would mean the end of their friendship forever.

Malak tells me that Haroun stopped hosting his wild parties when he decided to run for political office on an anticorruption platform, which still makes me chuckle because I remember one evening when he cynically explained to me how he does business in Egypt: "You meet a politician and with one hand, you shake his hand over the table and tell him how much you respect his honesty and lack of corruption, while with your other hand you pass him a sack of money under the table." But Haroun is still best friends with belly-dancer-loving Farouq, so Malak thinks it unlikely that he has become entirely chaste, just that he has had to be more discreet than ever before about his (literally) underground lifestyle and his links with Cairo's demimonde.

Farouq and Alia remain friends, and through Farouq, Alia and Haroun keep distant tabs on each other. Now in her late forties, Alia remains a strikingly beautiful woman. Sometimes she entertains a vague hope that one day she and Haroun will reunite. They were clearly, she says, fated to be together. Fate notwithstanding, she still has a lively social life, going out to the hottest current bars and restaurants late at night after work with her banker colleagues, most of whom are men. Yet she claims to have not had any sexual relationship with any man since Haroun. Perhaps she hopes that story will get back to Haroun and convince him of her undying commitment to him. Perhaps her love for Haroun was so life-changing that she can never love or desire another.

Nellie and Ahmed

Nellie and Ahmed, the couple whose future Ayah doubted because Ahmed showed no signs of controlling jealousy, are now married and have children. Nobody comments on Ahmed's lack of jealousy any more, proving that jealousy is not proof of love for all Egyptians.

Notes

Chapter 6

1. Portions of this chapter's analysis, and some of the ethnographic narrative in chapters 1 and 3, previously appeared in *American Sexuality Magazine* (Wynn 2008a).

2. There is a small but growing body of research on *'urfi* marriages in Egypt: see Abaza 2001; Singerman and Ibrahim 2003; El-Tawila and Khedr 2004; Rashad, Osman, and Roudi-Fahimi 2005; Hasso 2010; Salem 2011; and Wynn 2016. Another interesting point of comparison for paramarital relationships in the region is the Iranian "temporary" (*muta'a* or *sigha*) marriage (I thank an anonymous reviewer for this insight). Rania Salem (2011, 2) notes, "Popular concern with the high cost of marriage has found expression in Egyptian culture since the 1920s (Kholoussy 2010a). Today, references to the social repercussions of high marriage costs appear frequently in television dramas, movies, novels, and newspaper articles. Some commentators in the Egyptian media have characterized young people's inability to marry in a timely manner a 'marriage crisis' (Rashed 2006). Mosque sermons often denounce the materialism and ostentation of high marriage expenditures, but at the same time maintain that unions must conform to the *shari'a*'s requirement of cash gifts to the bride." For more on the cultural and economic issues associated with marriage in Egypt, see Singerman 1995; Hoodfar 1997; and Singerman and Ibrahim 2003 in addition to Salem's (2011) dissertation.

Chapter 8

1. It is also very late in the book that Lévi-Strauss (1969, 489) mentions love: "Marriage is thus a dramatic encounter between nature and culture, between alliance and kinship. . . . Thus, marriage is an arbitration between two loves, parental and conjugal. Nevertheless, they are both forms of love, and the instant the marriage takes place, considered in isolation, the two meet and merge."

2. The anthropology of kinship literature is vast. A few key publications are those of David Schneider (1984), who reevaluates his (and others') earlier approaches to kinship, reconsidering the centrality of sexual procreation in American kinship systems and showing how its dominance in the anthropology of kinship is the product of Eurocentric cultural assumptions; Adam Kuper (1988), who writes the history of kinship studies in anthropology since the eighteenth century; Michael Peletz (1995), who reviews the changes in kinship studies since the 1970s; Kath Weston (1997), who looks at gay and lesbian kinship; Marilyn Strathern (1992) and Faye Ginsburg and Rayna Rapp (1995), who were among the earliest anthropologists to address the implications of new reproductive technologies for kinship theory (see also Inhorn and Birenbaum-Carmeli 2008 for a recent review of this literature); and Janet Carsten (2000), who crucially argued that kinship studies need to take into account emic perspectives on relatedness. Some of the key researchers examining reproductive health technologies and kinship in the Middle East are Marcia Inhorn (1996, 2003, 2006), Susan Kahn (2000), Morgan Clarke (2009), and Angel Foster (2016).

3. For those who would like to sample the genre, *Beyond Heaving Bosoms* is Sarah Wendell and Candy Tan's (2009) critical but enthusiastic introduction to the evolution of the romance novel, and a couple of anthropologists who write historical romances are Elizabeth Hoyt (e.g., *The Raven Prince*, 2006) and Meredith Duran (e.g., *The Duke of Shadows*, 2010).

Chapter 9

1. At http://www.youtube.com/watch?v=WvBPvIjg8xI (in Arabic), accessed May 30, 2013; site discontinued.

2. "Egyptians Protest 'Virginity Test' Acquittal," *Daily Beast*, accessed May 30, 2013, http://www.thedailybeast.com/cheats/2012/03/16/egytians-pro test-virginity-test-acquittal.html.

3. For images of 2013 efforts to form a protective human shield around female protesters in Tahrir Square, see Hall 2013. Egyptian volunteer organizations that work against sexual harassment during demonstrations include Operation Anti-Sexual Harassment (Quwwa Didd al-Taharrush, @OpAntiSH) and Egypt's Girls Are a Red Line (Banat Misr Khatt Ahmar). For a powerful feminist analysis of the violence against women in Tahrir Square by Egyptian organizations, see "Brutal Sexual Assaults in the Vicinity of Tahrir Square and an Unprecedentedly Shameful Reaction from the Egyptian Authorities: 101 Incidents of Sexual Assaults during the Events of June 30th 2013," a joint statement issued on July 3, 2013, by seven organizations: Nazra for Feminist Studies, Egyptian Initiative for Personal Rights, El Nadeem Center for Rehabilitation of Victims of Violence, New Woman Foundation, Operation Anti-Sexual Harassment, Tahrir Bodyguard, and Women and Memory Forum, accessed July 3, 2013, http://nazra.org/en/node/244.

4. Arwa Gaballa, "Man Dresses as Woman to Experience Egypt's Sexual harassment," *Aswat Masriya*, May 6, 2013, accessed May 30, 2013, http://

en.aswatmasriya.com/news/view.aspx?id=01cb45cf-e7ea-49e0-9a10-9a03bc32 b3db (in Arabic).

5. "What Men Say to Men Who Harass Women on the Streets," YouTube video, June 13, 2012, Arabic with English subtitles, accessed May 30, 2013, http://www.youtube.com/watch?v=72RGtkwRMqU.

References

Abaza, Mona. 2001. "Perceptions of 'Urfi Marriage in the Egyptian Press." Institute for the Study of Islam in the Modern World (ISIM) newsletter 7, no. 1: 20–21.

Abdel-Malek, Anouar. 1963. "Orientalism in Crisis." *Diogenes* 11: 103–140.

Abu-Lughod, Lila. 1986. *Veiled Sentiments: Honor and Poetry in a Bedouin Society*. Berkeley, Los Angeles: University of California Press.

———. 1990. "The Romance of Resistance: Tracing Transformations of Power through Bedouin Women." *American Ethnologist* 17, no. 1: 41–55.

———. 1991. "Writing against Culture." In *Recapturing Anthropology: Working in the Present*, ed. Richard Fox, 137–162. Santa Fe, NM: School of American Research.

———. 1993. *Writing Women's Worlds*. Berkeley, Los Angeles: University of California Press.

———, ed. 1998. *Remaking Women: Feminism and Modernity in the Middle East*. Princeton: Princeton Studies in Culture/Power/History, Princeton University Press.

———. 2005. *Dramas of Nationhood: The Politics of Television in Egypt*. Chicago: University of Chicago Press.

———. 2010. "The Active Social Life of 'Muslim Women's Rights': A Plea for Ethnography, Not Polemic, with Cases from Egypt and Palestine." *Journal of Middle East Women's Studies* 6, no. 1: 1–45.

———. 2013. *Do Muslim Women Need Saving?* Cambridge, MA: Harvard University Press.

Abu-Odeh, Lama. 1997. "Comparatively Speaking: The 'Honor' of the 'East' and the 'Passion' of the 'West.'" *Utah Legal Review* 2: 287–307.

Abu-Zeid, A. 1965. "Honour and Shame among the Bedouins of Egypt." In *Honour and Shame*, ed. Jean G. Peristiany, 243–260. London: Weidenfeld and Nicolson.

Adams, Vincanne. 1996. *Tigers of the Snow and Other Virtual Sherpas: An Ethnography of Himalayan Encounters*. Princeton: Princeton University Press.

Al-Ali, Nadje S. 2000. *Secularism, Gender and the State in the Middle East: The Egyptian Women's Movement*. Cambridge: Cambridge University Press.

Alloula, Malek. 1986. *The Colonial Harem*. Translation by Myrna Godzich and Wlad Godzich. Introduction by Barbara Harlow. Minneapolis: University of Minnesota Press.

Amar, Paul. 2011. "Turning the Gendered Politics of the Security State Inside Out?" *International Feminist Journal of Politics* 13, no. 3: 299–328.

Appadurai, Arjun. 1997. "Discussion: Fieldwork in the Era of Globalization." *Anthropology and Humanism* 22(1): 115–118.

Aristotle. 1917. *Poetics*. Edited with critical notes and a translation by S. H. Butcher. London: Macmillan.

Armbrust, Walter. 1996. *Mass Culture and Modernism in Egypt*. Cambridge: Cambridge University Press.

Auerbach, Erich. 1953. *Mimesis: The Representation of Reality in Western Literature*. Princeton: Princeton University Press.

Badran, Margot. 2009. *Feminism in Islam: Secular and Religious Convergences*. Oxford: Oneworld Publications.

Baron, Beth. 1997. *The Women's Awakening in Egypt: Culture, Society, and the Press*. New Haven: Yale University Press.

Baudrillard, Jean. 1984. "The Precession of Simulacra." In *Art after Modernism: Rethinking Representation*, ed. Brian Wallis, 253–281. New York: New Museum.

———. 1988. "Simulacra and Simulations." In *Jean Baudrillard, Selected Writings*, ed. Mark Poster, 166–184. Palo Alto, CA: Stanford University Press.

Beatty, Andrew. 2005. "Emotions in the Field: What Are We Talking About?" *Journal of the Royal Anthropological Institute* 11: 17–37.

Benjamin, Walter. 1968. "The Work of Art in the Age of Mechanical Reproduction." In *Illuminations: Essays and Reflections*, ed. Hannah Arendt, 217–251. New York: Schochen Books.

———. 1978. "On the Mimetic Faculty." In *Reflections: Essays, Aphorisms, Autobiographical Writings*, ed. Peter Demetz, 333–336. New York: Schochen Books.

Berlant, Lauren. 2006. "Cruel Optimism." *Differences* 17, no. 5: 21–36.

———. 2012. *Desire/Love*. Brooklyn, NY: punctum books.

Bernstein, Elizabeth. 2013. *Temporarily Yours: Intimacy, Authenticity, and the Commerce of Sex*. Chicago, London: University of Chicago Press.

Besnier, Niko. 2009. *Gossip and the Everyday Production of Politics*. Honolulu: University of Hawai'i Press.

Bhabha, Homi K. 1994. *The Location of Culture*. London, New York: Routledge.

Biddle, Jennifer. 1993. "The Anthropologist's Body, or What It Means to Break Your Neck in the Field." *The Australian Journal of Anthropology* 4, no. 3: 184–197.

Biehl, João. 1995. *Vita: Life in a Zone of Social Abandonment*. Berkeley, Los Angeles: University of California Press.

Biehl, João, Byron Good, and Arthur Kleinman, eds. 2007. *Subjectivity: Ethnographic Investigations*. Berkeley, Los Angeles: University of California Press.

Biehl, João, and Peter Locke. 2010. "Deleuze and the Anthropology of Becoming." *Current Anthropology* 51, no. 3: 317–349.

Bier, Laura. 2011. *Revolutionary Womanhood: Feminisms, Modernity, and the State in Nasser's Egypt*. Stanford: Stanford University Press.

Boon, James. 1999. *Verging on Extra-Vagance: Anthropology, History, Religion, Literature, Arts . . . Showbiz*. Princeton: Princeton University Press.

Booth, Marilyn. 1998. "The Egyptian Lives of Jeanne d'Arc." In *Remaking Women: Feminism and Modernity in the Middle East*, ed. Lila Abu Lughod, 171–211. Princeton: Princeton University Press.

Borneman, John, and Abdellah Hammoudi. 2009. *Being There: The Fieldwork Encounter and the Making of Truth*. Berkeley, Los Angeles: University of California Press.

Bourdieu, Pierre. 1977. *Outline of a Theory of Practice*. Translation by Richard Nice. Cambridge: Cambridge University Press.

Bourgois, Philippe. 1995. *In Search of Respect: Selling Crack in El Barrio*. Cambridge: Cambridge University Press.

Bowman, Glenn. 1989. "Fucking Tourists: Sexual Relations and Tourism in Jerusalem's Old City." *Critique of Anthropology* 9, no. 2: 77–93.

Brennan, Denise. 2004. *What's Love Got to Do with It? Transnational Desires and Sex Tourism in the Dominican Republic*. Durham, NC: Duke University Press.

Briggs, Jean. 1970. *Never in Anger: Portrait of an Eskimo Family*. Cambridge, MA: Harvard University Press.

Bruner, Edward. 2004. *Culture on Tour: Ethnographies of Travel*. Chicago: University of Chicago Press.

Burnham, Gilbert, Riyadh Lafta, Shannon Doocy, and Les Roberts. 2006. "Mortality after the 2003 Invasion of Iraq: A Cross-Sectional Cluster Sample Survey." *Lancet* 368: 1421–1428.

Butler, Judith. 1999. *Gender Trouble: Feminism and the Subversion of Identity*. London, New York: Routledge.

Cahn, Michael. 1984. "Subversive Mimesis: Theodor Adorno and the Modern Impasse of Critique." In *Mimesis in Contemporary Theory*, ed. Mihai Spariosu, 27–64. Amsterdam: John Benjamins.

Carsten, Janet, ed. 2000. *Cultures of Relatedness: New Approaches to the Study of Kinship*. Cambridge: Cambridge University Press.

Cerwonka, Allaine, and Liisa Malkki. 2007. *Improvising Theory: Process and Temporality in Ethnographic Fieldwork*. Chicago: University of Chicago Press.

Clancy, Kathryn B. H., Robin G. Nelson, Julienne N. Rutherford, and Katie Hinde. 2014. "Survey of Academic Field Experiences (SAFE): Trainees Report Harassment and Assault." *PLOS One* 9, no. 7. https://doi.org/10.1371/journal.pone.0102172.

Clarke, Morgan. 2009. *Islam and the New Kinship: Reproductive Technology and the Shariah in Lebanon*. New York, Oxford: Berghahn Books.

Clifford, James. 1997. *Routes, Travel and Translation in the Late Twentieth Century*. Cambridge, MA: Harvard University Press.

Clifford, James, and George Marcus. 1986. *Writing Culture: The Poetics and Politics of Ethnography*. Berkeley, Los Angeles: University of California Press.

Coffey, Amanda. 1999. *The Ethnographic Self: Fieldwork and the Representation of Identity*. London: Sage.

Cole, Jennifer. 2009. "Love, Money, and Economies of Intimacy in Tamatave, Madagascar." In *Love in Africa*, ed. Jennifer Cole and Lynn M. Thomas, 105–134. Chicago: University of Chicago Press.

Comaroff, John L., and Jean Comaroff. 2009. *Ethnicity Inc.* Chicago: University of Chicago Press.

Connell, R. W. 1995. *Masculinities*. Berkeley, Los Angeles: University of California Press.

Connell, R. W., and James W. Messerschmidt. 2005. "Hegemonic Masculinity: Rethinking the Concept." *Gender and Society* 19, no. 6: 829–859.

Crick, Malcolm. 1985. "'Tracing' the Anthropological Self: Quizzical Reflections on Field Work, Tourism, and the Ludic." *Social Analysis: The International Journal of Social and Cultural Practice* 17: 71–92.

Csordas, Thomas J. 1994. *The Sacred Self: A Cultural Phenomenology of Charismatic Healing*. Berkeley, Los Angeles: University of California Press.

Culler, Jonathan. 1981. "The Semiotics of Tourism." *American Journal of Semiotics* 1, no. 1: 127–140.

Das, Veena. 2007. *Life and Words: Violence and the Descent into the Ordinary*. Berkeley, Los Angeles: University of California Press.

———. 2008. "Violence, Gender, and Subjectivity." *Annual Review of Anthropology* 37: 283–299.

Davis, John. 1977. *People of the Mediterranean*. London: Routledge.

de Certeau, Michel. 1984. *The Practice of Everyday Life*. Translation by Steven Rendall. Berkeley, Los Angeles: University of California Press.

Delaney, Carol. 1987. "Seeds of Honor, Fields of Shame." In *Honor and Shame and the Unity of the Mediterranean*, ed. David Gilmore, 35–48. American Anthropological Association special publication 22. Washington, DC: American Anthropological Association.

Deleuze, Gilles. 2006. *Two Regimes of Madness: Texts and Interviews 1975–1995*. Los Angeles: Semiotext(e).

Deleuze, Gilles, and Felix Guattari. 1987. *A Thousand Plateaus: Capitalism and Schizophrenia*. Translation by Brian Massumi. Minneapolis: University of Minnesota Press.

Desjarlais, Robert, and Jason Throop. 2011. "Phenomenological Approaches in Anthropology." *Annual Review of Anthropology* 40: 87–102.

Douglas, Mary, and Baron Isherwood. 1979. *The World of Goods*. New York: Basic Books.

Dunne, Bruce. 1996. "Sexuality and the 'Civilizing Process' in Modern Egypt." PhD diss., Georgetown University.

Duran, Meredith. 2010. *The Duke of Shadows*. New York: Simon and Schuster.

Eltahawy, Mona. 2012. "Why Do They Hate Us? The Real War on Women Is in the Middle East." *Foreign Policy*, April 23. Accessed September 22, 2017. http://foreignpolicy.com/2012/04/23/why-do-they-hate-us/.

Errazzouki, Samia. 2012. "Dear Mona Eltahawy, You Do Not Represent 'Us.'" *Al-Monitor*, April 24. Accessed September 22, 2017. http://www.al-monitor .com/pulse/originals/2012/al-monitor/dear-mona-eltahawy-you-do-not-re .html.

Fahmy, Khaled. 2002. "Prostitution in Egypt in the Nineteenth Century." In *Outside In: Marginality in the Modern Middle East*, ed. Eugene Rogan, 77–103. London: I. B. Tauris.

Faier, Lieba. 2007. "Filipina Migrants in Rural Japan and Their Professions of Love." *American Ethnologist* 34, no. 1: 148–162.

Fassin, Didier, Frédéric Le Marcis, and Todd Lethata. 2008. "Life and Times of Magda A: Telling a Story of Violence in South Africa." *Current Anthropology* 49, no. 2: 225–246.

Fekete, Liz. 2006. "Enlightened Fundamentalism? Immigration, Feminism and the Right." *Race and Class* 48, no. 2: 1–22.

Ferguson, James G. 2002. "Of Mimicry and Membership: Africans and the 'New World Society.'" *Cultural Anthropology* 17, no. 4: 551–569.

Flaubert, Gustave. 1996. *Flaubert in Egypt: A Sensibility on Tour.* Translation by Francis Steegmuller. New York: Penguin Classics.

Foster, Angel M. 2016. "Mifepristone in Tunisia: A Model for Expanding Access to Medication Abortion." In *Abortion Pills, Test Tube Babies, and Sex Toys: Emerging Sexual and Reproductive Health Technologies in the Middle East and North Africa*, ed. L. L. Wynn and Angel M. Foster, 44–57. Nashville, TN: Vanderbilt University Press.

Foster, Angel M., and L. L. Wynn. 2016. "Sexuality, Reproductive Health, and Medical Technologies in the Middle East and North Africa." In *Abortion Pills, Test Tube Babies, and Sex Toys: Emerging Sexual and Reproductive Health Technologies in the Middle East and North Africa*, ed. L. L. Wynn and Angel M. Foster, 1–12. Nashville, TN: Vanderbilt University Press.

Frohlick, Susan. 2013. *Sexuality, Women, and Tourism: Cross-Border Desires through Contemporary Travel.* New York, London: Routledge.

Gebauer, Gunter, and Christoph Wulf. 1995. *Mimesis: Culture, Art, Society.* Translation by Don Reneau. Berkeley, Los Angeles: University of California Press.

Gerstenzang, James, and Lisa Getter. 2001. "Laura Bush Addresses State of Afghan Women." *Los Angeles Times*, November 18. Accessed September 22, 2017. http://articles.latimes.com/2001/nov/18/news/mn-5602.

Ghannam, Farha. 2013. *Live and Die Like a Man: Gender Dynamics in Urban Egypt.* Stanford: Stanford University Press.

Giddens, Anthony. 1992. *The Transformation of Intimacy: Sexuality, Love and Eroticism.* Cambridge: Polity Press.

Gieryn, Thomas F. 1983. "Boundary-Work and the Demarcation of Science from Non-science: Strains and Interests in Professional Ideologies of Scientists." *American Sociological Review* 48, no. 6: 781–795.

Gilmore, David D. 1987. "Introduction: The Shame of Dishonor." In *Honor and Shame and the Unity of the Mediterranean*, ed. David Gilmore, 2–21. American Anthropological Association special publication 22. Washington, DC: American Anthropological Association.

Ginsburg, Faye, and Rayna Rapp. 1995. *Conceiving the New World Order: The Global Politics of Reproduction.* Berkeley, Los Angeles: University of California Press.

Gluckman, Max. 1963. "Gossip and Scandal." *Current Anthropology* 4, no. 3: 307–316.

Goffman, Erving. 1959. *The Presentation of Self in Everyday Life.* Garden City, NY: Doubleday.

Golde, Peggy. 1986. "Odyssey of Encounter." In *Women in the Field: Anthropo-*

logical Experiences, ed. P. Golde, 67–96. Berkeley, Los Angeles: University of California Press.

Haddon, Malcolm. 2003. "The Nectar of Translation: Conversion, Mimesis, and Cultural Translation in Krishna Consciousness." PhD diss., Macquarie University.

Haeri, Shahla. 1989. *Law of Desire: Temporary Marriage in Shi'i Iran*. Syracuse, NY: Syracuse University Press.

Hage, Ghassan. 2013. "Towards a Critical Arab Social Science: The Arab Social Sciences and Two Critical Traditions." Keynote presented to the inaugural conference of the Arab Council of Social Sciences, Beirut, March.

Hall, Elli. 2013. "Amazing Human Shield Forms around Women Protesters in Tahrir Square." *BuzzFeed News*, July 2. Accessed July 3, 2013. http://www.buzzfeed.com/ellievhall/amazing-human-shield-forms-around-women-protestors-in-tahrir.

Hammoudi, Abdellah. 2006. *A Season in Mecca: Narrative of a Pilgrimage*. New York: Polity Press.

Harrendorf, S., M. Heiskanen, and S. Malby. 2010. *International Statistics on Crime and Justice*. Helsinki: European Institute for Crime Prevention and Control and UNODC.

Hartsock, Nancy. 1998. *The Feminist Standpoint Revisited, and Other Essays*. Boulder, CO: Westview Press.

Hassan, Omar. 2010. "Real Queer Arabs: The Tension between Colonialism and Homosexuality in Egyptian Cinema." *Film International* 8, no. 1: 18.

Hasso, Francis. 2010. *Consuming Desires: Family Crisis and the State in the Middle East*. Stanford: Stanford University Press.

Herzfeld, Michael. 1980. "Honour and Shame: Problems in the Comparative Analysis of Moral Systems." *Man*, n.s., 15, no. 2: 339–351.

Hirsch, Jennifer, and Holly Wardlow, eds. 2006. *Modern Loves: The Anthropology of Romantic Courtship and Companionate Marriage*. Ann Arbor: University of Michigan Press.

Hirschman, Albert O. 1998. *Crossing Boundaries: Selected Writings*. New York: Zone Books.

Hochschild, Arlie R. 1983. *The Managed Heart: The Commercialization of Human Feeling*. Berkeley, Los Angeles: University of California Press.

Hoodfar, Homa. 1997. *Between Marriage and the Market: Intimate Politics and Survival in Cairo*. Berkeley, Los Angeles: University of California Press.

Hossain, Sara, and Lynn Welchman, eds. 2005. *Honour: Crimes, Paradigms and Violence against Women*. New York, London: Zed Books.

Hout, Syrine. 2012. *Post-War Anglophone Lebanese Fiction: Home Matters in the Diaspora*. Edinburgh: Edinburgh University Press.

Hoyt, Elizabeth. 2006. *The Raven Prince*. New York: Grand Central Publishing.

Huggan, Graham. 1997. "(Post)Colonialism, Anthropology, and the Magic of Mimesis." *Cultural Critique* 38 (Winter 1997–1998): 91–106.

Huhn, Thomas, ed. 2004. *The Cambridge Companion to Adorno*. Cambridge: Cambridge University Press.

Hunter, Mark. 2002. "The Materiality of Everyday Sex: Thinking Beyond 'Prostitution.'" *African Studies* 61, no. 1: 99–120.

————. 2009. "Providing Love: Sex and Exchange in Twentieth-Century South Africa." In *Love in Africa*, ed. Jennifer Cole and Lynn M. Thomas, 135–156. Chicago, University of Chicago Press.

Hussein, Shakira. 2013. "From Rescue Missions to Discipline: Post-9/11 Western Political Discourse on Muslim Women." *Australian Feminist Studies* 28, no. 76: 144–154.

Hyde, Lewis. 1983. *The Gift: Imagination and the Erotic Life of Property.* New York: Vintage Books.

Ingold, Tim. 2000. *The Perception of the Environment: Essays on Livelihood, Dwelling and Skill.* London: Routledge.

Inhorn, Marcia C. 1996. *Infertility and Patriarchy: The Cultural Politics of Gender and Family Life in Egypt.* Philadelphia: University of Pennsylvania Press.

————. 2003. *Local Babies, Global Science: Gender, Religion, and In Vitro Fertilization in Egypt.* New York: Routledge.

————, ed. 2006. *Reproductive Disruptions: Gender, Technology, and Biopolitics in the New Millennium.* New York, Oxford: Berghahn Books.

————. 2012. *The New Arab Man: Emergent Masculinities, Technologies, and Islam in the Middle East.* Princeton: Princeton University Press.

Inhorn, Marcia C., and Daphna Birenbaum-Carmeli. 2008. "Assisted Reproductive Technologies and Cultural Change." *Annual Review of Anthropology* 37: 177–196.

Irigaray, Luce. 1985. *This Sex Which Is Not One.* Translation by Catherine Porter. Ithaca, NY: Cornell University Press.

Jackson, Michael. 1983. "Knowledge of the Body." *Man*, n.s., 18, no. 2: 327–345.

————, ed. 1996. *Things as They Are: New Directions in Phenomenological Anthropology.* Bloomington: Indiana University Press.

Jacob, Wilson. 2011. *Working Out Egypt: Effendi Masculinity and Subject Formation in Colonial Modernity, 1870–1940.* Durham, NC: Duke University Press.

Jankowiak, William R., ed. 2008. *Intimacies: Love and Sex across Cultures.* New York: Columbia University Press.

Jankowiak, William R., and Edward F. Fischer. 1992. "A Cross-Cultural Perspective on Romantic Love." *Ethnology* 31, no. 2: 149–155.

Jeffreys, Elaine. 2004. "Feminist Prostitution Debates: Are There Any Sex Workers in China?" In *Chinese Women: Living and Working*, ed. Anne E. McLaren, 83–107. London, New York: RoutledgeCurzon.

Joseph, Suad. 1999. "Brother-Sister Relationships: Connectivity, Love, and Power in the Reproduction of Patriarchy in Lebanon." In *Intimate Selving in Arab Families: Gender, Self, and Identity*, ed. S. Joseph, 113–140. Syracuse, NY: Syracuse University Press.

Kabbani, Rana. 1986. *Europe's Myths of Orient.* Bloomington: Indiana University Press.

Kahn, Susan. 2000. *Reproducing Jews: A Cultural Account of Assisted Conception in Israel.* Durham, NC: Duke University Press.

Kareem, Mona. 2013. "Egyptian Men: The New Savages?" *Al-Akhbar English*, May 16. Accessed May 21, 2013. http://english.al-akhbar.com/blogs /subaltern/egyptian-men-new-savages.

Katz, Jack, and Thomas J. Csordas. 2003. "Phenomenological Ethnography in Sociology and Anthropology." *Ethnography* 4, no. 3: 275–288.

Kholoussy, Hanan. 2010a. *For Better, for Worse: The Marriage Crisis That Made Modern Egypt.* Stanford: Stanford University Press.

———. 2010b. "Monitoring and Medicalising Male Sexuality in Semi-Colonial Egypt." *Gender and History* 22, no. 3: 677–691.

Kleinman, Arthur. 1988. *The Illness Narratives: Suffering, Healing, and the Human Condition.* New York: Basic Books.

———. 2006. *What Really Matters: Living a Moral Life amidst Uncertainty and Danger.* Oxford: Oxford University Press.

Kleypas, Lisa. 2006. *Devil in Winter.* New York: Avon Books.

Knab, Timothy J. 1995. *A War of Witches: A Journey into the Underworld of the Contemporary Aztec.* San Francisco: Harper.

Kozma, Liat. 2013. "'We, the Sexologists . . . ': Arabic Medical Writing on Sexuality, 1879–1943." *Journal of the History of Sexuality* 22, no. 3: 426–445.

Kreil, Aymon. 2016a. "Finding Words for Sexual Harassment in Egypt: The Vicissitudes of Translation of a Legal Category." *Critique Internationale* 70, no. 1: 101–114.

———. 2016b. "The Price of Love: Valentine's Day in Egypt and Its Enemies." *Arab Studies Journal* 24, no. 2: 128–147.

Kulick, Don, and Margaret Willson. 1995. *Taboo: Sex, Identity, and Erotic Subjectivity in Anthropological Fieldwork.* New York: Routledge.

Kuper, Adam. 1988. *The Invention of Primitive Society: Transformations of an Illusion.* New York, London: Routledge.

Langohr, Vickie. 2015. "Women's Rights Movements during Political Transitions: Activism against Public Sexual Violence in Egypt." *International Journal of Middle East Studies* 47, no. 1: 131–135.

Lawlor, Leonard. 2002. "*Verflechtung*: The Triple Significance of Merleau Ponty's Course Notes on Husserl's 'The Origin of Geometry.'" In *Husserl at the Limits of Phenomenology,* ed. L. Lawlor and B. Bergo, ix–xxxviii. Evanston, IL: Northwestern University Press.

Lederman, Rena. 2006. "The Perils of Working at Home: IRB 'Mission Creep' as Context and Content for an Ethnography of Disciplinary Knowledges." *American Ethnologist* 33, no. 4: 482–491.

Lepani, Katherine. 2012. *Islands of Love, Islands of Risk: Culture and HIV in the Trobriands.* Nashville, TN: Vanderbilt University Press.

Lévi-Strauss, Claude. 1969. *The Elementary Structures of Kinship.* Translation by J. H. Bell, J. R. von Sturmer, and Rodney Needham. Boston: Beacon Press.

Lindholm, Charles. 1998. "Love and Structure." *Theory, Culture and Society* 15, no. 3: 243–263.

Lindsey, Ursula. 2011. "Egyptian Court Bans Army's 'Virginity Tests,' Calls Them Degrading." *Daily Beast,* December 27. Accessed May 30, 2013. http://www.thedailybeast.com/articles/2011/12/27/egyptian-court-bans-army-s-virginity-tests-calls-them-degrading.html.

Lyttleton, Christopher. 2014. *Intimate Economies of Development: Mobility, Sexuality and Health in Asia.* New York, London: Routledge.

Mahally, Farid. n.d. "A Study of the Word 'Love' in the Qur'an." Accessed July 3, 2013. http://www.answering-islam.org/Quran/Themes/love.htm.

Mahdavi, Pardis. 2008. *Passionate Uprisings: Iran's Sexual Revolution*. Palo Alto, CA: Stanford University Press.

Mahmood, Cynthia K. 2008. "Anthropology from the Bones: A Memoir of Fieldwork, Survival, and Commitment." *Anthropology and Humanism* 33, nos. 1–2: 1–11.

Malinowski, Bronislaw. 1929. *The Sexual Life of Savages*. Boston: Beacon Press.

Malmström, Maria Frederika. 2016. *The Politics of Female Circumcision in Egypt: Gender, Sexuality and the Construction of Identity*. London: I. B. Tauris.

Markowitz, Fran, and Michael Ashkenazi, eds. 1999. *Sex, Sexuality, and the Anthropologist*. Urbana-Champaign: University of Illinois Press.

Massad, Joseph A. 2007. *Desiring Arabs*. Chicago: University of Chicago Press.

Mauss, Marcel. 1966. *Essay on the Gift: Forms and Functions of Exchange in Archaic Societies*. Translation by Ian Cunnison. London: Cohen and West.

Mead, Margaret. 1928. *Coming of Age in Samoa*. New York: William Morrow.

Merleau-Ponty, Maurice. 1962. *Phenomenology of Perception*. Translation by Colin Smith. New York: Routledge.

Mernissi, Fatima. 1975. *Beyond the Veil*. Cambridge, MA: Schenkman.

Miller, Laura. 1997. "Not Just Weapons of the Weak: Gender Harassment as a Form of Protest for Army Men." *Social Psychology Quarterly* 60, no. 1: 32–51.

Mishra, Smeeta. 2007. "'Saving' Muslim Women and Fighting Muslim Men: Analysis of Representations in the *New York Times*." *Global Media Journal* 6, no. 11: 1–20.

Mitchell, Timothy. 1995. "Worlds Apart: An Egyptian Village and the International Tourism Industry." *Middle East Report* 196(25/5): 8–11, 23.

———. 2002. *Rule of Experts: Egypt, Techno-Politics, Modernity*. Berkeley, Los Angeles: University of California Press.

Nader, Laura. 1972. "Up the Anthropologist: Perspectives Gained from Studying Up." In *Reinventing Anthropology*, ed. Dell Hymes, 284–311. New York: Pantheon.

———. 1989. "Orientalism, Occidentalism, and the Control of Women." *Cultural Dynamics* 2: 323–355.

Naguib, Nefissa. 2015. *Nurturing Masculinities: Men, Food, and Family in Contemporary Egypt*. Austin: University of Texas Press.

Newton, Esther. 1993. "My Best Informant's Dress: The Erotic Equation in Fieldwork." *Cultural Anthropology* 8, no. 1: 3–23.

Okely, Judith. 2007. "Fieldwork Embodied." Supplement, *Sociological Review* 55, no. S1: 65–79.

Oldani, Michael. 2004. "Thick Prescriptions: Toward an Interpretation of Pharmaceutical Sales Practices." *Medical Anthropology Quarterly* 18, no. 3: 325–356.

Ortner, Sherry. 1978. "The Virgin and the State." *Feminist Studies* 4, no. 3: 19–35.

Padilla, Mark B. 2007. "'Western Union Daddies' and Their Quest for Authenticity: An Ethnographic Study of the Dominican Gay Sex Tourism Industry." *Journal of Homosexuality* 53, nos. 1–2: 241–275.

Peletz, Michael G. 1987. "The Exchange of Men in Nineteenth-Century Negeri Sembilan (Malaya)." *American Ethnologist* 14, no. 3: 449–469.

———. 1995. "Kinship Studies in Late Twentieth-Century Anthropology." *Annual Review of Anthropology* 24: 343–372.

Peristiany, Jean G., ed. 1965. *Honour and Shame: The Values of a Mediterranean Society*. London: Weidenfeld and Nicolson.

Pinto, Sarah. 2014. "Rehabilitating Ammi: Life at the End of the Asylum." Chap. 4 in *Daughters of Parvati: Women and Madness in Contemporary India*. Philadelphia: University of Pennsylvania Press.

Pitt-Rivers, Julian. 1965. "Honour and Social Status." In *Honour and Shame*, ed. Jean G. Peristiany, 19–78. London: Weidenfeld and Nicolson.

Plato. 1945. *The Republic of Plato*. Translation, introduction, and notes by Francis Macdonald Cornford. London: Oxford University Press.

Quraishi, Asifa, and Frank Vogel, eds. 2009. *The Islamic Marriage Contract: Case Studies in Islamic Family Law*. Cambridge, MA: Islamic Legal Studies Program, Harvard Law School.

Rabinow, Paul. 1977. *Reflections on Fieldwork in Morocco*. Berkeley, Los Angeles: University of California Press.

RAINN (Rape, Abuse, and Incest National Network). n.d. "Victims of Sexual Violence: Statistics." Accessed September 22, 2017. https://www.rainn.org/statistics/victims-sexual-violence.

Ramberg, Lucinda. 2014. *Given to the Goddess: South Indian Devadasis and the Sexuality of Religion*. Durham, NC: Duke University Press.

Rashad, Hoda, Magued Osman, and Farzaneh Roudi-Fahimi. 2005. "Marriage in the Arab World." *Population Reference Bureau MENA Policy Brief*. Accessed December 9, 2017. http://www.prb.org/pdf05/MarriageInArabWorld_Eng.pdf.

Rashed, Dena. 2006. "Legally Yours." *Al-Ahram Weekly*, 1–7 June.

Ratliff, Eric A. 1999. "Women as 'Sex Workers,' Men as 'Boyfriends': Shifting Identities in Philippine Go-Go Bars and Their Significance in STD/AIDS Control." *Anthropology and Medicine* 6, no. 1: 79–101.

Razack, Sherene H. 2005. "How Is White Supremacy Embodied? Sexualized Racial Violence at Abu Ghraib." *Canadian Journal of Women and the Law* 17, no. 2: 341–363.

Rebhun, L. A. 1999. *The Heart Is Unknown Country: Love in the Changing Economy of Northeast Brazil*. Stanford: Stanford University Press.

Ricoeur, Paul. 1981. *Hermeneutics and the Human Sciences*. Edited and translated by John B. Thompson. Cambridge: Cambridge University Press.

Rofel, Lisa. 2007. *Desiring China: Experiments in Neoliberalism, Sexuality, and Public Culture*. Durham, NC: Duke University Press.

Rosaldo, Michelle Zimbalist, and Louise Lamphere. 1974. "Introduction." In *Women, Culture, and Society*, ed. Michelle Zimbalist Rosaldo and Louise Lamphere, 1–16. Stanford: Stanford University Press.

Rubenstein, Steven L. 2004. "Fieldwork and the Erotic Economy on the Colonial Frontier." *Signs: Journal of Women in Culture and Society* 29, no. 4: 1041–1071.

Rubin, Gayle. 1975. "The Traffic in Women: Notes on the 'Political Economy' of Sex." In *Toward an Anthropology of Women*, ed. Rayna Reiter, 157–210. New York: Monthly Review Press.

Ryzova, Lucie. 2004–2005. "'I Am a Whore but I Will Be a Good Mother': On the Production and Consumption of the Female Body in Modern Egypt." *Arab Studies Journal* 12–13, no. 2/1: 80–122.

Said, Edward. 1978. *Orientalism*. New York: Vintage Books.

———. 2001. "Homage to a Belly Dancer." In *Reflections on Exile and Other Essays*, 346–355. Cambridge, MA: Harvard University Press.

Salem, Rania. 2011. "Economies of Courtship: Matrimonial Transactions and the Construction of Gender and Class Inequalities in Egypt." PhD diss., Princeton University.

al-Sayyid, Ridwan. 2004. "Commentary." In *Penser l'Orient: Traditions et actualité des orientalismes français et allemand*, ed. Youssef Courgabe and Manfred Kropp, 95–102. New ed. (online). Beirut, Lebanon: Presses de l'Ifpo, 2004. Accessed August 30, 2014. http://books.openedition.org/ifpo/175.

Scheper-Hughes, Nancy. 1992. *Death without Weeping: The Violence of Everyday Life in Brazil*. Berkeley and Los Angeles: University of California Press.

Schielke, Samuli. 2015. *Egypt in the Future Tense: Hope, Frustration, and Ambivalence before and after 2011*. Bloomington: Indiana University Press.

Schneider, David. 1984. *A Critique of the Study of Kinship*. Ann Arbor: University of Michigan Press.

Schneider, Jane. 1971. "Of Vigilance and Virgins." *Ethnology* 10: 1–24.

Scott, James C. 1987. *Weapons of the Weak: Everyday Forms of Peasant Resistance*. New Haven: Yale University Press.

Sedgwick, Eve Kosofsky. 1987. "A Poem Is Being Written." *Representations* 17 (Winter): 110–143.

Seizer, Susan. 2005. *Stigmas of the Tamil Stage: An Ethnography of Special Drama Artists in South India*. Durham, NC: Duke University Press.

Sen, Purna. 2005. "'Crimes of Honour,' Value and Meaning." In *Honour: Crimes, Paradigms and Violence against Women*, ed. Sara Hossain and Lynn Welchman, 42–63. New York, London: Zed Books.

Shay, Anthony, and Barbara Sellers-Young. 2005. *Belly Dance: Orientalism, Transnationalism, and Harem Fantasy*. Costa Mesa, CA: Mazda Publishers.

Singerman, Diane. 1995. *Avenues of Participation: Family, Politics, and Networks in Urban Quarters of Cairo*. Princeton: Princeton University Press.

Singerman, Diane, and Barbara Ibrahim. 2003. "The Cost of Marriage in Egypt: A Hidden Variable in the New Arab Demography." *Cairo Papers in Social Science* 24: 80–116.

Smith, Daniel J. 2006. "Love and the Risk of HIV: Courtship, Marriage, and Infidelity in Southeastern Nigeria." In *Modern Loves: The Anthropology of Romantic Courtship and Companionate Marriage*, ed. H. Wardlow and J. S. Hirsch, 135–156. Ann Arbor: University of Michigan Press.

Spivak, G. C. 1994. "Can the Subaltern Speak?" In *Colonial Discourse and Post-Colonial Theory: A Reader*, ed. P. Williams and L. Chrisman, 66–111. Hemel Hempstead, UK: Harvester-Wheatsheaf.

Stewart, Kathleen. 1996. *A Space on the Side of the Road: Cultural Poetics in an "Other" America*. Princeton: Princeton University Press.

Strathern, Marylin. 1981. "Self-Interest and the Social Good: Some Implications of Hagen Gender Imagery." In *Sexual Meanings*, ed. Sherry B. Ortner and Harriet Whitehead, 174–223. Cambridge: Cambridge University Press.

———. 1992. *After Nature: English Kinship in the Late Twentieth Century*. Cambridge: Cambridge University Press.

Taussig, Michael. 1993. *Mimesis and Alterity: A Particular History of the Senses*. New York, London: Routledge.

El-Tawila, Sahar, and Zeinab Khedr. 2004. *Models of Marriage and Family Formation among Youths in Egypt*. Cairo: National Population Council and Faculty of Economics and Political Sciences Cairo University.

Teo, Hsu-Ming. 2012. *Desert Passions: Orientalism and Romance Novels*. Austin: University of Texas Press.

Thompson, Fred. 2007. "America, Saving Muslim Women's Lives." *National Review Online*, May 3. Accessed December 10, 2017. https://www.aei.org /publication/america-saving-muslim-womens-lives/.

Tober, Diane M. 2001. "Semen as Gift, Semen as Goods: Reproductive Workers and the Market in Altruism." *Body and Society* 7, nos. 2–3: 137–160.

Transfeld, Mareike. 2014. "The New Orientalism: Westerners Working and Living in the Middle East." *Muftah*, July 12. Accessed July 21, 2014. http:// muftah.org/new-orientalism-westerners-working-living-middle-east/# .U8HsRBZuqoK.

Trawick, Margaret. 1990. *Notes on Love in a Tamil Family*. Berkeley, Los Angeles: University of California Press.

Tucker, Judith. 1985. *Women in Nineteenth Century Egypt*. Cambridge: Cambridge University Press.

Van Nieuwkerk, Karin. 2005. *"A Trade Like Any Other": Female Singers and Dancers in Egypt*. Austin: University of Texas Press.

Wallace, Anthony F. C. 2009. "Epilogue: On the Organization of Diversity." *Ethos* 37, no. 2: 251–255.

Wardlow, Holly. 2006. *Wayward Women: Sexuality and Agency in a New Guinea Society*. Berkeley, Los Angeles: University of California Press.

Warr, Deborah, and Priscilla Pyett. 1999. "Women at Risk in Sex Work." *Journal of Sociology* 35, no. 2: 183–197.

Weitzer, Ronald. 2009. "Sociology of Sex Work." *Annual Review of Sociology* 35: 213–234.

Welchman, Lynn, and Sara Hossain. 2005. "Introduction: 'Honour,' Rights and Wrongs." In *Honour: Crimes, Paradigms and Violence against Women*, ed. Sara Hossain and Lynn Welchman, 1–21. New York, London: Zed Books.

Wendell, Sarah, and Candy Tan. 2009. *Beyond Heaving Bosoms: The Smart Bitches' Guide to Romance Novels*. New York: Simon and Schuster.

Weston, Kath. 1997. *Families We Choose: Lesbians, Gays, Kinship*. New York: Columbia University Press.

Wikan, Unni. 1984. "Shame and Honour: A Contestable Pair." *Man*, n.s., 19, no. 4: 635–652.

———. 1996. *Tomorrow, God Willing: Self-Made Destinies in Cairo*. Chicago: University of Chicago Press.

Wilson, Ara. 2004. *The Intimate Economies of Bangkok: Tomboys, Tycoons, and Avon Ladies in the Global City*. Berkeley, Los Angeles: University of California Press.

Wynn, L. L. 1997. "The Romance of Tahliyya Street: Youth Culture, Commodities and the Use of Public Space in Jiddah." *Middle East Report* 204(30): 30–31.

———. 2007. *Pyramids and Nightclubs: A Travel-Ethnography of Arab and Western Imaginations of Egypt, from a Colony of Atlantis to Rumors of Sex Orgies, Urban Legends about a Marauding Prince, and Blonde Belly Dancers.* Austin: University of Texas Press.

———. 2008a. "In Egypt, 'Prostitute' Is a Slippery Term." *American Sexuality Magazine*, June 26, 2008. Reproduced on AlterNet.org. Accessed July 8, 2013. http://www.alternet.org/story/89597/in_egypt%2C_%22prostitute%22 _is_a_slippery_term.

———. 2008b. "Shape-Shifting Lizard People, Israelite Slaves, and Other Theories of Pyramid-Building: Notes on Labor, Nationalism, and Archaeology in Egypt." *Journal of Social Archaeology* 8, no. 2: 272–295.

———. 2015. "Writing Affect, Love and Desire into Ethnography." In *Phenomenology and Anthropology*, ed. K. Ram and C. Houston, 224–247. Bloomington: Indiana University Press.

———. 2016. "'Like a Virgin': Hymenoplasty and Secret Marriage in Egypt." *Medical Anthropology* 35, no. 6: 547–559.

Wynn, L. L., and Saffaa Hassanein. 2017. "Hymenoplasty, Virginity Testing, and the Simulacra of Female Respectability." *Signs: Journal of Women in Culture and Society* 42, no. 4: 893–917.

Zatz, Noah D. 1997. "Sex Work / Sex Act: Law, Labor, and Desire in Constructions of Prostitution." *Signs: Journal of Women in Culture and Society* 22, no. 2: 277–308.

Zelizer, Viviana. 1994. *The Purchase of Intimacy.* Princeton: Princeton University Press.

Zhang, Everett. 2005. "Rethinking Sexual Repression in Maoist China: Ideology, Structure, and the Ownership of the Body." *Body and Society* 11, no. 3: 1–25.

Zoepf, Katherine. 2008. "To Eye of Saudi Beholders, Camels Make Them Swoon." *New York Times*, March 16.

Index

Abdou, Fifi, 56, 190. *See also* belly dancers, belly dancing
abortion, 186, 219. *See also* pregnancy
Abu-Lughod, Lila, 31, 37, 94, 176, 179, 189, 191, 199, 200, 201
Abu-Odeh, Lama, 185
Adams, Vincanne, 90, 91, 96
Adorno, Theodore, 89. *See also* mimesis
affairs. *See* extra-marital affairs
affect. *See* kinship theory: affect in; love: as affect; love and desire: as emotion; love and desire: power of affect/attachment; tourist hustlers: affect and economic self-interest for
agency. *See* kinship theory: and agency and subjectivity; love and desire: diversity in practice of; respectability: claiming
'*aiza* (desire), 32. *See also* desire; love and desire: boundaries of
al-taharrush (harassment), 4. *See also* sexual harassment
"America, Saving Muslim Women's Lives" (2007), 188
Appadurai, Arjun, 198
'*ar* (shame), 174, 177. *See also* honor and shame
Aristotle, 89
Armbrust, Walter, 57
Auerbach, Erich, 76, 97

ayb (shameful), 56–57, 155, 177, 178. *See also* honor and shame

Barmawi, Yasmine al-, 205
Baudrillard, Jean, 8, 36, 89, 90, 98, 136, 173. *See also* simulacra, simulacrum
Bayeh, Jumana, 75–76
Beatty, Andrew, 40
behavior: constraint of women's, 9–10, 33, 53, 72–73, 110, 113–114, 176, 178; courtship rituals and scripts, 30–31, 85–88, 97–98, 172; and economic class, 9, 42, 112, 145; and gender bias, 10–11, 26, 38, 164–165, 178, 184; idealized versus actual, 7, 8, 27, 53, 181, 190–192; nonnormative openness, 101–107, 108–109, 138, 141–142, 146–148; social stigma of womens', 11, 54, 57, 127. *See also* codes; gender roles; norms and ideals; "prostitute" label, prostitution: and female behavior, judgment of; respectability; talk: and judgment
beity (homey), 132. *See also* respectability: residence and
belly dancers, belly dancing, 55–58, 59–65, 221–222; as actors, 56; and economic class, 64–65, 190; femme fatale stereotype of, 57, 63; foreign dancers, 58, 62, 117–118, 221–